C000139396

Phillip is Island-born and educated, first ʑ
then Newport Grammar School from whe
sity. He studied chemistry at Queen Mary College taking his first degree and
then a doctorate. He began his teaching career in Falmouth then went on
to Rugby and finally at Nailsea in Somerset. Still only thirty two, he became
science adviser for Somerset Education Authority before moving to County
of Avon as a senior adviser. Later he worked as an Ofsted inspector and retired to live in a Victorian rectory just outside Worcester, where he continues
to surround himself with books, maps and prints of the Isle of Wight.

It was whilst working in Somerset that he published his first book, com-
bining a lifelong interest in historic maps and prints with his Isle of Wight
background. Phillip's *A Bibliography of George Brannon's 'Vectis Scenery', 1820–
1857* is about the life and work of the acclaimed Irish-born Isle of Wight
artist, printmaker and publisher whose etchings of scenes of the Island in the
1800s were collected and catalogued by Phillip for the first time, and it was
Brannon's grandson who became a founder of the Isle of Wight County Press.

This work is dedicated to Mary, my wife.

First published by Beachy Books in 2019
www.beachybooks.com

Copyright © 2019 Phillip Armitage

1

The right of Phillip Armitage to be identified as the author of this work has been asserted in accordance with the
Copyrights, Designs and Patents Act 1988.

All rights reserved. No part of this book may be reprinted or reproduced or utilised in any form or by any electronic, mechanical or other means, now known or hereafter invented, including photocopying and recording, or in any information storage or retrieval system, without the permission in writing from the publisher.

ISBN: 9781999728328

Set in Adobe Caslon Pro

PERSONAE VECTENSES

ISLE OF WIGHT NOTABLES

PHILLIP ARMITAGE

BEACHY BOOKS

PERSONAE VECTENSES

ISLE OF WIGHT
NOTABLES

PHILLIP ARMITAGE

Contents

Apologia

Throughout this book, I have adopted the same terminology as was reported of the heroine, Fanny, in Jane Austin's *Mansfield Park*:

> '*She thinks of nothing but the Isle of Wight, and she calls it THE Island as if there were no other island in the world.*'

The reader might think, that with all the books about the Island that have been published, why another? My excuse is that, with a few notable exceptions, these books have been about places, events and scenery related to the Island. Some, particularly the histories, do concern themselves to a limited extent with the people that one-way or another helped mould our wider society. Good examples of this latter genre would be *The Isle of Wight* by J and J Jones; *The Oglander Memoirs* edited by Long; localised publications, such as *Shalfleet, Isle of Wight* by Sprake; The series of three (East Cowes and Whippingham etc) by Rosetta Brading and *The Enchanted Isle* by C W R Winter, but even this latter worthy book only concerns itself with eight of the most notable families, some of whom were not significantly involved in life outside the Island itself.

There are, of course, publications which provide biographies of Island born individuals such as that for Admiral Holmes (*Man of War*) and Robert Hooke (a large range of publications) and a few others. More recently (1996) saw the publication of *People of Wight* that looks at a range of people in different employments on the Island.

Then, using the same publisher, and both in 2006, came Ian Williams' *Remarkable Islanders* and Jan Tom's *Pushing up the Daisies*. This latter work concerned itself with those who have a memorial, or have been buried, on the Island even if, like many of the seafarers who came to grief on its shores, they never lived there. It represents a massive input of time and research and deserves a wider audience.

This present work is a determined attempt to supplement this by looking at some of the individuals who were born or lived on the Island and who have had significance beyond the Island itself. There are a vast number of publications about, for example, Queen Victoria and there is little point in too much of this being repeated here. But who has heard of Queen Osburga, of John or William Hutt, of Robert Newland or William Keeling? Inevitably there will be someone that has been omitted from a work of this nature, someone who should have been included, and I tender my apologies to those but also to anyone who is frustrated by my lack of detail in some of the entries. For those latter readers, I direct them to the Bibliography (page 210). Each of the works listed there provides greater detail and, although most of them are out of print, all but very few can be found with the help of Island secondhand book dealers or, as in the case of early wills, through the National Archive.

Further, I have deliberately ignored people, famous in their own right, whose actual link to the Island is, at best, tenuous. In this group I would include four significant figures: the future Lord Palmerston, the future Lord Melbourne, the Duke of Wellington and George Canning. All four of these men became Prime Ministers. Their link was simply that, for a limited period, they represented the Island at Parliament in London as a result of being an MP either for Newport or for the 'rotten borough' of Newtown. It is not clear whether any of them spent any significant time visiting the Island; they certainly never resided on it! (Palmerston spent time as MP for Newport under the express prohibition that he must never visit the borough!) Others might be such as Karl Marx who came to the Island a number of times for medical treatment, Emperor Haile Selassie of Ethiopia who came here as a war refugee, Winston Churchill who, as a young boy, holidayed here, or David Niven who, as a teenager, sometimes holidayed at his divorced mother's house in Bembridge but he wasn't Island born.

This work is set out alphabetically under each epoch, with each person's birthdate as the locater. Many of the players in this view of Island history are so often intertwined that it would be difficult to present it in any other form without the separate stories losing some of their impact.

Whenever quotations are used that were originally written in 17th century, or earlier, English (in wills and manuscripts, for example), I have normally taken the liberty of bringing the spelling up-to-date without, I hope, detracting from the intended meaning. Similarly, I have used the title 'manor' in its original sense to denote an area of land or an estate so that, often, my references to 'manor of' do not necessarily refer to existing structures. This is particularly so when considering the Island prior to 1600.

If a person is referred to in an entry that is not their own (e.g. John Gassiot, who has his own entry and is mentioned in that for William Amherst) their name is in **bold**.

As one might expect of any island inhabitants, many of the people referred to here 'went down to the sea in ships'. Whenever a sea-going craft is mentioned, its name is in *italics*.

EPOCH 1, 810–1600

Carey, George (1547–1603)

This son of lord Hunsdon, who was cousin to Queen Elizabeth, and was also her Lord Chamberlain, was born in London where he received a private education. He matriculated from Trinity College, Cambridge aged only thirteen! As with most of his fellows, he joined the army and in 1569, displayed such bravery during fighting at the Northern Rebellion, that he was knighted 'in the field' at Dunbar.

George served four terms as MP for Hampshire during the 1580s and in 1583 was appointed 'Captain of the Island'. In this post he energetically revitalised the Island defences to face the anticipated Spanish invasion. He also secured a surprising six MPs to represent the Island, two each for Yarmouth, Newport and Newtown. In 1596 his father died and George assumed the title of Lord Hunsdon as well as that of Lord Chamberlain. That year, he obtained permission (and the money) for the fortification of Carisbrooke Castle and employed the Italian military engineer Gianibelli to undertake the work which began in 1597. George was a keen patron of the arts and he gave support to the professional London theatre group 'The Lord Chamberlain's Men', which included William Shakespeare both as a writer and actor. He died the same year as Queen Elizabeth and was buried in London.

Cole, Henry (1504–1579)

Born at Godshill and probably educated by the priest there (the Godshill Free Grammar School established by Lady Anne Worsley at Godshill was not yet in place, funding for its foundation came from her will, proved in 1567), Henry attended Winchester College from 1519 and then New College, Oxford from where he graduated in 1527. Soon after graduating, he spent seven years in Italy, principally Padua. On his return to Queen Mary's Catholic England, he very quickly obtained significant, and well-paid, posts such as Warden of New College (1542–1551), Provost of Eton (1554–1559) and Dean of St Paul's Cathedral (1556–1559), having become Doctor of Divinity in 1540.

Upon Elizabeth becoming queen and the change of religion, Henry, at first, conformed to Anglicanism but reverted to Catholicism in 1557 and, in doing so, lost all of his benefices in 1559. He was heavily fined because of his beliefs and, in 1559, was the initial speaker in what became known as 'Discussions begun at Westminster' where high-ranking members of the church argued about the schism with Rome — Henry defending the use of Latin in the liturgy. Because of his strong stance defending others who were seen as a threat to the queen, Henry was sent to The Tower of London in early 1560 and, a year later, to Fleet Prison where, after eighteen years, he died. As was the case with deaths in this prison, no record of his internment exists.

Edes, Richard (1550–1604)

Born in Newport, the eldest son of clothier, Laurence Edes, Richard graduated from Christchurch College, Oxford in 1571. He spent some years as Rector of Freshwater and, by 1586, was Chaplain to Queen Elizabeth I. The family clearly had connections with this western end of the Island because records show that in 1597 a John Edes owned, and the family gave its name to, what is now Eades Farm, south-west of Newbridge. (Before this property came under the ownership of this family it was called 'Hampton'. In his will dated 1585 Richard's father, Laurence, refers to the leased property called Hampton when he bequeaths it to another of his sons, Edward.)

Richard became Dean of Worcester Cathedral in 1596 and, in 1603, was asked by King James to be one of the translators of the Bible, but he died before the task was begun. He is distinguished by being one of three Islanders who served Queen Elizabeth I at one and the same time.

In speaking to her lady-in-waiting Lady Walsingham, Queen Elizabeth is reported as saying of the three:

> 'one was for her sowle (Edes the priest), the other for her body (James the physician) and the third for her goods (Fleming the solicitor)'.

The three men were related.

Richard Ede's mother was Alice James, and **Thomas Fleming** (see page 15) married his own cousin, Mary James (Alice's niece), at Newport Church in 1570. This Mary was sister to Richard James. Somehow the advancement of all three was undoubtedly connected to Sir Francis Walsingham who had married the Island widow of **Sir Richard Worsley** (see page 37). Sir Francis himself was close to the queen, as was his wife. There must have been a close connection between the Island families of Worsley and James, which itself deserves further study. The Edes family were still significant figures in Newport because, in 1609, a John Edes was elected Mayor of the town — was this the John Edes of Eades Farm?

Erlesman, Thomas (c1470–1531)

Thomas was born at Newport where his family were of some consequence. (In 1499, King Henry VII stayed at the Newport house of the Erlesman family, and a later generation, in 1540, provided King Henry VIII with a John Erlesman who was one of a panel of Newport worthies asked to look at the state of repair of the chapel at Carisbrooke Castle.) Thomas received his basic education there, probably under the guidance of his father, and then went first to Winchester College and then Oxford University from where he graduated around 1491.

He reappears in 1511 when he was appointed Headmaster of Eton College, a post he held until 1515. He was then appointed head of his old school, Winchester, until, in 1525, he retired back to the Island, settling at

Whippingham. It is worth remembering that at this time, 'Whippingham' refers to the whole parish of that name, a huge area that ran down the east side of the Medina from Norris and Osborne in the north to Shide, south of Newport.

As Thomas maintained a link to Winchester College, it is most likely that his home was in the north of the parish of Whippingham not far from the church itself. This is evidenced in his will where he gives the profit from land that he owns to his family, referring to 'Lands called Clavells'. Kokeritz in his *Place-names of the Isle of Wight* says 'Clavell's Copse appears to be all that is left of the old manor of Clavells' which is referred to in documents from Winchester College of 1448 (the College owned this area of the Island at this time). It was in the hamlet of Whippingham itself and is now part of the Barton Manor lands. An 1841 Tithe map of Whippingham shows 'Cavell's Copse', 'Heath' and 'Marsh' due east of 'Padmore' and the 'Rectory'. Did the college sell the property to its ex-headmaster?

This location, within walking distance of the parish church, would make travel over to the mainland and Winchester College less of a problem as the nearby riverfront at East Shamblord (a place somewhere yet uncertain in what is now East Cowes) was a significant shipping area to the mainland and had been so since at least 1303.

In his will of 1531, Thomas expresses the wish that

> 'my body to be buried before Saint Mildred in the chancel of Whippingham if I die in Wight'.

(Which he did!)

He appears not to have married. At this time, to be a headmaster of distinguised establishments such as Eton or Winchester, Thomas would have had the full training of a celibate priest. It seems evident that, at some time between the years 1490 to 1511, he filled just such a role as, in his will, he remembered one of his earlier parishes because he bequeathed St Nicholas Church at North Stoneham, money and:

> 'Vestements of redd satten'.

In addition to Winchester College being left the (then) princely sum of six pounds, the main beneficiary of his will was his sister, Agnes, with whom he presumably lived. She not only received the income from land that he owned, but also money and:

'two featherbeds with ye blankets... and one of my best candles'.

Two of Thomas's male relatives acted as witnesses to the document, one of these presumably being the father of the Thomas Erlesman (of Calbourne) mentioned below. It is worth remembering that at this time, for people other than nobility, buildings and land did not normally figure in wills or bequests. Most wills of this period dealt with the disposal of movable goods and chattels, ownership of land normally passing to the eldest son or nearest male heir (although widows, not sisters, retained a one third share of it).

Another of Thomas's sisters, Ellen, had married a John Pocock. In 1524 a national subsidy was called for in order to pay the cost of a continuing war with France. It affected anyone on the Island whose worth was over £40. John Pocock of Claybrook, Whippingham (this includes the area now called Binfield Farm) was amongst the thirty-one Islanders named. So here, if it were needed, is further evidence that Thomas and other female members of his family lived in, or close to, the hamlet of Whippingham itself. This family connection also explains why, in his will, Thomas leaves 'iiis' three shillings (a lot of money then, but 15p today) to each of the daughters of the Pocock family — they were, after all, his nieces.

Other members of this family lived in or near Calbourne. In 1572, another Thomas Erlesman (of Calbourne) married twenty-four-year-old Dorothy Fleming of Haseley, sister of **Lord Chief Justice Fleming** (see page 15). A John Erlesman of Calbourne had his will proved in 1600. As late as 1622, Robert Dillington purchased Westover Estate (which is near Calbourne) from a 'Mr Erlesman' so the Calbourne side of the family were still significant landowners at that time.

In 1617, the son of Justice Fleming, another Sir Thomas, together with a John Erlesman (probably the son of the Calbourne Thomas and wife Dorothy Fleming) acted as co-executors for the Fleming estate. They granted the citizens of Newport the old Chantry House in Pyle Street for use as the town's first grammar school. This came with land in Shideford and a property in Lugley Street to help defray costs. In 1619, John Erlesman's widow, Agnes, released thirty-four acres of land at Honeyhill, near Newport, as a further endowment for this school.

Further, the 1637 will of **Robert Newland** (see page 25) refers to an orchard in Carisbrooke which he 'bought from **Sir Thomas Fleming**' (see page 15) and 'Mr Erlesman' (probably the Richard Erlesman who, in 1609, was elected Mayor of Newport). If nothing else, this shows that these two families remained close over many years.

Fleming, Thomas (1544–1613)

Born in Newport, son of the Bailiff, John, of the town, Thomas was educated at school at Godshill, then Winchester and finally Oxford. He followed a career in Law, first in Winchester and, later in London. He married his cousin, Mary James (daughter of Dr James, Queen Elizabeth's physician) at Newport, in 1571. For three years the couple lived at Carisbrooke Priory, the lease of which Thomas had purchased from the Secretary of State, Francis Walsingham (who, by this time, had established an Island link by his marriage to the recently widowed Lady Worsley). Thomas was called to the Bar at Lincoln's Inn in 1574 and represented Winchester as an MP from 1584 until 1601, becoming Solicitor General in 1595. He was knighted in 1603, and became Lord Chief Justice of England in that year. The most significant trial in which he took a leading role was that of Guy Fawkes in 1605.

Thomas was clearly well regarded and, by 1609, was wealthy enough to purchase land near Southampton and to increase his holdings on the Island such that he eventually owned some 4000 acres that included Binstead, part of Wootton, Arreton, Newchurch and Godshill. In total, the Fleming estate occupied over 15000 acres. Thomas died at his home near Southampton. Haseley Manor was the Island home of the family and the Island estates remained in the Fleming family until 1956. A statue of Sir Thomas is in Newport Town Hall.

Fortibus, Isabella de (1237–1293)

Born Isabella de Redvers, she was married aged twelve to William de Fortibus, Count of Albemarle and Lord of Holderness. He died when she was twenty-three and so did their eldest and only remaining son. Her unmarried brother, **Baldwin de Redvers (Reviers)** (see page 35), was Lord of the Isle of Wight and Devon and he died only two years later. As the only remaining member of the noble de Redvers family, Isabella inherited all her brother's lands and titles in addition to those of her deceased husband and so became immensely rich as well as being hereditary owner of the Island. Her land ownership on the Island encompassing all but parts around Yarmouth owned by her mother and various estates owned by religious orders such as at Quarr. In her time she was the richest woman in England and, probably, in Europe.

Isabella chose to live at Carisbrooke Castle, and she did much to improve and extend the buildings. She seemed to enjoy litigation because, at one time, she was simultaneously in dispute with the Burgesses of Newport, the Abbott of Quarr, her own mother and the Prior of Carisbrooke! The Abbott of Quarr appealed to the King (Edward I), asking him to stop Isabella's costly legal harassments, which he did.

As Lord of the Island, Isabella claimed the 'right of wreck' around the Island coast. At this time, should a shipwreck have no survivors, any value arising from salvaged cargo or the ship itself belonged to the Crown, and this was seen as an important source of royal income. Edward I decided that Isabella's claim to 'right of wreck' around the Island was just too much for him to permit and, in 1280, he issued a command that she attend a hearing before judges at Winchester in order to justify her claim. It says a great deal for her that, at a time when the King had virtually absolute power, she was prepared to stand her ground. Her defence was that

> *'she and all her ancestors from the time of King Richard,*
> *and also before that time, have had their wreck of the sea*
> *in her fee on the Isle of Wight without any interruption'.*

She had a point: King Henry I had bestowed the lordship of the Island on his adherent Richard de Redvers in 1102 and the family had enjoyed the privilege of 'right of wreck' since that time. The wording of this king's grant was a repeat of that of William the Conquerer who gave the Island to one of his followers in 1068. That earlier grant said the Island was:

> *'to be held as fully as I myself hold the Realm of England'.*

She won her case, to King Edward's displeasure.

Only on her deathbed did she show weakness. She had no close heirs and, under some pressure from Bishops (who were the King's people), she sold her rights to the Island for a mere 6000 marks (about £4,200). She was buried at Breamore Priory, Hampshire, where she had fallen ill, returning from a visit to Canterbury Cathedral.

Gibbons, William (1586–1646)

Very little is known about Gibbons' early life but it has been suggested he was born in London. He first appears in history when he accompanied his cousin, Thomas Button, on the latter's 1613 voyage aboard *Discovery* in search of the Northwest Passage. A search for this sea route was considered vital in order to shorten the journey times to the Orient.

In 1614, Gibbons himself was captain of the *Discovery* (which in its time had also been Henry Hudson's ship) and, under commission from the Prince of Wales, he set sail 'vitaled for 2 months', again, in search of the Northwest Passage. He sailed up the coast of Labrador with William Baffin (after whom Baffin Island is named) as his pilot but became ice-bound for ten weeks, near Saglek (about 58.5° N). He returned with little to show for his efforts but he was typical of the brave adventurers who did so much to establish Britain's command of the sea and, ultimately, the British Empire.

Around 1641 he retired to the Island, living near Ryde. On his death, he was buried at Binstead Church.

Hareslade, Robert de (1230–1280)

Actually born Robert Carpenter, this Robert's early education is a mystery. As it was said of him that he was no scholar of Latin, his education was unlikely to be through the normal channel of the church. Born at what is now Haslett Farm (but in the 13th Century known as Hareslade), just east of Shorwell, he became an associate of the de Lisle family that, at this time, lived at nearby West Court. The de Lisles owned huge tracts of land on the Island and, by the mid 1250s, Robert was acting as their bailiff.

It seems very likely that Robert accompanied William de Lisle when the latter went to Winchester in 1258 to investigate the revenues of the Bishopric.

In this work, John de Wyvill, an Island judge who lived at Whitefield near Brading, joined them.

From 1259 until 1263 (the year that Wyvill died), Robert appears to have worked as this judge's clerk and travelled with him when he was 'on Eyre', that is, providing a travelling court around the Island. In 1265, Robert worked for a short time at Westminster and would have had access to the legal papers lodged there, including the all-important Magna Carta, a copy of which Robert added to his manuscript. It was around this time that this upwardly mobile man altered his name to the more 'professional' name of de Hareslade, the name of his Shorwell home at this time. On his return to the Island, Robert acted as a 'hundred juror' for the court dealing with legal issues arising from West Medine, making good use of the work he had done under Judge Wyvill, and did so until at least 1279; this involved regular trips to Southampton, where the court was held. It is most likely that Robert was buried at Shorwell.

What makes Robert remarkable is that he created a manuscript detailing many elements of medieval law as well as advice on the preparation of manorial accounts. Many such documents may have been created at this time, but that of Robert is the only known extant example held by the library of Gonville and Caius College, Cambridge. Although the material it contains became obsolete by the beginning of the 14th Century because of changes in both law and legal procedures, it gives students of both medieval law and medieval accounting their only insight relating to this period. It has been said that his manuscript provides a definition of law without parallel, expanding upon the framework of Magna Carta, which itself was created in 1215, only some fifty years earlier.

Horsey, Edward (1525–1583)

Something of a 'wild card', Edward was born and educated in Devon. He soon became involved in a plot to overthrow Queen Mary and her intended husband, Philip of Spain. As a result he was exiled to France in 1556 where he met, and became friends with, Robert Dudley, later to become Earl of Leicester. Whilst in France, Edward married a local girl. During his time in France he provided Dudley with details of French activities in the Channel.

This spying activity led, under Queen Elizabeth, to Edward being allowed to return to England and given several minor posts. In 1562, Dudley, by then Earl of Leicester and of importance in the Court, arranged for him to be charged with the defence of both Dieppe and Rouen, which at this time were both important English outposts in France.

Soon after his return to England, Edward was made Captain of the Island (1565) as a reward for his work in France and, because of the threat of a Spanish invasion, he immediately began to strengthen the defences of both Carisbrooke and Cowes Castles. He was made JP for Hampshire and the Island in 1569, a post he retained until his death. Edward is credited with encouraging the importation of saltpetre to England, so as to make our forces less dependent on others for the all-important gunpowder.

Because of his knowledge of French and his continuing friendship with the Earl of Leicester, in 1576 Edward was asked to be English Ambassador to Austria, in order to deal with problems in the (then) Spanish Netherlands. He must have been successful because, on his return in 1577, he was knighted. Despite having married when he was in France, he came back to the Island around 1578 and, by 1580, was a permanent resident of Haseley Manor, near Arreton village, the home of a Northern lady called Dowsabell Mills. **Sir John Oglander** (see page 30), in his memoirs, says of them:

> '*he was not without some tax of incontinency, for nothing stop't their marriage save that he had a wife alive in France*'.

Despite this somewhat unusual arrangement, the local gentry warmly received their partnership and Haseley was, for a time, the centre of Island society. When he died, Sir Edward was buried in Newport Parish Church where there is an effigy of him above his tomb.

James, Dr John (1549–1601)

Born in Newport, the son of Mark James, a merchant and bailiff of the town, John graduated from Oxford in 1568. His studies there would have coincided with those of his two cousins, **Richard Edes** (see page 11) and **Thomas Fleming** (see page 15), helping to cement their relationship (Thomas

Fleming married Mary James, John's younger sister at Newport in 1571). In 1578 John became the first student from England to attend the prestigious medical school at Leiden in the Netherlands.

Soon after his return to England, Lord Walsingham arranged for him to become Court Master of Requests, a post that involved recovering state papers that were in private hands. It also gave him unrivalled contacts within Elizabeth's court. In 1595 he was appointed 'Physition in Ordinary' to Queen Elizabeth I and one of his more unusual duties, in addition to tending to her medical needs, was that 'he daily redd to the queen.' He is thought to have retired back to the Island in 1600, possibly to Newport, where he died.

James, Dr Thomas (c1572–1629)

Born in Newport, Thomas was a nephew of **Dr John James** (see above) and **Thomas Fleming** (see page 15). He studied first at Winchester College and then New College, Oxford, becoming a Fellow of that college in 1593. He developed a wide knowledge of books as well as skill in deciphering old manuscripts. In 1600, he published a catalogue of all the manuscripts then held by Oxford and Cambridge Universities (*Ecloga Oxonia-Cantabrigiensis*). This, together with his good 'eye' for detecting forgeries, led Sir Thomas Bodley, in 1602, to appoint him as the first librarian to the new Bodleian Library in Oxford. Thomas was created Rector of St Aldgate's Church in the city and, by 1605, had created the first catalogue of the library's holdings.

In about 1609, Thomas suggested to Bodley that the library should enter into an agreement with the Stationer's Company in London such that the library would be sent a copy of each book 'entered' at Stationer's Hall. This 'entering' was a process that, at this time, gave copyright to authors. This link was agreed in 1610 and, slowly at first, books were added to the Bodleian library by this process. Failing health forced Thomas to retire in 1620, and he died in Oxford in 1629. By his foresight, he had helped to establish the Bodleian library as possibly the world's most important repository of books and manuscripts.

It is perhaps worth noting that the James family continued to be of significance in Newport. Richard James was Mayor of Newport in 1618, as was his brother Andrew in 1622. This Andrew was the owner of Cosham Manor, a rambling Elizabethan building that was on the road known as Church Litten (the site is now occupied by a supermarket). In 1618, Andrew entertained **King Charles 1** (see page 56) there when the monarch came to the Island to inspect troops.

Keeling, William (1578–1620)

William's origins are lost in the mists of time but it is most likely that he was born in London. In 1604 (so still only twenty-six!) he was the captain of the East India Company's 240-ton *Susan*, in what was that company's second only voyage to the East Indies (the East India Company had only been set up in 1600). On the return voyage from Sumatra, William changed ships to the 300-ton *Hector* when her captain died and, after taking nine months to reach the Cape of Good Hope, his crew were emaciated and *Susan* lost. Nonetheless William brought back a large cargo of pepper and this helped to establish both his personal fortune and the regard in which he was held.

On returning from a later voyage to the East India Company's post at Bantam (N E Java) in 1609, he discovered the Cocos Islands (nearly midway between Australia and Sri Lanka) naming the largest of the group of twenty-seven small islands, Keeling Island. His sailors called the group 'Cocos' because of the profusion of coconuts growing there.

Very unusually for his time, William was fluent in both Arabic and Malayalam (the language of Malaya). The Malayalam would result from his two trips to Java and his facility with Arabic, suggesting that at some time in his early twenties he had served with the Levant Company. (This London-based group of merchants began in 1581, trading with Arabic-speaking Turkey.) His skill with these languages made him a valued leader of the East India Company's expedition of 1615. On this occasion, the Company sent Sir Thomas Roe (who is a direct ancestor of **Alliot Verdon Roe** (see page 173), the aviator), son of the then Lord Mayor of London, to establish the first British diplomatic mission at Agra, the capital of Jahangir, the Great Mughul, the Arabic speaking Muslim ruler of India. Having helped establish this far-reaching link that, centuries later, was to be pivotal to the British Empire, William sailed on to Malaya. There he fell ill, probably with malaria, and was grudgingly released by the company around August 1616, arriving back in England in May 1617.

Soon after his arrival, and still in 1617, his contacts in the East India Company arranged for him to be made Captain of Cowes Castle, a position that was something of a sinecure at this time. **Sir John Oglander** (see page 30) reported in his memoirs that William was famous for his generous, even extravagant, entertainments there and at his home. William clearly never shook off whatever sickness he had contracted in Malaya and this must have contributed to his relatively early death, aged only forty-two. Samuel Purchas published some details about his voyages in his book *Hakluytus Posthumus* (1625).

His travels had made him very rich. His household included seven servants and he had valuable shares in the East India Company. In his will he was also able to dispose:

> *'gold and silver plate and Jewels'*

to his wife, Ann (nee Bromefield) as well as providing each servant with a sizeable bequest.

William lived near Carisbrooke and was buried in the parish church there. His will says:

> *'I, William Keeling, of The Park within the parish of Carisbrooke...'*

And this suggests that his home was, as suggested by Hockey, in his *Insula Vecta*, the estate that could be reconstituted by putting together the present Great Park, Park Green, Park Place and New Park, just over 350 acres in all, due west of Newport but still in the parish of Carisbrooke. At this time, the estate was one of the more valuable Island properties still owned by the Crown, so perhaps William's powerful friends in the East India Company arranged for him to lease it. Later in this same century, this 'Park' property belonged to another famous sea-going Islander, **Robert Holmes** (see page 50). In the hearth tax return for 1664 this property was assessed for eleven chimneys — the main house was very large!

William's ornate monument in Carisbrooke church, erected by his wife Ann, erroneously gives the date of his death as September 1619 — strange this, when his signed, witnessed and proved will is dated October 1620! As she remarried in London early in 1621 (according to **Sir John Oglander** (see page 30)); perhaps she wished to present herself as having been a widow of sixteen — rather than four — months!

Leigh, Gilbert Captain (16th Cent.)

To date, very little has been uncovered about Captain Leigh, but he was very significant in his time. His ship was the 80-ton *Rat of Wight*. It is this ship name, and the name Leigh that strongly suggest an Isle of Wight origin. The Leigh family were very wealthy Island landowners (at various times the members of the family owned Appuldercombe, Arreton, Wolverton, Thorley and other manors). It is possible that Gilbert was a brother of Barnaby Leigh (1560–1625) who, at various times in the early 1600s, was Mayor of Yarmouth. This would make sense as Yarmouth was known as a hotbed of piracy and, if he lived in the area, Gilbert would 'be among friends'.

Gilbert's boat was most likely to have been built on the Island — but where? In the 1580s, Island boatbuilding was mostly limited to small, coastal craft, but one site provided ideal conditions for sea-going construction. Newport was a busy port (as its name makes clear!) but was too far from open water, though shipbuilding was present there. Bembridge, around this time, was silting up as a harbour and was only useful to small craft. The same was true of Wootton Creek, a narrow seaway that exposed huge areas of mud at low tide; although shipbuilding was carried out here, it was of small, coastal craft. (However, by the early 1800s, James and Daniel List operated a successful shipbuilding yard at the mouth of the creek, building, for example, a 36-gun sloop *Magicienne* there.) Only Cowes, and then, only the east side of the river, provided the conditions for construction of an 80-ton, seagoing vessel. Evidence for considerable marine activity at what is now East Cowes is supported by the fact that, as early as 1575, a 'Customs House' was based there and was only moved to the west bank of the river in the 1830s. This eastern bank of the river Medina also suffers from mud, but a few yards to the north of the present 'floating bridge' is an area of hard shingle, just where the old 'Gridiron' yard once stood. This would have been an ideal spot for shipbuilding, and indeed, in the 1620s is the first recorded example of a large — for those times — ship being built in this very area.

Gilbert first appears in our tale in 1588; working under a commission from the King of Navarre (the future King Henry IV of France), he undertook piratical attacks on English (!) shipping. In April of that year, he captured an English trader with a cargo of wine, promptly took the wine to the Island and sold it to the grateful inhabitants!

Gilbert (said he) had been collecting cargo at various Mediterranean ports when, in late June 1588, he passed the Spanish port of Cadiz, to find the Armada of 'over 120 ships' had left port on its way to attack England and more specifically, as he believed, land first, on the Isle of Wight. He must have done everything in his power to make good speed because, on July 5th, he arrived in Portsmouth Harbour and was able to report what he had seen. Exactly what the authorities felt whilst dealing with a known pirate, and one who had so recently been in the pay of the French, is not recorded. His report gave the English over two weeks warning of what was heading their way, and the Armada itself came into view from the Island on July 25th, already being harried by ships from Plymouth and, better still for the English, becalmed. The *Rat of Wight* was one of four Island boats that kept up the attack on the Spanish fleet, presumably still under the captaincy of Leigh.

The outcome is well known and of little relevance to the Island. Captain Leigh disappears from history for the moment but his dash back to home waters provided a much appreciated opportunity for pre-laid plans to be brought into a high state of readiness.

Mohun, Phillipa de (?1373–1431)

Born at Dunster Castle, Somerset, where her father enjoyed a barony, her precise date of birth is unclear. As her first marriage was in 1385 and, at this time, female children of the nobility were often married at age twelve, a birth date of 1373 is probable. Her first two husbands died while she was still young and, by 1396 (that is, she was still only twenty-three!), she had married Edward Plantagenet. In 1402 Edward became the second Duke of York and she, Duchess of York. In 1409 Edward was put in charge of the Island and remained so until his death. That the nobility were involved with the Island at this time is a reflection of the fear that, being an island with accessible beaches, it would be an obvious place for the French to launch an invasion.

Edward died at the Battle of Agincourt (1415) and that year, Phillipa moved to the Island, living at Carisbrooke Castle. An effigy (somewhat mutilated) of her, in Westminster Abbey where she is buried, shows her in a mantle, veil and pleated barbette, the attire of a vowess (a widow living under religious rule), possibly linked to the nearby Carisbrooke Priory. In her time, she was referred to as 'The Lady of Wight'.

Morville, Hugh de (?1138–1204)

Hugh de Morville was one of the Knights who, in 1170, murdered Archbishop Thomas à Becket at Canterbury. The story says he was never tried for his crime and, for several years after the deed, appears to have hidden. Possibly a legend, some earlier writers have suggested that, like King John after the signing of the Magna Carta, Hugh fled to the Island. For someone who was Lord of Westmorland, this seems a long way from home! Interestingly though, the de Morvilles did own land at or near the estate of Knighton Gorges (almost midway between Newport and Brading on the south side of the 'Downs') at the time of Henry III (1216–1272) and possibly before this. More unusual is the fact that Newport St Thomas's Church, built in 1172, was dedicated to Thomas a Becket (it was pulled down in 1853 and rebuilt). Further, in the year of Hugh's death, 1204, his son-in-law also built a chapel at Newchurch (where Hugh is said to have been buried). It has been suggested that these building activities were an attempt by the family to pay penance for the earlier crime.

Newland, Robert (?1570–1637)

The name Robert Newland does not mean much on the Island today. He was Island born, as were his large family and he became possibly the most significant Island merchant of the 17th Century. Based in Newport, he owned swathes of land in Carisbrooke, Newport (the areas that, in his will, he referred to as Shishpoole and Whitepitt) and East Cowes. His forebears had been farmers in the Newchurch and Arreton areas and later, merchants of Newport.

About 1616, he was involved with **Richard Worsley** (see page 37) and others in funding and provisioning settlers, under the leadership of a Captain Christopher Lawne, to continue the colonisation of Virginia begun by other Islanders in 1605. They settled in an area known by the local Indians as Warrosquoyacke, which was on the south bank of what is now known as the James River. Early American records show that both Robert and Sir Richard Worsley visited the settlers in 1619. The plantation begun by the settlers is still known as 'Lawne's Creek' and, once the Virginia Company had accepted the group's patent, the area was called, and is to this day, Isle of Wight County, an area of some 350 square miles. Very unusually, this area of Virginia not only shared its name with the Island but also shared a Governor, Lord Culpeper. He was Governor of the Island in 1661 and 1669–1670 and, when he left for the settlement in Virginia in 1672, he owned much of the Shenandoah Valley there, and was made the settlement's governor

In the reign of James I (reigned 1603–1625), Robert was engaged in litigation with the corporation of Newport. He had built a quay at East Cowes to land goods. (This was almost certainly just to the north of the present floating bridge, close to, and perhaps on the site of, the old Gridiron works where, instead of mud and 'blue slipper' clay, there was an area of firm shingle.) This meant that ships no longer had to travel up the Medina to unload and, as a consequence, Newport's decline as a trading centre began in earnest. The Burgesses of Newport appealed to the King in an attempt to stop the quay's construction but failed. In the struggle with Newport, Newland had a friend in **Sir John Oglander** (see page 30) who, in his memoirs, wrote:

> *'It is the best policy for the gentlemen of the Island strongly to maintain the now growing Birth of The Cowes'.*

The link between John Oglander and the Newland family deserves further investigation. During the Commonwealth, and before he was imprisoned, John, in his role of Justice of the Peace, authorised a marriage. Newport records show:

'William Newland, son of William of Newport, merchant married Frances Kidden of Arreton before Mr John Oglander, Justice. June 1654'.

And, despite any rancour remaining between the Newland family and the town of Newport, resulting from the dispute over the quay at East Cowes, the burgesses of the town elected a George Newland their Mayor in 1670.

The extent of Robert Newland's activities can be judged by the bequests made in his will (dated 1637):

'...all my houses at shishpoole in Newport with the warehouses, yards, wharfs and gardens lying there together...'

(note that everything is in the plural!)
In Carisbrooke, his land included:

'my orchard in Castle Hold which I purchased from **Sir Thomas Fleming** *and* **Thomas Erlesman***'.*

But it is his holdings at East Cowes that speak volumes:

'To my said son Benjamin and Sara his lawful wife a third part of the yearly rent and profit from the aforesaid Inn at East Cowes and the said wine therein'.

(This early Inn was called The Dolphin.)

Again:

'I give and bequeath to my son Benjamin my water-works and mast pond at East Cowes'.

The reference to a mast pond is unequivocal evidence for shipbuilding. It was close to the waters edge and was fed by the stream that flowed past what was later to become St James's Church. (Mast ponds were used to season logs by sinking them in water and, after several months, allowing them to dry slowly. This prevented the trunks from splitting prior to use as ship's masts.)

And, at the end of the will:

> *'my sons hereunder named shall make an equal division*
> *between them all of my shipping and boats and all*
> *things thereto belonging'.*

(Robert had four sons Robert, William, John and Benjamin; all were treated generously in the will, as were his wife, daughters and sisters.)

Interestingly, the will makes no mention of the land in Virginia that Robert was given in 1621 by the Virginia Company as a mark of that company's thanks for his help.

The company records say:

> *'The five shares of land granted to Mr Newland as a*
> *free gift of the company in record of his extraordinary*
> *pains taken in their service in taking care of shipping*
> *their people in the Abigail at the Isle of Wight being*
> *now put to the question, was confirmed upon condition*
> *that he sell them not away.'*

The reference to 'five shares' suggests that he was given 250 acres of land for his efforts as each new settler was provided with fifty acres, that is, a share.

This absence in the will suggests that Robert had already given this land to his eldest son, perhaps as part of a marriage settlement because, in this son's will of 1644, this land in America does appear and it is passed on to Robert's grandson, another Robert. It was to another grandson, Benjamin Newland's house in East Cowes, that the Dutch artist Willem Schellinks came and dined in 1662. This Benjamin was clearly a wealthy man. (He was knighted in 1679 and became an Alderman of the City of London in 1683.) The Hearth Tax returns for 1665 show that his main house had ten chimneys, but he was also liable in respect of twenty other chimneys which presumably represented the numerous small properties that he let out for rent in East Cowes. (For comparison, Mr Mann, who lived at the original, large Osborne house was assessed for nine chimneys.) As an aside, it is this Benjamin who, in 1642, paid £10 for a bronze statue of **King Charles 1** (see page 56) that had been 'liberated' from Winchester Cathedral by parliamentary forces. For eighteen years he had it buried somewhere in East Cowes and, on the Restoration, sold it back to the cathedral, where it now resides, for £100.

In a mortgage of 1677, Benjamin leases a property from a Newport grocer. Documents refer to:

> *'the farmhouse or Grange called East Shamblers, also 120 acres of arable land, bounded by lands of the Warden of Winton on south; Broadfields and Slatwood on North; lands formerly called the Fryary and Osborne on east; and the haven on west'.*

Incidentally, this statement helps to locate the mysterious 'Shamblord' estate as it clearly defines three sides of it. Only the precise extent of lands belonging to the 'Warden of Winton' (Winton was a Monastery near Salisbury and within the see of Winchester) is unsure, the 'Fryary' being a reference to what later became Barton Manor. The 'haven' is the River Medina. One very strong possibility is that this southern boundary is what is now known as Victoria Grove. It would create a parcel of land in which The Grange is central, just where Grange Road School (as was) is sited. It would also allow a clear passage from there to the parish church of Whippingham and delineate an estate of just over 120 acres!

Another Benjamin Newland (who married Katherine Kind at Newport in 1713), perhaps the son of the earlier Benjamin, owned this property as late as 1721, when the Governor of the Island gave to the owner of The Grange (Mr Newland) on behalf of the Crown, the right to operate a ferry across the Medina at East Cowes, and to appoint the ferryman. This implies that the Shamblers estate included the area that encompasses the present 'floating bridge' landing site, as this spot has always been the location of a ferry across the Medina and confirms the above reference to 'the haven'.

Another grandson, Christopher, surfaces in the estate of **Robert Hooke** (see page 52). Captain Christopher Newland of East Cowes had the responsibility of collecting rent from two Island properties owned by Hooke, and getting the money safely to him in London (from about 1670 until Hooke's death in 1703).

So here is an Island man, owning a great deal of property and ships. He was heavily involved in the early history of English settlements in America and his family continued as people of significance outside of the Island. Yet about this family so little has been written. Perhaps my gentle rummaging will stir others into giving Robert Newland and his family greater notice?

Oglander, John (1) (1585–1655)

Remembered primarily as a diarist, John was born at the ancestral home of the family, Nunwell, near Brading. He attended Winchester College and then Balliol College Oxford but left in 1603 without taking a degree (as was often the case with the children of wealthy families). He became friends with **Henry, Earl Wriothesley** (see page 39) when, in that year, the earl became Captain of The Wight. These two were the principal financiers of Lord Weymouth's 1605 expedition that began the English colonisation of Virginia.

John was knighted in 1615 and, in 1620, was appointed Deputy Governor of Portsmouth. He became MP for Yarmouth, 1625, 1626 and 1628–29 and, in 1632, was made Sheriff of Hampshire. He became an ally of **King Charles I** (see page 56) and this caused him to be thrown into prison (during which time his wife died) and to be heavily fined. After the civil war, when the King fled to the Island, it was to John that he initially turned for help. John assisted with a number of failed attempts to get the King freed from his imprisonment at Carisbrooke.

Sir John died at Nunwell and his tomb is in nearby Brading Church. He was a chronicler of his times. **W H Long** (see page 137) acted as editor of his voluminous papers and published them as *The Oglander Memoirs* (1888), material that relates to the Island in the period 1595 to 1648. They provide a rare view of life on the Island at this time of great change. However, John was not strong on chronology and, too often, he also took much that was rumour as if it were fact.

Queen Osburga (c813–854)

Osburga was the daughter of Oslac, Saxon Thane of the Isle of Wight, and he is known to have owned the manor of Arreton where Osburga is most likely to have been born. Asser, in his *Life of King Alfred* (written around 893AD) says:

'The mother of Alfred was named Osburga, a religious woman, noble by birth and by nature; she was the daughter of Oslac'.

Aged twenty, Osburga married King Aethelwulf of Wessex, bearing him four sons and a daughter. At this time, the saxon tribes did not use the term 'queen' but rather 'king-wife' but, as the wife of a king, we would recognize her as a queen. The daughter married the King of Kent and the four sons were, in turn, all Kings of Wessex. The youngest, and last of the four to become King, was Alfred the Great (847–899) who reigned from 871 until 899.

In his will, King Alfred left the manor of Arreton to his youngest son Aethelweard, which is proof of a continuing link between the family and this manor and substantiates the idea that Osburga was born there. Kokeritz provides another possible link between this royal family and this part of the Island when he traces the derivation of the name 'Alverstone' — the hamlet near Brading — to 'Alfred's Farm'. The close proximity of Arreton and this Alverstone (there are two Alverstones on the Island) adds weight to the idea that this whole area of the Island was, in Saxon times, one large estate in the ownership of Oslac, then Aethelwulf and Osburga and, later, Oslac's grandson King Alfred and that this estate probably extended as far as Brading and its haven and possibly encompassed the whole of the early-medieval parish of Brading.

These first parishes, of which there were six (Freshwater, Shalfleet, Calbourne, Carisbrooke, Newchurch and Brading) ran north-south from coast to coast so that each had a variety of soil types, allowing the production of a range of crops in each. At this time, the sea's encroachment went further inland than it does now. It seems almost certain that around the year 860 this Alverstone was itself on the water's edge (the land around the eastern River Yar, as it passes Alverstone on its way to Brading harbour, is presently just less than one metre above sea level) so this extensive Arreton estate would have had its own landing stage. A recent BBC *Time Team* investigation at nearby Yaverland produced firm evidence that as late as 800 AD, and for some time after that, what is now Brading haven was open to the sea from the north and the south, leaving the present Bembridge and Yaverland as a separate Islet and with the area of Sandown, near the present zoo, under the sea. This would make sense, as a senior figure such as Oslac would require easy access to the sea to enable fast movement between his home and the Wessex Court at Winchester at a time when roads were virtually non-existent.

From as early as 686, Brading had also been the most important centre for Christianity on the Island. This could help explain the devout nature of Osburga and her family if their lands encompassed any early Island centre of Christianity.

The date of Osburga's death is given variously as 850, 854 and 'after 876' this latter date being ill informed. In 855 Aethelwulf, together with his youngest son Alfred, went on a pilgrimage to Rome 'on the death of his wife' (i.e. Osburga) and, returning via Paris in 856, married Judith the twelve-year-old daughter of the Frankish King, Charles the Bald. This would suggest that Osburga died in 854.

Plantagenet, Cecily (Cecily of York) (1469–1507)

Cecily Plantagenet was King Edward IV's second daughter. Because Richard III had effectively usurped the throne on the death of his brother Edward, Cecily had to take sanctuary with her mother and sisters in Westminster Cathedral (Cecily's mother was Elizabeth Woodville, sometimes spelt Wydeville). Cecily's two brothers were the 'Princes in the Tower' whose murder was almost certainly orchestrated by Richard or someone close to him from the Lancastrian camp, so the women of this Yorkist family had reason to be fearful.

Once Richard was unassailable as King, he swore in public that

> *'Elizabeth and her daughters would not be harmed nor ravished and they would not be imprisoned in the Tower of London or any other prison'.*

The King also promised to provide the daughters with marriage 'portions' and to marry them to 'gentlemen borne'.

The family rejoined court life, leaving sanctuary in 1484 with Cecily, after only a short betrothal, being briefly married to a Ralph Scrope. The King did not approve of this union for dynastic reasons and had the marriage annulled. Instead, he had this desirable young woman married to the much older Lord Wells, a close relation to the house of Lancaster. Some ten years later Lord Wells died and, shortly after, so did their two young daughters.

Cecily was named, along with Sir Reynold Bray, as an executor to her husband's extensive will.

Cecily was now a very wealthy young widow with many family connections to royalty. When Henry VII's eldest son, Arthur, married Catherine of Aragon in 1501 Cecily, who was reported as 'one of the loveliest things in Britain', performed 'two bass dances' with the bridegroom during the festivities.

Very soon after this, possibly in 1502, Cecily married a commoner. His name is given variously as Richard Keen or Kyme and he came originally from Lincolnshire. It seems most probable that it was Richard Keynes of Keynes Court, Niton (Kokeritz gives an alternative spelling of Caines Court). They rented and lived at Great East Standen Manor, near Arreton, and were known to **Sir John Oglander** (see page 30) of Nunwell who, in one of his manuscripts, wrote:

> *'Richard Keene of this family lived in Henry the Seventh's reign, and was written Esqr; He married Cicely, one of the daughters of Edward the 4th, King of England, being her last husband; he was a very p'sonable man, and lived here in the Island with his wife at East Stannum'.*

(The comment 'and was written Esqr.' was Oglander's polite way of saying that Richard was not titled in any way.)

Henry VII did not recognise the marriage, perhaps because Richard was not 'a gentleman borne', but it was a happy union, producing two children, Richard and Margerie. The King denied Cecily her considerable inheritance from Lord Welles, and the family lived 'comfortably' rather than in royal style. Cecily died in her sleep at her Island home.

Some writers have doubted that Cecily ever had children from this third marriage. However, Island-born children of Cecily are mentioned in the 1602 enhanced copy of the 1576 Heraldic Visitation of Hampshire. This alone suggests that not only did they exist but married and had children themselves. Further, there is a record of an Island marriage between a Margaret Kyme and a John Wetherby around 1525.

The link between the Plantagenets and the Island is significant and of considerable duration. The wife of Edward Plantagenet, 2nd Duke of York, was known as 'Lady of the Isle of Wight' from 1415 until her death in 1431.

Anthony Woodville (2nd Earl Rivers) had responsibility as Lieutenant of the Island from 1466 until 1483, and then his brother Sir Edward Woodville followed from 1485 to 1488 (when, leading an ill-judged attack on France, he was killed along with some 400 of the Island nobility and gentry). These two men just happen to be brothers to Elizabeth, Cecily's mother (who, in 1464, became Queen Consort to King Edward IV and the first commoner to marry into English royalty). So, possibly, Cecily knew the Island and, perhaps even, Richard Keynes, through visits to one or both of her uncles there.

An additional reason for choosing the Island as her home might lie in the fact that the co-executor of her husband's will, Sir Reynold Bray, was, at the time of Cecily's marriage to Richard Keynes, Lord of the Isle of Wight (from 1495 to 1503). Bray was also a significant landowner in the county of Lincolnshire — was this a further link to Richard Keynes whose family originally hailed from that county? Bray had received this position of Island Lordship, in addition to other honours, for the seminal role he had played in arranging the 1486 marriage of his master, King Henry VII, to Elizabeth (1465–1503), Cecily's elder sister; a union that finally united the two warring houses of Lancaster and York. Bray must have been someone who, in uncertain and difficult times, Cecily both knew well and trusted.

It was in 1499 (August 9th to 23rd), that King Henry VII spent time on the Island, sleeping at Carisbrooke Castle (guest of Sir Reynold Bray?), Nunwell (guest of the Oglanders), Wootton (guest of the Lisles), Brooke (guest of the Bowermans) and finally, Newport ('in ye house by ye bullring' — guest of the Erlesmans).

Because the King did not recognise the marriage, Cecily's two children, though having one king as grandparent, another as an uncle and a queen as an aunt, were allowed no 'royal titles, lands or positions in Court.' This, presumably, was because the two children represented a direct line to the House of York, the losers in the Wars of the Roses. By imposing this prohibition, the King was simply strengthening the Lancastrian claim to the throne.

Cecily was buried at Quarr Abbey but the grave site disappeared upon the Dissolution and the destruction of the original building. She was one of very few women to be buried in this male bastion. **Queen Victoria** (see page 121) asked the architect **Percy Stone** (see page 147) to locate the site of the grave, but he was unable to do so, in part, because of a misunderstanding with the (French-speaking) monks. **Sir John Oglander** (see page 30) had written:

'The Lord Abbot of Quarr desired that they might have the honour to have her (Cecily) interred in their Church, which was performed with honour and state by the convent and gentry of the whole Island, who attended the corpse from Stannum (East Standen) to Quarr, where the Lord Abbot preached at her funeral.'

Cecily's particular significance is that, as a princess, she was the last of the Plantagenets, a family that had had such an influence on this Country, and she left children on the Island who themselves raised families.

Reviers, Baldwin de (c 1090–1155)

Baldwin was Island born, probably at Carisbrooke Castle. He was the elder son of Richard, Count of Reviers in Normandy and on who's death, in 1107, Baldwin assumed the ancestral lands and title of 'Count' (the family later anglised their name to 'Redvers').

Baldwin appears to have lived on the Island as he appears in many documents of the period. For example, donating land for the construction of Quarr Abbey (1131) and a charter for Eremuth (Yarmouth) (1132), making it the first municipality on the Island. By 1135 he was caught up in the battle for the English throne between Stephen (c1097–1154) and Stephen's cousin, the Empress Matilda (1102–1167). Matilda, sometimes called Maud, was an Empress having been widowed by the death of her first husband, Henry V of France, then Holy Roman Emperor. She later married Henry I of England and bore him a son, on whose behalf she rightly claimed the throne.

Having sided with Matilda, Baldwin first defended Exeter and then retreated to Carisbrooke where, after much bitter fighting, he was forced to surrender through lack of water. He and his family were allowed to take refuge at the court of the French Count of Anjou (Matilda had been married to a member of this family) and only on Stephen's death was Baldwin restored to his titles and was made Earl of Devon. He and his wife Aldezira lived on at Carisbrooke and both were buried at Quarr.

Roche, William (c1491–1553)

Many writers suggest that the family by this name came to the Island as followers of William of Normandy in 1066. This is entirely possible but, as yet, unproved. This particular William was almost certainly born on the Island and, in some way, connected with the Island's flourishing wool trade because, by 1515, he was a member of the Draper's Company of London. The city at this time had woollen cloth as its principal export, so this company was of major significance. In 1540, William was elected as Lord Mayor of London. This was a difficult time: Thomas Cromwell, chief advisor to King Henry VIII, was first ennobled to be Earl of Essex and, later the same year (1540), he was executed!

Full details of William's funeral arrangements can be found in the Draper's Company Archives. He died in London in 1553 (not 1523 as suggested by others!) and was buried at St Peter the Poor's Church, Broad Street there. It was around this time that the family took possession of the Arreton Manor estate and were still the owners into the 20th Century. The family still play a significant role in Island life, either as the original 'Roche' or the more recent 'Roach' branches.

Ross, Alexander (1591–1654)

Alexander was born and educated in Aberdeen. According to **Sir John Oglander** (see page 30), he was, for many years, headmaster of the free school at Southampton. In 1634, he was given the living at Carisbrooke parish church, and he remained there for most of his life, but for a short period during the English Civil War. He married the daughter of William Bowerman of Brook. He was a prodigious author, publishing nearly thirty works but now most are forgotten. He was immortalised as 'Alexander Ross' in Butler's *Hudibras*. Alexander's most widely read work was *A View of all Religions of the World* which ran to several editions. He died at Bramshill, Hampshire at the home of a friend, where he is buried.

Seymour, Margaret (c1478–1517)

Born at Wolfhall, Wiltshire, Margaret was aunt to the ill-fated Queen Jane Seymour. She became the second wife of Sir Nicholas Wadham who, in 1509, became Captain of the Isle of Wight, a post he held until 1520 (he was also Steward of Crown Lands). They lived at Carisbrooke Castle and, during her stay, Elizabeth founded an Island hospital for the infirm, though its location is uncertain; it might well have been at the same location as the 13th century Leper hospital at Gunville that had been maintained by the monks from Carisbrooke Priory. Margaret is buried in Carisbrooke church where there is a monument to her.

Stokesley, John (1475–1539)

John was born in Northamptonshire and educated at Magdalen School then Magdalen College, Oxford, graduating in 1500. By 1506 he was vice president of the college and then entered the Church. After an ecclesiastical career in Warwickshire and then Gloucestershire, John became Rector of Brighstone (1518–1524). He was made royal confessor (to Henry VIII) in 1517 and royal chaplain in 1519. In this latter role, he joined the King at 'The Field of the Cloth of Gold' in 1520.

John played a major role in convincing both the law and divinity faculties of the University of Paris to determine in favour of King Henry in his dispute with Rome. He was a prime mover in all the legislation that abolished papal authority in England. John was rewarded for his unstinting support of the King's cause when, in 1530, he was made Bishop of London. He died in London.

Worsley, James (1491–1538) and his son Richard (1516–1565)

The Worsley family have its origins in Lancashire. James was a page at the court of King Henry VII and was the same age as the King's second son (who was to become King Henry VIII). James was elected to be this young

Prince Henry's 'whipping boy'. At this time a law made it a criminal offence to strike a royal prince so, in order to get round this restriction, teachers and others who might have good reason to punish a prince for boyish misdemeanours meted out punishments to the whipping boy on his behalf. When Henry became King, he knighted James and made him Captain of Wight (from 1520 until his death in 1538), doubtless in recognition of this earlier service! James was also created 'Master of the Robes'. In this office, he was responsible for arranging the famous 'Field of the Cloth of Gold' in 1520, the vast display of wealth that Henry VIII devised to outshine Francis I, the King of France. James married Anne Leigh, heiress to Appuldercombe and, on the death of her father, he became the owner of the estate and also the richest man on the Island and began the Island-based Worsley dynasty.

When James died, his eldest son, Richard, became the master of the family estates. This Richard was ultimately given, by King Henry VIII, the post of Captain of the Wight and charged with improving the Island defences, a task he completed with great skill, re-fortifying Carisbrooke Castle and then building new fortifications at Sandown, East and West Cowes as well as a structure on the cliffs to the west of Yarmouth (known to this day as 'Worsley's Tower').

The *Mary Rose* catastrophe in 1545 led to further demands for security. Richard was charged with building a fort at the remaining Island port, Yarmouth. In addition, he armed the local militia and insisted that each parish should purchase and maintain its own cannon and that practice sessions on their discharge be a regular feature in the training of the Militia.

Two years after his death, his two young sons were killed in an explosion at Appuldercombe (the servants tried drying gunpowder in front of an open fire! — the boy's classroom was immediately above.) His widow remarried, her second husband being Sir Francis Walsingham, Secretary of State to Queen Elizabeth and the new Lady Walsingham became the Queen's lady-in-waiting (see **Richard Edes** page 11). The estates eventually passed to another Richard (1588–1621). He was the grandson of John, brother of the first Richard and the inheritance was his when he was just fifteen. Aged twenty, he met and married Frances Neville whose father was sufficiently influential to have Richard first knighted (in 1610) and then given a barony (in 1611). According to early records from Virginia (USA), it was this Sir Richard who travelled with **Robert Newland** (see page 25) in 1619 to visit the newly established colony in America.

In what was a later member of this family, Sir Richard Worsley (1730–1805) undertook to write the classic *History of the Isle of Wight* (1781). He was a widely travelled diplomat and filled his house, Appuldurcombe, with treasures from around the world. It was this family member who had the deer park of Appuldurcombe redesigned by Capability Brown in 1781.

Wriothesley, Henry (1573–1624), Earl of Southampton

Henry became the 3rd Earl of Southampton when he was seven years old. He then became a royal ward under the guardianship of Lord Burleigh who saw to his early education. Aged twelve, Henry was admitted to St John's College Cambridge and left with a degree of MA aged only sixteen. He took part in the Earl of Essex's successful expedition to Cadiz (1596) but was imprisoned in the Fleet Gaol in 1598 and again in late 1601. This latter jailing was for his involvement in reviving Shakespeare's *Richard II* that was seen as an attempt to incite the London public with a stage production showing the deposition of a King. His imprisonment for this lasted until 1603 and, on the accession of James I, Henry was released and very soon made Captain of the Wight (1603–1624).

During his time in this role, Henry lived at Great East Standen Manor, south east of Newport. Every Tuesday and Thursday he would meet with important Islanders such as **Sir John Oglander** (see page 30), who wrote in his memoirs:

> 'I have seen with my Lord of Southampton on St George's Down at bowls, from 30 to 40 knights ....
> and we had an ordinary (a meal) there, and cards and tables'.

(In his memoirs, Sir John Oglander lists nearly forty Island worthies who attended these gatherings.)

Henry helped to finance expeditions to begin the colonisation of America. These were the *Concord* out of Dartmouth, which landed at Cape Cod (then called *Cuttyhunk*, a native American Wampanoag word meaning 'end of land') in 1602. This was arranged in 1601 whilst he was out of prison and, while he was Captain of the Wight, he joined Sir John Oglander of Nunwell to finance Lord Weymouth's expedition to Virginia (1605) that began the English colonisation of the area, later supported by **Robert Newland** (see page 25). It was at this time that he made a generous donation to the recently formed Bodleian Library at Oxford that enabled the purchase of some 400 rare books. Henry also helped to equip Henry Hudson's expedition of 1610 to find the Northwest Passage. He was active at court until, in 1624, he went to Holland with his son to support the Dutch against the Spanish army. Soon after landing on the continent, father and son died, Henry, of a heart attack or, possibly, plague.

EPOCH 2, 1600–1775

Amherst, William (1732–1781)

William was born in Sevenoaks, Kent and joined the army as an Ensign in the 1st Regiment of Foot Guards in 1755 (his older brother Jeffrey also joined the forces, becoming a peer in 1776 and, ultimately, Commander-in-chief of the army. The city of Amherst in Nova Scotia is named after this Jeffrey). William quickly rose through the ranks, being a Lt Col by 1762 and Lt Gen by 1779. His fast promotion resulted from a significant victory he achieved in 1762. This was the Battle of Signal Hill where he defeated the French forces holding St John's, Canada. It was the final battle against the French and signalled the end of the Seven Years War in North America. The victory meant that the British held the whole of eastern North America and it led, ultimately, to the British domination of the whole of North America. (This, aptly named, Signal Hill was to become famous some 140 years later when, in an area near the battlefield, **Marconi** (see page 166) used it to build a receiving station for his newly developed 'wireless communicator'. It received the first-ever transatlantic radio signal from a transmitter sited at Poldhu Cove, Cornwall.)

William returned to England in 1765 and became MP for Hythe, Kent in 1766 and, in 1769, purchased land from the grandson of **Henry Player** (see page 64) and had a house built close to, and east of, Ryde on the Island. In 1774, he was appointed Lt-Governor of Portsmouth and took up residence at his Island home, St John's, named after his earlier victory. He lived there for some six years, but it was whilst staying with his brother in Sevenoaks that he died. William is buried in the family vault there. It was this St John's estate that **John Gassiot** (see page 89) purchased in 1871. Only in 2009 was William remembered by having Amherst Close, in the Elmfield area of Ryde, named after him.

Auldjo, Thomas (1757–1823)

Thomas was a trader based at East Cowes, and it is likely that he was of Maltese extraction. From a map of East Cowes of 1841, land still belonging to the family lay north of church path at its junction with Castle Street, as well as the family owning riverside warehouses and the Slatwoods estate that had belonged to William Arnold.

Thomas was an importer and exporter of wine and spirits such as brandy and much of his trade involved the supply of these to the American colonies, mostly from East Cowes to New York. His particular claim to fame is that he became a spy! He also entertained Thomas Jefferson, the future third President of the USA, 1801 to 1809, for an extended period in 1788 when Jefferson was returning to America from France. So impressed by Auldjo's attentions was Jefferson that, when he returned to America, he wrote:

> 'Mr Auldjo has given me every possible attention and friendly assistance'.

In 1790 Jefferson (who at that time was responsible for 'Foreign Affairs') wrote to him formally giving him a commission from President Washington to be American Consul in East Cowes. This sounds a trivial post today but, in the period 1610 to at least 1830, East Cowes was an important link between America and the whole of Europe. Most of American tobacco, cotton, wheat and rice imports came to Europe through the town and the 18th Century Navigation Acts meant that a wide range of goods (known as enumerated goods), whether from America or from Britain itself, had to pay customs duty before they could be shipped to any continental market. In addition, East Cowes had been a favourite port of embarkation for English and European settlers leaving for America since the involvement of Robert

Newland in the early 1600s. Only the advent of reliable steam-powered vessels signalled the end of much of this trade that had, to a large extent, relied on the protection from adverse winds afforded by the Solent. In addition, the Island farms were able to provision ships at a cost far below those being charged in London.

Because Thomas was a merchant he must have had regular contact with William Arnold in the latter's role as collector of excise, particularly so in view of his wine business with America. In addition, of course, they were also near neighbours (in a letter of 1800 to his brother-in-law in America, William refers to 'my neighbour Auldjo').

Jefferson's letter to Auldjo asked that he provide:

> 'Patronage of our commerce and its liberation from embarrassments in the British dominions'.

He was also charged with:

> 'Protecting the interests of all American citizens engaged in work'.

Tellingly he was also asked to provide intelligence and to send:

> 'from time to time, regular information from you of whatever occurs within your notice interesting to the United States'.

Although records concerning Thomas are sparse, it is known that he was elected Mayor of Newtown in 1797. It is unclear what his connections with this 'rotten borough' were. From 1806 until his death he was a churchwarden at Whippingham. In 1812, when the Arnold family finally left the Island, Thomas purchased their estate, Slatwoods, and lived there until 1822. He was clearly a very successful businessman because, amongst other sizeable bequests in his will, he left £1,500 to each of his sisters living in Scotland. This sum would have the purchasing power of nearly £100,000 in today's money! He died at Portsea near Portsmouth where he wrote the final codicil to his will, resulting from the death of his younger brother, Alexander (who had been a beneficiary in his original will). Thomas was buried at Whippingham.

Buncombe, John (1748–1827)

Probably born in London, John was in Newport by 1794 working as a schoolmaster and in lodgings in the high street. At this time, the Island was effectively a huge military base with regiments from all over the kingdom based there in expectation of an invasion by Napoleon. John was adept at creating silhouette images and very soon had officers coming to him to have their image produced in cameo form, usually with their distinctive uniforms picked out in colour. The first of these images dates from 1795. They became immensely popular and very soon, 'Buncombe silhouettes' were a 'must have' item for officers, of whom there were many!

He continued with this business until 1825, the date of his last known cameo. John died in the Newport Workhouse, which is both inexplicable for a successful artist and ironic, in view of the huge prices now paid for examples of his work (one sold at auction in 2002 for £6,000!). Newport Corporation minutes have an entry under 1830 in which his son, 'a poor orphan', be apprenticed in London until he was twenty one. Other artists from all over England soon copied the concept of cameo silhouettes using sitters of all types. John was responsible for a considerable national industry and many forgeries of his work exist.

Caldwell, James (1770–1863)

Born at Greenwich, where he received his schooling, James joined the Royal Madras Engineers in 1788. He was a 2nd lieutenant by 1789 and fought alongside Lord Cornwallis at the 1792 Seige of Seringapatam during which conflict he received serious injuries. He was a Colonel by 1824 and major general by 1836. James left India around 1840 and moved to the Island, buying Beachlands House, Ryde, soon after (the 1851 census shows him living there with his widowed daughter and fourteen servants!). He was elected to the Grand Order of the Bath (GCB) in 1848 and knighted in 1854, that year becoming a general and at the same time having the distinction of being the oldest serving officer in the army. James was very generous with his considerable wealth. He was a founder of the Royal Victoria Yacht Club (originally based in Ryde, now at Fishbourne) and was the largest contributor and founder of the Royal IOW Infirmary. He died at his home and is buried in Ryde.

Christian, Hugh (1747–1798)

Hugh, a distant relative of Fletcher Christian, the well known mutineer, was born at Hook Norton, Oxfordshire. The son of a naval officer, he naturally followed suit, joining the Navy in 1761. By 1767 he was a lieutenant and based at Portsmouth. A Navy rule at this time was that a sailor had to spend six years 'before the mast' before they could be considered for promotion, so to do so in the minimum time was unusual. He obviously visited the Island, becasue, by 1774, he had purchased land in Cowes and had a house built (it was called West Hill 'Cottage', even though it was one of the largest houses in the town at the time). In 1775 Hugh married an Island girl (Anne Leigh of Thorley) and the property became their family home.

He was promoted to captain in 1778 and was fighting the French off Martinique that year. As captain of the 74-gun *Suffolk* he was heavily involved in the capture of Grenada, St Lucia and St Vincent and made commander-in-chief of the West Indies station. By 1780, Hugh captained a captured French 40-gun sloop, the *Fortunee*, seeing action off Chesapeake (1781) during the American War of Independence and off St Kitts (1782). The Treaty of Versailles in 1783 ended the fighting and Hugh returned to England, remaining at his Island home (on half pay) until 1790.

He was promoted to Rear Admiral of the *Blue* in 1795 and his flag was aboard the 98-gun *Prince George*. In this warship, he led a squadron of 200 transports from Portsmouth carrying troops bound for the West Indies. The fleet encountered a fierce storm and was scattered off the south coast with a massive loss of life, *Prince George* being badly damaged but able to limp back to port. Hugh was honoured with the Order of the Bath in 1796 and, in 1797, sent to the Cape of Good Hope as second-in-command of the troops based there. He was again promoted to become Commander-in-Chief in 1798 but died of a heart attack after a few months in post. In his will he asked that he be buried at Northwood (at this time, Cowes had only a chapel of rest and Northwood had the nearest church to his family home). His wife, Anne, died at their home in the same year and is also buried at Northwood.

The house eventually became the home of one of the sisters of **George Ward** (see page 69), but was demolished in 1907.

Davenant, William (1605–1668)

Born in Oxford, he attended Lincoln College but did not complete a degree. In 1629 he published a tragedy, *Albovine*, and this brought him to the attention of critics. Somewhat surprisingly he was appointed unofficial 'poet laureate' in 1638 on the death of the previous incumbent, Ben Johnson. William was a strong royalist and, on the outbreak of the civil war, fought with honour for the royalists such that, at The Battle of Gloucester (1643), he was knighted by **King Charles I** (see page 56). Once the King had been executed, William left for France and served there in the French royal court. In 1646, he sailed from La Rochelle (France) intending to settle in Virginia. Unfortunately, parliamentary ships intercepted him; he was captured and imprisoned on the Island from 1650 to 1652 at West Cowes Castle, although it was more like a house arrest than full imprisonment. Most significantly however, his enforced stay gave him the time to write his most notable work, *Gondibert*, in 1651. He was pardoned in 1654 and began to organize clandestine stage productions (this was still a puritan society and they abhorred such activities). At the restoration, Davenant was allowed to form a company of players who performed at Lincoln's Inn Field.

Dingley, Robert (1619–1659)

Robert was the son of Sir John Dingley (1588–1668) and his mother was Jane Hammond (1595–?) who was Aunt to Col. Hammond (who was later to become Governor of the Island and Jailer to **King Charles I** (see page 56)). After a childhood at Woolverton Manor, Robert attended Magdalen College, Oxford, graduating in 1642. In 1643, he was appointed as Rector at Barnes, London and, after a short time in Lancashire, he was offered the living at Brighstone in 1653, a post he held until his death there in 1659. In his time he was recognised as one of the leading puritan divines. He published a number of pamphlets and sermons, the most radical of which was a discourse on 'divine optics'.

Such was the regard in which the puritan authorities held him that two Island parishioners were sent to Winchester prison for six months:

> *'charged with disturbing Robert Dingley during his sermon on the day of Humiliation, 1658'.*

Gordon, James Willoughby (1773–1851)

James was born in Hertfordshire and joined the army as an ensign in the 66th Regiment of Foot in 1783. By 1793 he was a lieutenant and volunteered to join Lord Hood's fleet at the Siege of Toulon. In command of the 85th Regiment, he took the city of Madeira. In 1812, he was made a colonel and given the post of Quarter Master General (QMG) to the forces in the Peninsular War. In this post he made a damaging decision that meant supplies were routed the wrong way, leaving a large body of troops with insufficient food and ammunition for some days during which time some 2,000 were killed through enemy action. His close friendship with the Duke of York meant that this error did not lead to his dismissal, though he did return to England suffering from 'fatigue' very shortly after this blunder. During The Peninsular War, he had been present at the capture of Madrid, the Siege of Burgos, and the earlier retreat into Portugal. James was created a Baronet in 1818 and moved to the Island in 1819, buying The Orchard, on the Undercliff.

James was appointed to The Privy Council in 1830 and, by 1841, became a full general. He retained the position of QMG of all British forces until his death. He had inherited the Northcourt estate near Shorwell in early 1817 (his baronetcy was gazetted as 'Baronet Gordon of Northcourt') but did not live there, letting his son Henry (1806–1876) and family do so. He also owned other Island properties including Chale Manor where, in 1845, he re-roofed the great hall. Unusually for a military man, he was a founder member of the Royal Geological Society (FRGS). He died in London.

Grose, Nash (1740–1814)

Born in London and educated at Tonbridge School, Nash attended Trinity Hall, Cambridge, from where he graduated LLB in 1768. He had already enrolled as a member of Lincoln's Inn in London (1766) and quickly rose through the legal hierarchy to become knighted and a judge on the King's Bench by 1787. In 1783 he married an Island girl, Mary Dennett (1761–1794), who was a distantly related orphan living as a companion to his widowed mother at The Priory, St Helens. His voluminous correspondence with his wife, written while he was acting as a circuit judge, makes it clear that their lives revolved around their home in London and St Helens. In 1799 he moved his remaining family to the Island. The property had previously been owned by Eton College and leased and then purchased by his father. Nash resigned from the bench in 1813 due to ill health, having established himself as a very capable legal administrator. Sir Nash died at a colleague's house at Petersfield, Hampshire and is buried at The Priory. One of his sons, Captain Edward Grose, was killed at the Battle of Quatre Bras, Waterloo (1815). Nash's house is now Priory Bay Hotel.

Hadfield, Joseph (1759–1851)

Born in Exeter, at the home of his mother's family, Joseph was the son of a wealthy Manchester silk merchant, John. He received his early education in that city. He joined his father's business aged about seventeen. Joseph was sent to America in 1785 (that is only two years after the end of the American war of independence!) in order to secure huge debts owed to his father. Whilst there, he not only met George Washington (before he became President) but other significant people, such as the Roosevelt family. The details of his visit were taken from notes in his journal and published in Canada, in 1933, under the title, *An Englishman in America*.

Joseph moved to the Island in 1800, bringing his father John (1720–1802) with him and built a home at Bonchurch, Upper Mount, now called Peacock Vane. Joseph and his wife and children lived at Ventnor Farm and, because of his interest in the area, he was known as 'Father of the Undercliff'. He died at Ventnor and is buried near his father at Bonchurch.

Henday, Anthony (1725–1762)

Anthony was christened at Shorwell church and so must have been born in the immediate vicinity. He only reappears in history in 1750 by which time he is employed by the Hudson Bay Company, Canada. He undertook fairly menial work until, in 1753, he volunteered to explore west from his base of York Fort on the banks of Hudson Bay.

With a small group of Indian guides, Anthony began an arduous trek on foot but did reach what is now known as Red Deer, Alberta. He mapped his journey, but also established trading links with the tribes he encountered and returned safely to York Fort. Because he was the first European to venture to this part of Canada, the Albertan administration has a number of civic works named after him. He continued to work for the Company until 1762 when he resigned, feeling that he was given too little credit for his exploits. He died that year and is thought to be buried near the fort.

Hobson, John (1642–1717)

Confusingly, John is sometimes referred to as 'John Hopson' and even 'John Hopsonn'. There is an oft repeated but unconfirmed story that John, who was an orphan born in Bonchurch and working as a tailor's apprentice at Niton, ran away to sea upon seeing the English fleet passing the South of the Island. Other sources claim he was the son of an impoverished sea captain who lived at Shalfleet. Whichever is the case, he certainly joined the Royal Navy around 1662.

John began as a cabin boy and, during an engagement with the French, he climbed the rigging of the French flagship and took down the Admiral's pennant. The other French ships took this as a sign of defeat and lay down their weapons, giving the day to the English. As thanks for his bravery, the English admiral took John into his care and saw to his preferment. He was a lieutenant by 1672 and captain by 1678. He later distinguished himself as a captain of a fifth rate ship, of the line at the Battle of Beachy Head, at the Battle of Rande (1702).

The English commander Admiral Rooke, having failed to capture any ships when he attacked Cadiz (Spain), heard that the 1702 Spanish treasure fleet had sailed from Cuba and had been diverted to Vigo. On approaching Vigo, Rooke found that the treasure fleet was protected by thirty warships (French and Spanish) and that a boom, consisting of masts lashed together, had fortified the harbour itself. In addition there were numerous shore guns facing out to sea.

Vice Admiral Hobson (as he was by then) was sent aboard his flagship *Torbay* to break the boom whilst troops were landed to secure the forts or, at least, limit their firepower. *Torbay* broke through the boom and, under murderous gunfire at the start, destroyed the combined French-Spanish fleet. At one stage, the *Torbay* was so badly damaged that John was forced to move his admiral's flag to the *Monmouth*. After ten hours, the battle was a complete victory for Rooke. The victors made off with booty, mostly silver and gold, said by some at the time to be to the value of £1,000,000 (there is a suspicion that the bulk of the treasure is still in Vigo Bay!) Hobson was knighted for his actions and, in addition to receiving a pension, was allowed to sell much of the snuff that was on board one of the Spanish vessels. This was sold in London as 'Spanish snuff', soon abbreviated to 'SP snuff'. The sudden arrival of a plentiful supply of the material helped to establish snuff taking in the country and this 'SP' brand is still one of the most popular to this day.

Such was the government's pleasure at so decisive a victory that silver and gold coins minted in 1702 and 1703 bear the word 'VIGO' to commemorate the battle.

Sir John had, for a time, served as MP for the 'rotten borough' of Newtown (1698–1702). He died at Weymouth.

Holmes, Robert (1622–1692)

Born in Mallow, County Cork, nothing is known of his early life but, to judge by his neat handwriting and clear use of language in his letters, it is evident he had the upbringing of a country gentleman. Robert has an unusual claim to fame being the only Englishman of recent times who single-handedly began not one, but two, wars. In 1646, he was serving as page to Prince Rupert whose royalist army was helping the French against the Spanish. During this action he became firm friends with the Prince, a friendship that paid many dividends later in his life. Holmes went with the Prince with the

1652 cruise to Barbados and the Guinea coast of Africa, and it was here that Holmes had his first taste of command of a ship — 'John', a small trader captured by the Prince.

Only after the Restoration of the monarchy (1660) does Robert make a significant reappearance as he was given command of the Medway guard ship Bramble and, very soon afterwards, command of Henrietta and its small squadron of four other Navy ships. In 1661, he was given orders to assist the staff of the Royal African Company but rather took things into his own hands by forcing a small Dutch fort, on the West African coast, to surrender. He also captured a Dutch man-of-war without a fight, simply by superb tactical forethought. It represented a valuable prize. Later, this was given as the cause of the second 'Dutch War' (1665–1667). The gold that Robert brought back from this expedition to the Guinea coast was minted into coins and introduced us to (the now obsolete) 'guinea' (£1.05 in today's money). It was around this time that he made an enemy of Samuel Pepys, who was a major figure in the Navy Board, by trying to seduce Mrs Pepys!

By 1666, Robert had been knighted, sent to the Tower of London (but only for some weeks) and then, with Prince Rupert's help, promoted to Rear Admiral of the Red! (At this time, the Navy operated under three 'colours', blue being the rear squadron, white at the centre and red at the head of any attack.) His most audacious action became known as 'Holmes's Bonfire'. Given intelligence by a Dutch traitor that the islands of Vlie and Schelling were poorly guarded, yet were the centre of Dutch trade with much of the world, Holmes was instructed to attack them. He did so in what was possibly the most successful single encounter of the century, destroying the greater part of the Dutch merchant fleet of over 100 ships as well as all the goods stored there. This, of course, was the reason for the start of the Third Dutch War!

By now Sir Robert was immensely wealthy. Not only did he receive a share of the spoils from the ships that he had captured, but also he had been given various land offices, Captain of Sandown Castle, etc, all of which generated a steady income. Further, the King granted him rental income from land both in Ireland and the county of Southampton. In 1668, he purchased the Governorship of the Island and soon set to repairing the forts there, at Carisbrooke, Cowes and Yarmouth, initially, at his own expense. He also built a house at Yarmouth where he was based; it is now The George Hotel. In the period 1679 to 1692, Robert was MP for Newport borough three times. There is evidence that, during his time as MP, he was engaged in what can only be described as 'piratical activities'.

He never married but, in 1678, did have an illegitimate daughter, Mary. All the evidence points to Mary's mother being Grace Hooke, **Robert Hooke's** (see page 52) eighteen-year-old niece, though this has not been fully established. (Grace had a lengthy confinement at a friend's house in Newport at this time, for 'measles'. The friend's father was the local physician and, because John, the father of Grace, had been Mayor of Newport, would doubtless be a friend of the doctor's family.)

In 1679, Sir Robert purchased Thorley Manor Farm for this daughter and her recently widowed grandmother (the wife of Robert Hooke's brother, John) and treated Mary as his only heir, insisting that when old enough, she should marry one of his nephews, so keeping wealth within his family. This wealth was considerable: not only did he own Thorley Manor and all its considerable lands and the principal house in Yarmouth but also at least two other Island estates (one being The Park, which had been leased from the crown by **William Keeling** (see page 21)), as well as a grand property in Whitehall, London; a large farm in North Wales (which generated a regular, sizeable income) and another house in Bath.

He died on the Island, and Yarmouth Church has a magnificent monument to him. It seems as if this monument had been created for a French nobleman and was some of the booty that Robert had collected. Such monuments were always delivered incomplete: the head was never carved so that, on receipt, the owner concerned could 'personalise' it, which is exactly what Robert did!

Hooke, Robert (1635–1703)

Robert was born at Freshwater where his father was priest. As a sickly child, he began his early education at home. (His father originally came to the Island as a teacher in the Oglander household at Nunwell in 1615, so Robert was in good hands). He appears to have had a relatively unfettered childhood and displayed remarkable modelling abilities. His biographer Waller reported that when he was only twelve:

'Much about the same time he made a small ship about a yard long, fitly shaping it, adding its rigging of ropes, pulleys masts etc. with a contrivance to make it fire off some small guns, as it was sailing cross a Haven of a pretty breadth'.

And again, having seen the workings of a brass clock, the young Robert constructed a working version from wood!

All these skills came into play later when he was appointed as an assistant to the youngest son of the Earl of Cork, Robert Boyle. He had studied at Westminster school and then, in 1653, Christchurch, Oxford, where, because he was not wealthy, he acted as 'servitor' to a wealthy student. Working for Boyle, first in Oxford, then later, London, in 1662, Robert became the first 'Curator of Experiments' to the newly formed Royal Society. This entailed having to devise novel experiments each week to be shown to the Society members.

This remarkable man has been quite overshadowed and ignored, in particular, because of his intense dislike of, and vitriolic disagreements with, Sir Isaac Newton. Most will remember him from Hooke's Law, learnt in Physics lessons at school, but this does a serious injustice to his undoubted genius. His most substantial published work was *Micrographia* (1665), a book that explained the use of a microscope but also, for the first time, showed the world details of a flea, looked at a sample of cork and used 'cell' to describe what was seen. But *Micrographia* contained far more than that! After a long discourse on light, Robert concluded (on page 56):

'light must therefore be a vibrating motion'.

— and this, long before Newton came to the same conclusion.

Robert also reported (1665) the patterns of refracted light, today known as 'Newton's rings'. He theorized that light travels faster in a solid medium, such as glass, and slower in a more fluid medium, such as air or water. Because of this variation of velocity in different media, the refraction caused by passing from one to another caused the front of the pulse to move in a way oblique to the direction of the beam. Robert decided this 'obliquity' to be the cause of colour.

Long before 1665, and so in time to be explained in his book, he had built an accurate barometer and used it to record the variation of atmospheric pressure with height (by taking the barometer to the top of St Paul's Cathedral). It was a further sixty years before this experiment was repeated and which finally established the idea of us living at the bottom of an ocean of air.

It was 1665 when Robert made his last lengthy visit to the Island to attend to the death of his mother. He used the opportunity to revisit his old haunt of Freshwater Bay and used his time to study the numerous fossils to be found there. Hooke Hill in Freshwater is the area where Robert was born and grew up. He would have met with his brother, John, who, in 1668 and again in 1676, was Mayor of Newport.

Robert was fascinated by mechanical systems and it is thanks to him that the famous clock and watchmaker, Thomas Tompion, created the very first 'pocket watch' that relied on an escapement mechanism. He also befriended the architect, Wren, and it may have been through this friendship that Robert was also in demand as an architect. He was responsible for Montague House (now the British Museum) and the original Bedlam Hospital among many fine buildings, not all of them in London. He was almost certainly the architect behind the Great Fire of London 'Monument' which is currently ascribed to Wren! He also served, with scrupulous honesty, as the surveyor with responsibility for the laying out and rebuilding of London after The Great Fire in 1666. This duty alone brought him enormous wealth.

Robert was a serious hypochondriac who 'enjoyed' every day of ill health that came his way! He never married, but his niece, Grace (1660–1687), the daughter of his brother John from Freshwater, came to live with him in London when she was twelve with visits back to the Island, until her death. His diary contains entries that indicate that she, as well as some of the servants, had intimate relationships with him. On a visit back to the Island, Grace came to the attention of **Robert Holmes** (see page 50) (on any visit back to the Island she is most likely to have landed at East Cowes, and would then pass through Newport and then Yarmouth, where Holmes lived, on her way to Freshwater, her mother's home) and it is most likely that, in 1678, Holmes sired an illegitimate daughter with her, though she claimed that her lengthy confinement at a friend's house in Newport, late in 1678, was the result of 'measles'. It is through this illegitimate daughter (Mary Holmes) that the Holmes family continued its influence on the Island because Robert, in his will, made it a condition that his fortune would pass to his nephew, only if the nephew married the girl, Mary.

Robert died in London and was buried at St Helen's, Bishopsgate. As the area was badly damaged in World War II, burials were moved to a communal grave at the City of London Cemetery. He was the first member of the Royal Society for whom it instructed all its fellows, then in London, to attend the funeral in full academic dress (Newton was the second), such was the debt the society felt it owed him.

Hoy, Michael (1758–1828)

Michael was born in London where his father was a merchant in the Piccadilly area. By 1786, he was a merchant himself, based in Moscow when he joined the Russia Company. His wife ran an 'English' shop there, selling 'English luxuries' and the pair appear to have lived in Moscow for some six years. Most of his trade must have been in furs and iron ore for, in 1792, he joined the Worshipful Company of Ironmongers in London. In 1798, he became a Freeman of the City of London and was elected as one of two sheriffs in 1812. Around 1809 he began to buy property on the Island, much of it purchased from the Earl of Yarborough. This included Chale and Walpen Manors and the property he rebuilt and lived in, presumably because of his interest in things Russian, The Hermitage (between Chale Green and Niton, a property that already had this name as shown in Worsley's 1775 map of the Island), in total, over 1600 acres. He also made investments in the Island, having shares in Ryde Pier and a financial interest in Ward's 'Steam Packets' that were to operate between Cowes and Southampton. (This is likely to be the result of Michael having known John Ward when the latter was a director of the London East India Dock Company, through whose facilities Michael would have imported most of his goods from Russia.)

Tsar Alexander I of Russia came to England in 1814 in celebration of the defeat of Napoleon. As a Sheriff of London, Michael may well have met him in his official capacity (and, after so long in Russia, doubtless could speak to the Tsar in his own tongue) and in celebration of this visit, Michael erected a monument on St Catherine's Down in his Hermitage estate overlooking Chale. Although he spent most of his retirement at The Hermitage he died at, and is buried close to, another of his properties, Thornhill, near Southampton.

The 'Hoy Monument', as it is known, is all that is left to remind us of Michael's time on the Island; his original house was burnt down around 1880 and rebuilt soon after. It is this monument that had an additional inscription added, probably by a relative of **Sophie Dawes** (see page 85).

King Charles I (1600–1649)

Born at Dunfermline Castle, Charles began his troubles by marrying a French Princess and allowing her to practice her Catholic religion so soon after the Guy Fawkes attempt on Parliament and while anti-Catholic sentiment was still very strong. He became King in 1625 and by this time had visited the Island a number of times, normally to visit troops or to inspect them, such as when he visited in 1618 and 1628. A number of parliaments were called and then quickly disbanded, as they would not tolerate the King's plans. For a further eleven years, he ruled in the absence of a Parliament and further alienated the country until a civil war was declared (1642–1645). Having finally been beaten at the Battle of Naseby, he made peace with the Scots, who handed him over to Parliament. He escaped to the Island and secretly negotiated with the Scots. Their defeat at Preston (1648) ended the war.

At the time, most Island gentry (led particularly by **Sir John Oglander** of Nunwell) (see page 30) were royalists, whilst the general population were for Parliament. To begin with, the King's presence on the Island was tolerated by Parliament, and Charles was free to stay with his friend at Nunwell, and to visit others that were adherents to his cause. Whilst Charles was visiting Billingham Manor, Colonel Hammond, who was in charge of Carisbrooke Castle, heard of a scheme to aid the King's escape to France and took action. Hammond immediately had the King arrested and escorted to Carisbrooke where his single room became a true prison.

In an effort to resolve this predicament — a ruling King being held a prisoner — a treaty was proposed and, during the negotiations, the King stayed in a house in Newport under guard. In the discussions, neither the King nor the parliamentary side were prepared to give ground and, after several weeks of fruitless meetings, right at the end of 1648 the parliamentary Army took over and moved Charles to Hurst Castle. Exactly a month later he was beheaded at Whitehall.

Lisle, John (1610–1664)

Born at Lisle Court, Wootton (not the existing building which is far more recent) and a scion of one of the oldest Island families of de Lisle, John was educated at Winchester College and then Magdalen Hall, Oxford from where he graduated aged sixteen. He was called to the bar in 1633 and became both recorder and then MP for Winchester. He was a staunch parliamentarian, sitting as a judge at the trial of **King Charles I** (see page 56) but was one of very few who refused to sign the death warrant. He served on Cromwell's Council of State and was the Officer with the responsibility of installing Cromwell as 'Lord Protector' as well as playing a significant role during the 'protectorate' itself.

Upon the restoration of The Crown in 1660, and despite his refusal over the death warrant, John was branded a regicide and had to flee the country. He settled in Switzerland, in a small village outside of Lausanne. Despite hiding in such a relatively out-of-the-way place, he was tracked down by a fanatical royalist and murdered as he left church.

Most of the late King's enemies had been pardoned in what was called 'The Act of Oblivion', but Sir John was specifically excluded so that the Crown seized all his property. His widowed second wife, Dame Alice, has the unfortunate honour of being the first victim of 'Hanging Judge Jefferies' (except she was beheaded!) for sheltering two men who had fought on the 'wrong' side in the Monmouth Rebellion.

McBride, John (1735–1800)

This Scottish-born man first went to sea in 1751, serving on merchant vessels. In 1754 he had enlisted in the Royal Navy. As a junior officer he saw action in the Seven Years War and the American War of Independence. By 1765 he was in command of the 32-gun HMS *Jason* and with this sloop was instrumental in establishing and securing a British settlement on the Falkland Islands.

In 1776 John was given command of the 64-gun HMS *Beinfaisant* and aboard her was involved in the relief of Gibraltar. Aboard her in 1777, he was in the thick of the fighting with the Dutch at the Battle of Cape St

Vincent. Once Fighting was over he was, like all senior officers, reduced to half pay. John assumed an interest in politics, becoming MP for the naval town of Plymouth (1784–1790) where there is a public house named after him. Around 1791 John had command of a guard flotilla along the south coast, based at Portsmouth, and this was when he purchased a property in Cowes. He was made Admiral of the Blue shortly before his death.

It was John's presence in Cowes that made his friend, the architect, **John Nash** (see page 58), visit Cowes in the period 1793–1798 and become so enthralled by the location that he purchased land there (and built East Cowes Castle). Admiral McBride died in a London coffee house.

Nash, John (1752–1835)

John was born in London and, at an early age, articled to the then well known architect, Sir Robert Taylor. Within ten years he had set up in private business but, in 1783, was declared bankrupt. He withdrew to Wales but continued working as an architect; one of his first works there being that at Carmarthen Church (1785). During his stay in Wales he made a number of visits to the Island to see on old friend from London (**Admiral John McBride** (see page 57)). John would have approached the Island from Southampton, and so had an unrivalled view of the wooded hill above, and just to the north-east of the town of East Cowes, a location that was eventually to become his home.

By 1798, John had become quite well known and much in demand for 'picturesque' designs. He was able to purchase land at East Cowes, initially some 30 acres, just to the south of the old road to Newport. He soon set to designing a house for himself and his wife. (Aged forty-six, John married the beautiful twenty-five-year-old Mary Bradley, and other writers have indicated it was a marriage of convenience and that she may have been one of the numerous mistresses of members of the Royalty). By 1802 the first stage of East Cowes Castle was complete and he took up residence there, buying a further forty acres from the next-door estate of Slatwoods. John and Mary had no children, but the house was enlivened by the presence of Mary's cousins, the Pennethorne family. Interestingly, it has been suggested that the unusual circular staircase that was in the centre of the castle was built on the foundations of the old windmill that once stood there.

In 1806, John purchased the manor of Ningwood that included the hamlet of Hamstead; there he remodelled the main house but also constructed a lime kiln and brick kilns, both serviced by a small railway that provided access to the nearby shore. He was now in a position to both design buildings and then supply the materials for their construction!

By now he was at the height of his popularity and the range of works for which he was responsible is enormous. They include:

Blaise Hamlet, Bristol (1810),
St Mildred's Church, Whippingham (1813),
The Guildhall, Newport (1814),
The Royal Pavilion, Brighton (1815),
Lough Cutra Castle, Co. Galway (1815),
sections of Regent Street, London (1817),
Haymarket Theatre, London (1820),
Buckingham Palace, London (from 1825),
St James's Church, East Cowes (1831).

A complete list of his country-wide works is given in the Bibliography, no.17 (see page 211).

Lough Cutra Castle is of interest because it was built for Charles Vereker MP, second Viscount Gort. When his son, the third Viscount moved to East Cowes Castle, he was amazed to find his new home there was so like his old home in Ireland.

Buckingham Palace became a massive problem for John because the Prince Regent kept asking for changes so that original cost estimates were soon exceeded. Despite pleading with the newly elected Prime Minister at the time, the Duke of Wellington, John was refused more funds and, in 1830, dismissed as the architect for the work.

Around this time, possibly under great strain from the dismissal, John suffered what was probably a mild heart attack and he began to spend more and more time at his Island home. He had always run an 'open' house and there was rarely a week when the house was free of visitors. One of his many personal contacts, through which he received a number of commissions, was with that of **George Ward** (see page 69) of West Cowes. It seems possible that John was responsible for the design of Ward's House, Northwood, although he did not live to see its construction.

He also developed the plans for St James's Church at East Cowes and building work began in 1831 when the Princess Victoria, aged twelve, together with her mother, the Duchess of Kent, laid the foundation stone (Victoria and her mother were, at the time, staying at Norris Castle, East Cowes). Near the end of his life, he faced a range of financial problems and was short of ready cash, because, as he wrote:

> 'My capital is embarked in houses and in materials for building, both of which, at the present time are most difficult to turn into cash'.

John died at East Cowes Castle and is buried in the churchyard of St James, East Cowes. His widow, Mary, and the Pennethorne family, left the castle and moved to Hamstead house, Ningwood, where Mary died in 1851.

Nye, Joseph (c1669–1753)

Almost certainly born in Portsmouth, Joseph appears to have completed a shipbuilding apprenticeship there in 1689 when his name first appears in the shipyard records. The record of his first marriage, in 1690, refers to both Joseph and his first wife, Mary Bedford, as 'of Portsmouth.' He finished his service there in 1693 and very soon after took over an existing yard at East Cowes. This yard, possibly immediately north of the existing chain ferry, had built ocean-going ships for the Virginia Company as early as 1620 and perhaps, for other tradesmen, before that (see the entry for **Captain Gilbert Leigh**, Epoch 1, page 23). The fact that East Cowes was a significant ship handling entity even as early as the mid-1500s is established by the presence of the customs house there from 1575. It was also the premier landing area for the Island, as evidenced by the palisade, or defence post, built there by order of the Privy Council in 1339 in order to guard the landing site whose earliest recorded use was to ship wheat to the army in Scotland in 1303.

Joseph quickly obtained Royal Navy orders — after all, he would be known to them through his work at Portsmouth. The earliest Cowes record is for the construction of a 32-gun 'Fifth-rate frigate line of battleship' this was launched by Joseph himself in 1696 and was called HMS *Poole*. This was followed in 1698 by the 46-gun, fourth rate, HMS *Jersey*. (It is worth remembering that the 'rating' of a ship depended only on its tonnage, the size of its crew and the number of guns it carried. It was not a reflection of its quality! For example, a sixth rate ship of the line carried 16 guns and had a crew of sixty-five, whereas a first rate carried 100 guns and a crew of 800. Further, 'frigate' was a reference to the style of construction, rather than to that of a role.) The Navy Board normally commissioned shipbuilding from the Royal Dockyards such as those at Woolwich, Deptford and Chatham but, such was the need for warships, the board had to look to private yards such as Nye's.

None other than the wealthy East Cowes businessman, Benjamin Newland, had recommended Joseph's work to The Board, and it was this recommendation that led to the building of HMS *Poole*:

'27 May 1695, Isle of Wight

Honble Sirs

*The bearer hereof, Mr Joseph Nye, Master Builder
in this Island understanding you have occasion to
build some fifth rate frigates has desired my letter of
recommendation by your discourse with him. You will
better know his great abilities and the conveniences
of his launching and other accommodations for his
building (of) ships here than I can represent it to you
Mr Nye desires to offer you his services so you shall
please to command him, and I recommend him to your
favour, being*

Honble Sir

Your Honours most faithfull friend and servant

Benjamin Newland'.

It cannot be a mere coincidence that an uncle of this Benjamin Newland was none other than Sir Benjamin Newland, a senior member of the Navy Board!

However, whilst Joseph was clearly an extremely competent shipbuilder, he was a poor accountant and, by early 1698, was heavily in debt, owing his group of shipwrights over £300. He left the Island in some secrecy and reappeared in London.

Joseph had clearly heard that Peter the Great, Tsar of Russia, was in London, specifically to study shipbuilding. (The Tsar stayed at the home of John Evelyn, the diarist, who was only too happy to see him leave!) His interest in the subject was such that, for most of his stay, he worked as a shipwright at Deptford in order better to understand the English method of ship construction. As there are Russian records that the Tsar paid money to 'shipbuilder Noy', it is clear that this is where the two men first met. It must be during this period of his life that his wife, Mary, died and he remarried — to a Deptford girl.

Peter's interest was driven by his need to thwart attacks in the south of Russia by the Tartars (the Turkish Empire). They had sailed up the river Don from the Black Sea and destroyed the city of Azov. Joseph, with others, saw their opportunity and agreed to service in the Russian forces. After the death in 1699 of John Deane, who had travelled with him as the senior of the two, Joseph became the chief shipbuilder, and was based at Voronezh, just north of Azov. After building at least six ships there, Joseph was moved to yards around St Petersburg. After only some ten years, he and his team had built a substantial fleet and this was the start of Russia's challenge to what then was Swedish domination of the Baltic.

This domination had meant that Russia's trade with Europe was in the hands of Sweden. By his efforts, Joseph had laid the foundation of the Russian Imperial Baltic Fleet and ultimate Russian domination of that area.

After receiving great honours from Peter and, after his death, from the Tsarina Catherine, Joseph left for England around 1737 complete with a sizeable pension. He settled in his second wife's home town of Deptford where he died and is buried. Despite the relatively short period that he was based in East Cowes, his influence remained for over a hundred years, as the yard that he used was still referred to as 'Nye's Yard' as late as 1802 when **Thomas White** (see page 70) purchased the area with that name.

Oglander, John (2) (1737–1794)

This second son of the fourth baronet was born at the ancestral home of Nunwell and was schooled at the Free Grammar School at Godshill, established by his forebears. After time at Winchester College, John attended New College, Oxford, being awarded his MA in 1765. He remained at the college, with visits home to see his parents, obtaining his degree of Bachelor of Divinity in 1770 and then Doctor of Divinity in 1774.

In 1768, John was appointed as Warden of the College, a post he held until his death. During this time he was a contemporary of James Woodforde who, in his *The Diary of a Country Parson, 1758-1802* refers to the impact of John. In addition to his strong religious inclination, John also had a deep interest in aspects of nature. The museum at the college has items donated by him: two Adam's globes, one celestial and one terrestrial, and a chest containing 'materia medica' what was, in effect, a 17th century chemistry set. John died at the college and is buried at Brading.

Pinhorn, John (1742–1831)

One of identical twins, John was born in Newport where his father was a grocer. He was educated locally and, probably around his 14th birthday, was apprenticed to a London tea dealer. He clearly served his time well because, by 1772, he was an independent tea dealer and a very successful one.

By 1784 he had made sufficient money to build Ningwood House (between Shalfleet and Yarmouth) and allowed his twin (Thomas, 1742–1824) to live there with his family. In 1795, he joined with other London merchants and opened a private bank ('Weston, Pinhorn, Golding, Newsome and Weston'), a past constituent of what is now, Royal Bank of Scotland. He was knighted in 1802 and in 1810 became that year's Master of the Worshipful Company of Grocers. Possibly around 1825, the year that he resigned from the bank, he returned to his Island house where he died. Sir John is believed to be buried at Shalfleet.

Pittis, Thomas (1636–1687)

Born at Niton, where his great-grandfather, William (1480–1559), settled having moved there with his family from Iffley, Oxfordshire (and his father, Thomas (1599–1670) also born at Niton, and was a captain in the Island militia). Thomas attended the Godshill Free Grammar School, then Winchester College. He graduated from Trinity College, Oxford in 1656 and, by 1662, was Rector of Newport. In 1666 he was appointed as Rector of St Cross, Southampton and in 1670, Thomas was awarded the degree of Doctor of Divinity by his university.

In 1678 he became Rector of St Botolph in London, a very significant church at the time, being one of the very few not destroyed in The Great Fire of 1666. Very soon after this appointment, Thomas became Royal Chaplain, a post he held until his death. He was buried at Niton.

Player, Henry (1650–1711)

Having made his fortune as a brewer in the Gosport area supplying beer to the wealthy and powerful East India Company, Henry moved to the Island and, in 1705, purchased a large tract of land in what are now Ryde and Ashey. He built a substantial house near the sea, but its precise location is not now known. Henry soon realised that the area had much to commend it, so he split the remaining land into a number of plots and put them up for sale; attracting interest from many wealthy and titled families, Ryde was born! For up to this time, the area contained small, rather mean, properties belonging to fishermen, pilots and others who relied on the sea.

The majority of sizeable houses were built above an escarpment; the area was known as 'Upper Ryde'. The majority of other houses, belonging to fishermen and sailors, were close to the sea in the area known, unsurprisingly, as 'lower Ryde'. A belt of some twelve acres of woodland separated the two. Henry's son, Thomas, built the first church there in 1719 and his grandson linked the two areas of Ryde with the construction of Union Street around 1780. The family remained as major contributors to the growth of Ryde until at least 1845. (Elizabeth Player (1764–1845), Henry's great-granddaughter, married Dr John Lind in 1789; he was the son of Dr James Lind who is called the 'Father of Naval Medicine', and it was he that was responsible for the Americans calling the English 'Limeys'.) Elizabeth and John lived in Ryde, building the house, Westmont, which is now part of Ryde School. The Lind family are remembered by the road to which they gave their name and they continued the expansion of the town, laying down strict building rules dictating what would be permitted in terms of size, style and materials used for any construction.

Powlett, Harry (1720–1794)

This second son of the Duke of Bolton joined the Navy in 1740. By means of preferment (his father, amongst other high offices, was a Lord of the Admiralty) he was captain of the *Oxford* by 1741! And this, at a time when promotion only followed after six years 'before the mast'. In this command, he played a successful part in the Siege of Toulon. Despite being court marshalled (and acquitted, though he was thereafter referred to as 'Captain Sternpost') for deserting the line at the commencement of another battle, his rise through the Navy was remarkable. On the suicide of his elder brother in 1765, he assumed the title of Duke of Bolton. He was appointed Privy Councillor in 1766 and at the same time made Governor of the Island. He rose to become Admiral of the White by 1775. During the period 1770 to 1782, he fell foul of the Prime Minister (George Grenville) who divested him of his Island position but, with a change of government, he was reinstated and served a second term as governor, 1782–1791. About 1768, he built his Island home: the magnificent Fernhill, on the western hill above Wotton. Lord Bolton lived at Fernhill during the summer months and died at a friend's house, Hackwood Park in Hampshire. Fernhill was destroyed by fire in the 1900s.

Richmond, Legh (1772–1827)

Born in Liverpool in 1772, Legh was educated first at home and later with a curate in Dorset. In 1789, he went to Trinity College, Cambridge and was ordained a Deacon in 1797. That year he married and became curate of the parishes of both Brading and Yaverland on the Island.

Legh worked in these parishes for seven years and, during this time, became acquainted with a very pious young, consumptive, Arreton-born girl, Elizabeth Wallbridge (1770–1800). Her circumstance, and that of others with whom he came into contact, led him to publish a number of religious tracts. The first, called *The Dairyman's Daughter*, about Elizabeth and first published in 1810, was soon followed by *The Negro Servant*, *Little Jane of Brading* and *The Young Cottager*. Collectively, they were called *Annals of the Poor*. Since the book's first publication, English language copies alone are estimated as in excess of two million.

In 1805, Legh worked for a short time at a London hospital and that year settled for over twenty years as a rector in Bedfordshire. He died in post after a short illness. Elizabeth's cottage still stands just south of Arreton church, and the local public house is called, rather strangely bearing in mind the very pious and abstemious nature of Elizabeth, The Dairyman's Daughter.

Seymour, Henry (1746–1830)

Born in London at his father's house, this second son of the Marquess of Hertford attended Eton and then Hertford College, Oxford, from where he received his MA in 1767. Family influence allowed him, while still a minor, to be elected as MP for Coventry in 1766, a post he held until 1774 when disagreements with the city's burghers had him deselected. He returned to politics in 1776 becoming member for Antrim in the Irish Parliament, holding that post until 1783.

The death of both his father and elder brother meant that he took the family title and on leaving Parliament was rewarded for his political work by being given a number of very lucrative posts that were, in effect, sinecures.

After spending some years travelling, Lord Seymour purchased Norris Farm, just east of East Cowes, and, in 1799, commissioned the architect James Wyatt to build a Gothic-style castle there, which was completed in 1805. He spent much of his time there improving the castle, its grounds and the associated farm. He died at the castle and there is a memorial to him in Whippingham church.

Stanley, Hans (1721–1780)

This grandson of Sir Hans Sloane, Queen Anne's physician and founder of the British Museum, was born at Owre, near Romsey. His education appears to have been by means of private tutors in London where his mother moved after the death of his father.

Hans first became a public figure when he was appointed MP for St Albans in 1742. Failing to be re-elected in 1747, Hans went to Paris and studied International Law. He returned to England in 1751 and was appointed MP for Southampton, a post he held until his death. He was appointed Lord of the Admiralty in 1757 and, after spending a somewhat wasted period in France attempting to complete negotiations over The Seven Years' War, was made a Privy Councillor in 1762.

In 1764 Hans enjoyed his first term as Governor of the Island. A change of government in 1767 terminated this honour, but another change in 1770 brought him back, this time as an appointment for life. In 1770 he built a 'cottage ornee', Steephill Cottage near St Lawrence. This was his home for ten years until Hans committed suicide on a visit to the home of his friend, Earl Spencer.

Stephens, William (1672–1753)

William was born at Bowcombe Manor, south-west of Newport. His family were wealthy, his father having been the first Lieutenant Governor of the Island (Sir William Stephens 1650–1697). William was educated at Winchester College and then Kings College, Cambridge. He studied Law but never practiced, becoming MP for Newport in 1702, a position he kept for twenty years. He then served five years as MP for Newtown. William was a colonel in the Isle of Wight Militia during this time but left the Island under a financial cloud and, because he had squandered his inheritance in the process, had to seek employment. One of his contacts was Colonel Horsey, MP, who needed a surveyor for a grant of land he had been given in South Carolina, America.

William took up this task, arriving in Carolina in 1736. Later that same year he became secretary for the new colony of Georgia. This position came with a useful salary and a 500-acre estate, Beaulieu, at the mouth of the Vernon River. In 1742 he published *State of the Province of Georgia* using a London publisher. By 1743 William was de facto Governor of Georgia and was instrumental in establishing the colony as an independent entity, separate from the parent colony of the Carolinas; unfortunately this was achieved only by the heavy use of slaves! William relinquished his post of Governor in 1750, retiring to his estate of Beaulieu where he died and is buried. He is particularly remembered for maintaining a personal journal, begun in 1737 and complete up to 1749. This journal and his earlier book on Georgia, between them, represent a unique source of early colonial history in America.

Sterne, Laurence (1713–1768)

Born in Ireland, the eldest of seven, Laurence moved to the Island in 1719. His father was an officer in the Duke of Marlborough's army and was stationed on the Island in preparation of an attack on Spain. Laurence stayed with his father until 1723 when he moved to Halifax where an uncle had estates and was Canon at York Cathedral. This short stay on the Island provided Laurence with an unrivalled opportunity to witness army life. Some of the soldiers with whom he had almost daily contact gave him the inspiration he was to use later in his most famous publication.

He went to Jesus College, Cambridge and was ordained in 1738. After some years as a parish priest, and with a number of financial problems, he published the first volume of *The Life and Opinions of Tristram Shandy, Gentleman* in 1759. To his huge surprise, the book was an immediate success and ultimately ran to nine volumes and many later editions. The comic individuals that are central to the story include Uncle Toby, Corporal Trim and Lieutenant Le Fever, characterisations all drawn from the soldiers Laurence had known as a child on the Island.

The dedication to the first edition (which was illustrated by Hogarth) sets the tone for the work:

> *'Sir, Never poor Wight of a dedicator had less hopes*
> *from his dedication than I have from this of mine; for*
> *it is written in a bye corner of the Kingdom, and in a*
> *retired thatch house, where I live in constant endeavour*

*to fence against the infirmities of ill health, and other
evils of life, by mirth.*

Stuart, Princess Elizabeth (1635–1650)

Born at St James's Palace, London this young woman spent most of her short life being guarded by the enemies of her father (who was **King Charles I** (see page 56)). She was a somewhat sickly child but very clever; it was reported that, by age eight, she could read and write in at least six languages, and was able to read the Bible in Greek! Along with her brother, she was allowed to meet with her father in London in 1650 shortly before he was beheaded. On the King's death and, in order to prevent her being seen or lionized by the public, she and her brother were shipped without delay to Carisbrooke Castle where both were, effectively, imprisoned. The Roundhead government had thoughts of marrying her off to a local young tradesman but, having spent time outside in bitterly cold weather in the castle grounds, she became ill, probably with influenza, and died.

She was buried in Newport (St Thomas's Church). Only when the church came to be rebuilt was her coffin found and it was realised that the princess had no monument so **Queen Victoria** (see page 121) paid for one to be erected.

Ward, George (1747–1829)

George came to Cowes in 1795 having retired as a successful London merchant. The family had had a controlling financial interest in the development of the East India Docks there and so had played a major role in securing London as the foremost port of Europe. Soon after his arrival on the Island, he purchased two estates, Debourne and Belle Vue, both close to Cowes.

In subsequent years he, and later his son, continued to buy tracts of land until they were by far the largest landowners around Cowes and owned most of Northwood parish. This included ownership of land and buildings that fronted Cowes harbour. In 1819 and, in collaboration with William

Fitzhugh, he demolished the waterside Dolphin Inn and used its harbour frontage to develop a secure landing area for steam packet boats. These two men, with financial backing from people such as **Michael Hoy** (see page 55) and **John Nash** (see page 58), then set up a regular steam packet connection between Cowes and Southampton and this was the precursor of the company now calling itself Red Funnel. Ward and Fitzhugh began a regular cross-Solent service in 1820 with *Prince of Coberg*.

Much of the building by the Ward family was done with the help of the architect John Nash, and the two families became close to the extent that, when Nash prepared his last will in 1834, George's son, George Henry Ward (1785–1849), was named as one of the executers. About 1815, Nash was commissioned to design the Regent's Canal in London (it opened in 1820) and George Ward was one of the principal financiers of the project. This could have been one of the earliest cases of cooperation between these two men that would continue until George's death. It was the son, George Henry Ward, who commissioned Nash to design a new house to be built as a replacement for, and on the site of, Belle Vue. The new building was called Northwood House and it sits, appropriately, on what is now called Ward Avenue. It is not clear whether the design of this superb building was the work of Nash himself, or of his close associate, James Pennethorne (the Pennethornes were cousins of Mrs Nash).

The Ward family continued to play a major role in the life of Cowes, the four daughters of George living at West Hill until the last of them, Emma, died there in 1880. They had paid for a number of improvements in the town as well as significant building work at St Mary's Church, Cowes, where they had a family vault.

White, Thomas (1773–1859)

The White family were a well-established family of ship builders based at Broadstairs, Kent. They had been building boats since the early 1700s and perhaps earlier. John White (1732–1801) published a book of hull designs in 1764, creating much interest, particularly as it contained designs for ships as large as frigates. Of his five sons, only Thomas followed into the family business, taking over the company on the death of his father in 1801.

Almost immediately Thomas heard that the Nye shipbuilding yard at East Cowes was for sale. Thomas could see that development at Broadstairs was limited, as the north-east Kent coast placed a limit on the draught of ships that could be built there, this at a time when the Navy Board were looking to construct larger ships. In 1802 Thomas purchased the Nye yard knowing that it had both a skilled workforce and, at the nearby New Forest, a plentiful supply of timber (at this time, the even closer forest at Parkhurst had been effectively stripped of useful trees). Cowes being so close to the home of the Royal Navy at Portsmouth would have been an extra bonus. Thomas's first Island-built ship was a 10-gun cutter called *Speedwell* and built for the Revenue Service — doubtless an order from the next-door East Cowes-based Revenue Office.

As early as 1815 the company's growth allowed Thomas to open the Thetis yard on the west bank of the river. This facility included a dry dock capable of taking ships of up to 800 tons burthen. In 1825 he continued expanding operations with the construction of the Falcon yard at East Cowes. The name 'Falcon' was taken from the name of the 351-ton yacht built by Thomas for the Baron Yarborough in 1815. This is evidence, were it needed, of a close link between White's yard and The Yacht Club (later to be renamed as the Royal Yacht Squadron) as the Baron was, at the time, the first commodore of The Yacht Club (he was elevated to Earl Yarborough in 1837).

A continued growth in the demand for new ships led Thomas, in the late 1820s, to develop land on the west bank of the river to the south of the Thetis yard (putting it immediately south of the present 'floating bridge'). This area of land, up to this point, had been marsh and mud flats, part of which had been used as salterns. His development of building slips along the water's edge allowed him to launch ships from both sides of the river.

One of the most celebrated ships at this time was the brigantine yacht, *Waterwitch*. This was launched at East Cowes in 1832 (but completed in 1834). She was 331 tons burthen and ninety feet long. The unique feature is that it lays claim to have been the first true 'clipper ship' ever built. The name 'clipper' was originally given to the unique bow design of the ship but later was applied to larger, often three-masted craft that employed this bow design. *Waterwitch* proved to be remarkably fast, stable in high seas and easily manoeuvrable. In 1834, she was purchased by the Royal Navy and underwent further extensive sea trials. In these, she demonstrated the total superiority of her design, leading to a statement in Parliament that year that all Royal Navy ships designed by others 'should be given the bows of Mr White's vessels.'

White's first steam-driven boat was another *Falcon*, a 325-ton paddle steamer, again built for the Revenue Service in 1817. This craft, much larger than any other conventional revenue sailing cutters, provided a huge margin of superiority in chasing smugglers, especially in calm conditions. At this time, White's had no foundry or engine shop and many of the engines they used, up to as late as 1865, were built by others, notably, Edward Bury of Liverpool, and later, and more significantly, George Belliss of Birmingham.

Sometime around 1845, Thomas's two sons, John (1810–1893) and Robert (1818–?1900), joined the company, and, on the west bank of the river, began the construction of self-righting lifeboats intended for service aboard ocean-going vessels. These were very successful and soon came to the attention of shore-based lifeboat stations. In 1860, the loss of a Royal Navy ship prompted the Admiralty to order over 500 lifeboats from White's for use on its vessels. These 'Lamb and White' lifeboats, as they were known, soon came into demand from foreign navies, but also from the group that was to become the Royal National Lifeboat Institution (RNLI). The link with the RNLI continued until 1964 when the last lifeboat was delivered to the Cromer station, Norfolk.

When Thomas died in 1859 his grandson, John Samuel (1838–1915), took over the running of the Falcon yard and was soon working in collaboration with the Birmingham engineer, George Belliss. Their intention was to develop more efficient steam engines for the variety of craft being constructed, particularly for the Royal Navy. Amongst all the ships built by White at this time was the wooden-hulled, paddle steamer, *Vectis* which was ordered by the Ward family's Southampton and Isle of Wight Royal Mail Steam Packet Co (the precursor to the present, Red Funnel Company), and this vessel came into service in 1866. Perhaps the greatest success of the company around this time was the design of high-speed torpedo boats. Those of White and Belliss easily outran and outmanoeuvred other designs. The 1885 *Swift* was the first of these and, capable of over twenty knots, also had the advantage of a vastly strong bow that would enable the craft to ram other torpedo boats with relative impunity. This led to an increase in orders, both from the Royal Navy and then from overseas.

1894 marked a significant point in the company's history: because of the success of the programme of torpedo boat construction, Whites were asked to build a new class of warship, the destroyer. Three were built using an Admiralty requirement of a very low profile (the first of these destroyers was the 'A' class HMS *Conflict*, launched just before Christmas 1894). This worked adequately until the Admiralty asked for ships with the same profile (inadequate freeboard, low in the water) and greater speed. John Samuel decided this was too dangerous and refused to tender for the work, feeling that greater speed would develop a bow wave that could endanger a ship that sat so low in the water. As a result the yards received no more Royal Navy orders for some seven years. His stand was vindicated when, in 1901, the two new destroyers HMS *Cobra* and sister ship HMS *Viper*, built by other yards to this new requirement, were both sunk with huge loss of life.

The build up of orders prior to the First World War were such that Whites continued to expand, buying up and reclaiming land along the west bank of the Medina and filling in redundant dry docks. It was here that the company installed the famous 'Hammer-head' crane. In 1912, John Samuel again demonstrated his interest in technological advance when the company opened its aircraft division and, with the guidance of Howard Wright who was a respected British aircraft designer, developed a series of floatplane craft called The Wight Navyplane. Seven were built and used by the Navy for anti-submarine patrols. These were used on the early carriers HMS *Argus* and HMS *Ark Royal*.

In an attack on the naval base at Smyrna, Turkey, in 1917, a converted Wight seaplane was the first aircraft ever to destroy a submarine, dropping a 100lb bomb. During the war, Whites produced 200 seaplanes of various designs. Still acting as company chairman, John Samuel White died at his home at Fishbourne in 1915. Immediately after the war, the family sold its interest in the works and so ended the link between the family and the shipbuilders. The company continued to thrive and for many years was the principal employer in the area. The huge hammer-head crane dominated the skyline, from its erection in 1911 until this day. Despite redevelopment of the old Whites works, the crane, one of very few of its type in England, has been given Grade II listed status and is now the subject of the attention of a local preservation society.

Wilkes, John (1726–1797)

Born in London, John became well known only after his marriage to a wealthy heiress with a large estate in Aylesbury. By 1757 he was MP for Aylesbury and this gave him a platform for his attacks on both the King (George III) and the Prime Minister of the time (the ineffectual Lord Bute). He published a journal, the *North Briton*, that ran from 1762–1764. It was seen as seditious, and in 1762 he spent time in prison and was expelled from The House (of Commons).

In 1763, John had to flee to Paris as he had been advised that he was about to be imprisoned again. He returned in 1768 and was promptly arrested. Soon after a crowd estimated at 15,000 was outside the prison, chanting for his release. The guards panicked and opened fire at what was to be known as the 'Massacre of St George's Fields'. He was re-elected as MP by the populace a number of times but Parliament refused to admit him. He became Lord Mayor of London in 1774 and finally returned to Parliament that year as MP for Aylesbury until 1790. It has been said of him that London has never had such an effective Lord Mayor.

John was very quick-witted; at one casual encounter, Earl Sandwich said to him:

> 'Sir, I do not know whether you will die on the gallows or of the pox'.

John immediately responded:

> 'That, sir, depends on whether I embrace your principles or your mistress'.

The Earl retired, speechless!

John had pushed for the end to 'rotten boroughs'. In a speech to the House of Commons in 1775, he said:

> 'That every free agent in this kingdom should, in my wish, be represented in Parliament. That the Metropolis, which contains in itself a ninth part of the people, and the Counties of Middlesex, York and others, which so greatly abound with inhabitants, should receive an increase in this representation. That the mean and

> *insignificant boroughs, so emphatically styled the rotten*
> *part of our constitution, should be lopped off, and the*
> *electors in them thrown into the Counties, and the rich,*
> *populous trading towns of Birmingham, Manchester,*
> *Sheffield, Leeds and others, be permitted to send deputies*
> *to the great council of the nation.'*

Typically, it took Parliament almost eighty years to recognise the democratic honesty of this proposal.

In 1788, at the end of his service as an MP, John retired to the Island, building a house at Sandown that he called 'My Villakin'. In the nine years he lived there, mostly during the summer months, he entertained many influential visitors as he was seen as a champion of both press freedom and of liberty for the working man. The house was demolished and others built on the site, one of which (in Wilkes Road) has a blue plaque marking the location of The Villakin. John died at his house in Westminster.

Worsley, Henry (1768–1841)

Although born at the family seat of Appuldurcombe, Henry was the son of the Rector of Chale who was a spur of that famous family. He received his early education at Godshill and, aged only twelve, left for India as an infantry cadet in the army run by the East India Company, landing at Madras. (This Henry is often confused with another, Henry Worsley (1783–1820), also Island-born, who served with Wellington in the Peninsular War and is a distant relative.)

By 1782, Henry was serving in Sumatra with the 30th Regiment and, by 1798, was a captain fighting in Oudh and at the Battle of Delhi. In 1806, Henry became adjutant-general of forces in India with the rank of lieutenant colonel. His meteoric rise was slowed in 1810 when he became very ill and had to return to England. Henry resumed his career in India in 1812 but the return of his illness in 1819 forced him finally to return to England. He resigned his commission but was retained by the company, being promoted by them to the rank of major general in 1830. Henry was knighted in 1831 and, soon after, retired to the Island, taking up residence at Shide where he died and is buried.

EPOCH 3, 1775–1810

Arnold, Thomas (1795–1842)

Thomas Arnold was born in West Cowes where his father, William, was Collector of Customs. William moved to this post on the Island with his family in 1777 and took on the arduous task of Collector at a time when England was in the throes of a war with the colonists in America, soon after to be at war with France, Spain and Holland as well! At this time smuggling was also a major problem all along the south coast of England.

The only suitable property William could find was on the west bank of the river Medina with the Custom's House on the east bank (it was first located there in 1575 and only moved to the west bank in 1834), requiring William to cross the river daily, no matter what the weather. Thomas was born in 1795, just as his father had purchased a twenty-acre site on the more convenient east side. A plaque marks Thomas Arnold's birthplace in West Cowes.

Writing to his brother-in-law in November 1795, William said:

> 'In a letter I wrote you some time ago, I mentioned a purchase of land I had made near East Cowes and that I was about building a house. It has now advanced as much as we could expect in the time'.

By 1796, the family had settled in East Cowes. William called the house Slatwoods (using an old 'field name' for the area). It was sited at the shore end, and to the north, of Old Road. (The estate is shown on the first edition of the one-inch Ordnance Survey map, post 1870, and was bounded by what are now the present Old Road, Cambridge Road and the sea). Interestingly, a biographer of Thomas, writing shortly after his death (A P Stanley, 1852, in *Life and Letters of Thomas Arnold*), said of the house's location that it was:

> *'built on the ground rising above the old Henry VIII castle site'*

— a location for 'The East Cow' that makes more sense than the alternative, commonly accepted, Castle Point. Further evidence for this site being that of the 'East Cow' comes from an early print of West Cowes castle that says that

> *'The castles have an good mile between them'.*

Slatwoods is just that, whereas Old Castle Point is nearly 1.7 miles distant!

When William died in 1801, his wife Martha (nee Delafield) was given the post of Deputy Postmistress of the Isle of Wight, a post she held until 1812 when the family moved to the mainland. She sold Slatwoods to her neighbour, Thomas Auldjo, and he lived there until 1822.

Slatwoods was demolished in the 1880s but overlooked Cowes Harbour and gave the young Thomas an opportunity that he recalled in later life:

> *'I was brought up in the Isle of Wight amidst the bustle of soldiers, and from childhood familiar with boats, ships, and the flags of half Europe, which gave me an instructive acquaintance with geography. I quite marvel to find in what a state of ignorance boys are at seventeen or eighteen who have lived all their lives in inland towns and parishes'.*

His early life at Slatwoods allowed him to receive the beginnings of his education under the guidance of both his mother and an aunt who lived with them.

Aged eight, Thomas went to a school in Warminster and then to Winchester before entering Oriel College, Oxford. There he graduated with a first class honours degree in Classics (1814). He became a Deacon of the Church of England in 1818 and moved to a parish, just outside of London, with his new wife. Whilst he was there, his tutor from Oxford days recommended him for the post of headteacher of Rugby School. He took up this post in 1828, having just been awarded his doctorate (in divinity). In addition to the task of headmastership, from 1831, Thomas took on the role of school chaplain. His influence on English school education whilst at Rugby cannot be overestimated and is the subject of a number of books.

He visited the Island for the last time in 1836. Writing to his sister about that visit, he said:

> *'I admired the interior of the Island, which people affect to sneer at, but which I think is very superior to most of the scenery of common countries. As for the Sandrock Hotel, it was most beautiful, and Bonchurch is the most beautiful thing I ever saw on the sea coast on this side of Genoa. Slatwoods was deeply interesting... the only home of my childhood.'*

In 1841, he became Regius Professor of Modern History at Oxford University (whilst still being full time at Rugby) and gave lectures that, unusual for the time, were attended by hundreds of students.

Thomas died at Rugby, still in post, after a short illness. His insistence on the importance of team games at Rugby School influenced Baron Pierre de Coubertin. The Baron is the man who, in 1896, revived the Olympic Games. In his book *L'Education en Angleterre* (1888), the Baron wrote:

> *'It was to Arnold that we turned, more or less consciously, for inspiration'*

because, whilst visiting Rugby School where Thomas's influence was still very strong, the Baron noted how:

> *'..organised sport can create moral and social strength.'*

So, Thomas helped to inspire the present Olympic movement!

Brannon, George (1784–1860)

George was born in Ireland and moved to London aged between ten and twelve, probably beginning as an indentured apprentice in the printing business. He moved to the Island with his new wife in 1813, first settling in Newport and then Wootton Common. He began work in the printing business and, by 1820, began to create rather naive views drawn from the scenery around him. He arranged for the local gentry to become subscribers to his venture and, with their help, the first set of views were created. They were popular enough to make him realise that there was a growing tourist market for such works. So began the publication that did so much for Island tourism, *Vectis Scenery*. In his first full year (1821) he created images of twenty-three different views, and this from someone who, in a later work, said he was self-taught!

The quality of his etchings improved quickly and, by the time of his death, he had created 173 plates used in different editions of his 'magnum opus'. During his life he created nine other tourist-enticing publications although two of these appeared in only one edition. His work did much to advertise the Island as a worthy destination, helped, no doubt, by **Queen Victoria** (see page 121) and the Poet Laureate (see page 103) both choosing the Island as a place to live and relax.

From 1837, his publications become interspersed with contributions by two of his sons, first from Philip (1816–1877) and then Alfred (1815–1893). It was Alfred who took on the business until, in 1875, he was partially blinded in a tree-lopping accident. At this point Alfred's son, George (1848–1938), took up the baton. George was recalled from London where he had gone to live and work. It was this George who was the principal proprietor of the launch, in 1884, of the current Island newspaper, the *Isle of Wight County Press*. In this guise the family continued its close link to the Island until the death, in 1980, of Colonel Wilfred Brannon, the last male Brannon, and great-grandson of the original, Irish, George.

Bromfield, William (1801–1851)

William was born at Boldre, Hampshire and, after attending schools in Tonbridge, Kent, took an MD degree at Glasgow University in 1823. He travelled widely, visiting Egypt and many parts of the Turkish Empire as well as much of sub-Saharan Africa and the West Indies. In 1835 he and his sister settled in Ryde. William had become interested in Botany as a result of attending lectures in Paris given by the famous botanist Professor M Dumal. He began collecting examples of Island flora (though qualified as a physician, he never practiced medicine as he was of independent means) and became a member of the London Botanical Society in 1843. William discovered a number of previously unrecorded Island plants, the most significant being wood calamint (clinopodium menthifolium) found only in one limited area on the Island and nowhere on the mainland. His intention was to publish a book of all Island plants, but he died of fever in Damascus before it was ready, despite having laboured over it for fourteen years!

In 1852, his sister, Eliza (1794–1877), bequeathed over 600 botanical books from his library as well as his herbarium (a systematic collection of dried plants) to Kew Gardens. This herbarium had received plant samples from an eclectic mix of amateur botanists and others. Amongst these contributors were John Stuart Mill (1806–1895) the great 19th Century philosopher, and Alexander More (1830–1895) who later became the Curator of the Natural History Museum, Dublin. A duplicate copy of this very herbarium only very recently (2009) found its way to Hampshire County Council Museum Service.

In 1856, William's friends Dr Hooker, and the Ryde physician and amateur botanist, Thomas Salter (1814–1858), arranged for the posthumous publication of his book *Flora Vectensis*, and then, in 1871, Alexander More created an index for it as well as publishing *A Supplement to Flora Vectensis*. Eliza's donation of William's books and herbarium was the start of Kew Garden's library that now ranks as one of the most complete botanic-related collections in the world and is an important centre for worldwide botanic research.

Cheape, John (1792–1875)

Born at Rossie, Flintshire, John was educated locally and then went to the military college at Woolwich. He joined the Bengal Engineers (part of the East India Company) in 1809 as a lieutenant and, as a captain, oversaw the victory at the Siege of Multan. He was a colonel by 1844. His most significant achievement was in Burma when, in 1853, his tactical skill ended a fierce battle and brought the Second Anglo-Burmese War to a close. In the year he was knighted, 1854, John left the army and moved his family to the Island at Old Park, at the Undercliff. Still employed by the East India Company, he was promoted to general in 1866. Sir John died at Old Park, as did his wife, Agnes, two years later. Both are buried at St Lawrence.

Clark, James (1788–1870)

Though not resident for any significant period on the Island, James deserves inclusion because he was responsible for the Victorian growth of Ventnor. He was born in the village of Callen, Bamffshire, and attended a nearby grammar school. After some time studying arts, he realised his interest was medicine, and he transferred to Edinburgh University. The Napoleonic Wars interrupted his studies, during which time he worked at Haslar Naval Hospital and, on a number of fighting ships, as their surgeon until 1815. He graduated from the university in 1817. He then obtained a post as companion to a man who suffered badly from consumption, travelling with him to the South of France and to Rome in 1818. During these travels, he noted the effect of climate upon his charge and, when the man eventually died, James set up a practice in Rome. There he came to the notice of Prince (later, King) Leopold of Belgium. He returned to England in 1826 and continued to run a successful practice and published the influential *Influence of Climate in Prevention and Cure of Chronic Diseases* in 1829; made a Fellow of the Royal Society (FRS) in 1832, he published *A Treatise on Pulmonary Consumption* in 1835.

James first visited the Island in 1845 at the behest of **Queen Victoria** (see page 121) (she had appointed him as her physician on her accession to the throne in 1837, the year in which he was also knighted) as she wished to be assured of the healthy nature of the Island climate. Then, and during subsequent visits, he realised that the area around Ventnor had its own 'micro-climate'. The first edition of his 1829 work made no mention of the Island, but the second edition, in 1846, extolled the virtue of the Ventnor environs particularly. As prints of the area, by people such as Brannon show, at this time Ventnor was no more than a few fishermen's huts, a farm and a water mill. James's medical publications changed that and, for some fifteen years, building in the area was both very fast and also lacking in any overall plan. Not only did the Queen enjoy the Island, but also this particular area was very healthy! It also led to the establishment of the world's first purpose-built hospital for consumptives (see the entry for **Arthur Hassall**, Epoch 4, see page 114). Sir James retired to Bagshott Park, Surrey, in 1860; this property being a gift to him from the Queen. He died there after a short illness.

Clifford, Augustus (1788–1877)

This illegitimate son of the 5th Duke of Devonshire was born in Rouen, France, where his mother, Lady Elizabeth Foster (1759–1824), had an estate (the Duke married her some years later). After private education, Augustus attended Harrow School (1796–1799) and, despite his hereditary deafness, joined the Navy as a midshipman in 1800 under the auspices of Earl Spencer who, at this time, was First Sea Lord. He also enjoyed a sizeable annual endowment from his younger half-brother, the (legitimate) 6th Duke.

He had an eventful life, fighting in the West Indies and with the Navy in the 1807 Anglo-Egyptian War. He was knighted in 1830 and appointed Black Rod in 1832 (Black Rod is an officer of Parliament responsible for security in the House of Lords), a post he held for an unprecedented forty-five years until his death. Augustus served twice as MP for Brandon Bridge (as a result of support from the 6th Duke). By 1848 he was a rear admiral and, having purchased Westfield in Ryde in 1843 (this was the house built by Earl Spencer), settled his family there. Augustus became an Admiral of the Red in 1864 by which time he had ceased active life in the Navy. His service as Black Rod was exemplarary and much commented upon at the time. He died at his lodgings in the House of Lords.

Cochrane, Thomas (1789–1872)

Born to a Scottish naval family, it is no surprise that Thomas joined the Navy — only that he did so aged seven! By 1805 he was a midshipman aboard the 18-gun sloop, *Nimrod* and, through an act of flagrant jobbery by his father (who by then was an admiral and commander-in-chief of a fleet), promoted to captain of the *Jason* while he was still only seventeen.

He was active against the French, capturing one of its fleet and, later against the Americans at both Washington and Baltimore, shelling the latter. Whilst on the American station, Thomas was appointed the first governor of Newfoundland (1825–1834). After further service in home waters, he was posted to the China Seas where he was second in command (1842–1845) and was involved in heavy fighting at Nanking. Soon after his return to England, he was knighted (1847) and became C-in-C Portsmouth (1852–1855).

He married in 1853 and set up home at his recently acquired Quarr Abbey House near Ryde. Made Admiral of the Fleet in 1865, Sir Thomas lived at Quarr until his death there. His wife, Rosetta, lived on at the house until her death in 1901.

Crozier, Richard (1803–1880)

Like his father (Rawsom B Crozier, 1775–1849), Richard was born at Bombay as the family had close ties to the East India Company. He was educated at the Royal Naval College, Chatham and joined the Navy in 1815.

By 1823, he was captain of the elderly 38-gun, 5th rate frigate, HMS *Lively* and, by 1834, captain of the 18-gun cruiser-class, brig-sloop HMS *Victor*. It was aboard this vessel that he made his mark. He was clearly someone well commended by the Admiralty board because in 1835 he was sailing Asiatic waters making surveys in order to improve earlier charts. When, in 1836, he was sent to Fiji to investigate the murder of four British crew of HMS *Active* he took the opportunity to update charts of the islands. He also carried out important work charting Australian ports. When visiting, what was then known as, the 'Swan River Colony' in Western Australia, the sheltered waters off Granite Island were named Victor Harbour after his ship.

Richard returned to England in 1838 and in 1839 married Julia Stone (1810–1883) setting up home at the house purchased by his father around 1830, West Hill at Norton. Their children, Mary and Richard, were born there. He continued working for the Admiralty, mostly employing his keen charting skills and, at some point, was promoted to the rank of admiral. His father and his wife came to England around 1845 and took up residence, along with Richard and his family, at Norton. There, the whole family were of some significance, and many of them died at the house and are buried at Freshwater. The area around Norton is still called West Hill and there is a Crozier Road there.

Dabell, Alexander (1808–1898)

Island people will know the name of Dabell from the soft furnishing shop in Newport. The family moved to the Island around 1823 coming from Nottingham where the father, William (1782–1852), had been a master lacemaker. The move to Newport was in response to the rapid growth of Mr Nunn's laceworks there. After spending a short time in London, where he ran a shop, Alexander joined his family on the Island helping to run the family's shops in Newport, Sandown and Ryde. He married a local girl, Edith Pierce, in Newport in 1834. By 1841 (when money was tight after the failure of two Newport banks) he had sufficient means to buy land at Blackgang.

In a storm in 1842, a huge whale was washed ashore near the Needles. Alexander bought the carcass at auction, sold off the blubber for a tidy profit, had the bones bleached clean and then moved the skeleton to Blackgang. By a degree of landscaping, and making the most of the spectacular views, Alexander had created an interesting tourist attraction — one where you could walk inside a whale! This was the beginning of the Blackgang Chine park that did much to attract visitors to the Island. It is believed to be the very first such 'amusement park' in the world. Interestingly, the original parcel of land bought by Alexander is no more, having been subject to sea erosion, particularly in 1978. Subsequent land purchases have allowed the site to thrive.

In 1844, Alexander produced a small publication *Dabell's Handbook to the Isle of Wight*.

The family still retain ownership of the Blackgang site and, in 1995, opened another at Robin Hill near Arreton, having bought the land from the Fleming estate — Alexander's entrepreneurial spirit lives on!

Dawes, Sophie (1792–1840)

Sophie was the daughter of an oystercatcher who lived in St Helens (the house where she was born faces out over St Helen's Green and sports a blue plaque). Her father was also a successful smuggler and so, despite this humble background, the family initially lived in modest comfort. The heavy drinking of her father changed this and, despite trying to keep their heads above water, mother and children had to move into the Newport 'House of Industry'— the dreaded 'workhouse'! This certainly did not suit Sophie who, after a short while, escaped to Portsmouth and eventually, in about 1816, London.

She tried various ways to earn an honest crust: orange seller, actress, etc, and, by this time, had begun to attract attention by virtue of her very clear skin, dark eyes and well proportioned body. It was not long before she found herself in demand in a Piccadilly brothel (some writers have modestly suggested that she was simply a servant there). One visitor was a servant of the exiled Duc de Bourbon who was so taken by her that he arranged for her to visit Bourbon at his home.

Bourbon was totally smitten. His infatuation was such that he paid huge sums of money to have her educated at his home while he took full advantage of her presence there. To disguise his actions Bourbon introduced her to an officer of his guards, Baron de Foucheres. The Baron soon fell in love with Sophie and they were married in 1818 just as Bourbon had planned, Sophie becoming Baroness de Foucheres. As such, she moved easily through French society, dining regularly with such notables as Talleyrand.

On the death of his father, Bourbon assumed the title of Prince de Conde and was in a position of great authority. Baron de Foucheres, having discovered Sophie's relationship with Conde, first whipped her and then divorced her. Sophie then spent the next ten years making the ailing Conde, who initially would have nothing more to do with her, entirely dependent on her and effectively forcing the old man to create a will that would make his nephew his only heir, which eventually he did. This meant that Conde's vast wealth and estates would go to allies of Sophie who had already indicated to her how well she would be rewarded in such an event.

In 1830, finding Conde dead one day, just before he was to make changes to his will and the disposition of his vast estates, the authorities accused Sophie of his murder. She was tried and acquitted (but almost certainly helped to plan the death and, according to one servant speaking on his own deathbed, she was personally involved in it), and she soon left France, along with one of her Island family, James Dawes, who, through her contacts, had been given a position under Conde and had the title Baron de Flassons. He is now buried at St Helen's Church with a headstone arranged by Sophie.

She came back with great wealth, at least twelve million francs in cash and gold, perhaps the equivalent of £20 million today, as well as owning at least three large and valuable estates in France. She bought an estate in Hampshire for herself and another on the Island for her cousin, Edward. She also sent Foucheres one million francs, a huge sum in those days. He refused the money, passing it on to a relative.

The Island property she purchased was The Hermitage, on the hills above Chale Green. Edward's nephew, Lieutenant William H Dawes (1806–1863), who died at the house, was an officer in the 43rd Regiment of Foot; he enrolled in 1831 and served mostly in India, and it is entirely possible that it was he that was responsible for the addition to Hoy's Monument that stands in the grounds of the Hermitage. This William had also inherited sufficient wealth from Sophie to own nearby Wydcombe and Gotten Manors.

Sophie died at lodgings in London (this despite owning a house in Hyde Park Square) where she had gone to see her solicitor. It has only recently been established that she is buried in the old cemetery at Kensal Green. She left the bulk of her huge wealth to Sophie Thananron, the daughter of her sister, Catherine.

Dennett, John (1790–1852)

The Dennett family have had a long connection with the Island, and it is likely that John was born in the village were he lived most of his life: New Village, between Carisbrooke and Newport. After early private experiments,

John was able to demonstrate a rocket system for firing rescue lines to ships in distress. It is entirely possible that in some military role he was involved in the use of rockets in the fighting against Bonaparte in the Peninsular War (the 2nd Rocket Troop of the Royal Horse Artillery did just this in 1813, using Congreve War Rockets). There exists a record that in 1826, when the Newport Volunteers were disbanded, Ensign Dennett was presented with the regiment's colours as:

'He had last had the honour of bearing them in the field'

— was this the same Dennett?

By 1826, John was able to provide a very good demonstration of his system that led the authorities to create three rocket stations on the Island at sites where shipwrecks were more likely to occur.

The breakthrough came in early October 1832. The *Bainbridge*, having crossed from Canada, came to grief on Atherfield Ledge, a notorious graveyard for ships. The nearby Atherfield rocket station was able to land a line on her and all crew were saved. The captain and mate of the *Bainbridge* wrote, only a few days after (once they had recovered!):

'We hereby certify that the Bainbridge From Halifax for London was wrecked during the heavy gale on the night of the 7–8th inst., on Atherfield rocks, at the back of the Isle of Wight, that four attempts were made with Captain Manby's apparatus to throw a line over the ship, without success, owing principally to the great distance she lay from the shore. A rocket of Mr Dennett's invention was then fired, and at once carried a line to its destination in the most complete manner, although the position of the ship was most unfavourable for such a manoeuvre, as she lay end on, with her stern to the shore.'

The Norfolk born Captain George Manby (1765–1854) had developed the world's first means of throwing a line from shore to a ship in distress. It had severely limited range and was difficult to use in storm conditions though, in its time, it had saved many lives. His system was first used successfully in 1808 when it saved the lives of all on board the brig *Elizabeth* off the Norfolk coast. It employed a mortar shell system that, once fired, had no further driving impulse and so, as in the case of the *Bainbridge*, the line often fell short.

In 1833, during one of her visits to the Island and having heard about the *Bainbridge* incident, Princess Victoria attended a demonstration of John's rocket system at the Earl of Yarborough's estate overlooking the sea at St Lawrence, at the Undercliff. This *Bainbridge* report meant that all coastguard stations would be fitted with a rocket system, and, by the early 1850s, over 120 such stations had Dennett rocket facilities. The system saved a huge number of lives though Dennett does not appear to have been given any public recognition. John died at his home.

By 1865, even this system was overtaken, and the rocket system of **Edward Boxer** (1822–1897) (see page 106) came to the fore. These used a two-stage rocket but also had a long stick attached to provide better stability. Boxer retired to the Island around 1875 and he and his wife died in Ryde.

It seems entirely fitting that Islanders should devise a system for helping distressed ships that forms the basis of the system used around the world to this day.

Fellows, Charles (1799–1860)

Charles was born just outside Nottingham where his father was a wealthy banker and dealer in silk. He always had an interest in foreign travel and, in 1827, discovered the ascent route to the top of Mont Blanc still used to this day. His wide reading of classical texts such as that by Pliny led him to begin exploring ancient Lydia (now part of Turkey), and in 1838 he established a base at Smyrna. Very soon he discovered the ruins of the region's ancient capital, Xanthus. He published *A Journal Written During an Excursion in Asia Minor* in 1839 and, with limited help from the government, mounted another expedition to the area having obtained the Turkish governor's permission to remove various artefacts and ruins. Using his own wealth, he donated his materials to the British Museum, most notably the Nereid Monument. For his contribution to archaeological understanding of this area he was knighted in 1845. Charles's much-acclaimed book *Travels in Lycia* (1847) brought him public recognition and, in 1849, he retired to Cowes. He was active in a variety of local societies and took an active role in aspects of community work. Beginning around 1854, he privately paid for the construction of Marine Parade at Cowes, a row of large sea-front properties, he himself living in one he called Terrace House. He fell ill in 1860 and died that year in London. His daughter, Elinor (1849–1867), is buried at Northwood.

Fitzgibbon, Elizabeth (1793–1879)

Born near Haslemere, Sussex, where her father, Sir Peter Burrell, had an estate, Elizabeth married the 2nd Earl of Clare in 1826, becoming Countess of Clare. Her husband was active in government, serving in the House of Lords. In 1830 he became a Privy Councillor and then, in 1831, was made Governor of Bombay, a post he held until 1835. It is safe to assume that Elizabeth accompanied him to India. Soon after their return to England they purchased Appley House, just outside of Ryde. She used their huge wealth, first to build St Mary's Roman Catholic Church at Ryde (1841), then a primary school (1848). She was well known for her largesse — recovering from an illness, she spent several weeks in a hotel at Sandown and was so thrilled with the area that she paid for all the children at 'her' school to spend the day there.

In 1867 the Countess paid for the construction of a Dominican Priory close to Carisbrooke Castle and, when she died at her home, she arranged to be buried — some say in a glass coffin — in the grounds of the Priory.

Gassiot, John (1797–1877)

John was born in London and at the earliest opportunity, possibly around 1813, became a midshipman in the Royal Navy. At this time even midshipmen received huge rewards (upwards of £500, perhaps £25,000 in today's money) if they had served on a ship that successfully attacked an enemy and collected the worth of both the craft itself and any cargo. This may have been the source of the money that John needed to set up in business.

In 1822 he formed a company with the Spaniard, Sebastian Martinez, to import cigars, sherry and port from Spain, and the income from this company formed the basis of his substantial wealth. He became a well-known amateur scientist and was elected as a Fellow of the Royal Society (FRS) in 1840. Soon after this, he was appointed Chairman of the Kew Observatory and used his own money to develop its activities. He also served as vice president of the Royal Society four times.

At his home on Clapham Common, he established a well-equipped laboratory. Such were the facilities there that, during the late 1850s and early 1860s, the house attracted many researchers, the most famous of whom included William Grove, Michael Faraday and James Clerk Maxwell. John worked with these people, both investigating photography (with Grove) and electricity (with Faraday and Maxwell).

In a well-recorded experimental demonstration in 1858, John showed his audience the deflection of an electric discharge in a tube holding rarefied gas. He showed that both a magnetic field and an electrostatic field had the effect of deflecting the discharge. This was the earliest demonstration of these effects that now form the basis of cathode ray displays, though scientific literature credits others with this discovery. In 1863 the Royal Society awarded him their 'gold medal' for his investigations of voltaic cells, an early means of generating electricity.

In 1871, John purchased the St John's estate near Ryde as his family home. He lived there until his death but gave the property to his youngest daughter, Anne, as a wedding present in 1877. Much later, the Isle of Wight County Council bought the property and it is now the main building of Bishop Lovett Middle School, as was. Oakfield primary school nearby was once called Gassiot School. There is a memorial stone over the main entrance to that effect, the building having been paid for by John's son as a memorial to his father.

Hammond, Graham (1779–1862)

Born in London to a naval family, Graham joined the Navy in 1785 — that is, at the age of five and a half! He acted as captain's servant under his father's own command. As a twelve-year-old midshipman aboard HMS *Phaeton* he assisted in the capture of a number of French vessels and, as a junior officer, received his share of a large pot of prize money. That year, he served aboard

Earl Howe's flagship during the battle that was dubbed 'The Glorious First of June'. Graham also took a major role in the blockade of Le Havre (1798) and that of Malta (1799).

In 1804, he was captain aboard the 38-gun frigate, HMS *Lively*, when he captured three Spanish treasure ships, each laden with gold and silver. His prize money on this occasion was huge: the equivalent of two million pounds in today's money!

He married in 1806 (Elizabeth Kimber of Fowey, Cornwall 1786–1855) and, for a time, was invalided and moved his family to the Island, buying Norton Grange just outside of Yarmouth in 1810. He was promoted to the rank of rear admiral in 1825, soon after resuming his duties, then vice admiral and, finally, only some weeks before his death at Norton, Admiral of the Fleet. He became 2nd baronet in 1828 upon the death of his father, and in 1831 he was honoured by the award of KCB (Knight Commander of the Order of the Bath).

The house still stands and is now the centre of a holiday village.

Huish, Mark (1808–1867)

Born in Nottingham where he received his education at Mr Taylor's School, High Pavement, Mark joined the East India Company army as a cadet in 1823. By 1825 he was a lieutenant and, after serving on the staff of the Governor-General, was appointed quartermaster at Chittagong in 1830. This post provided Mark with a firm grasp of management, which at the time was not available by normal means.

He was on leave in England when he was promoted to captain, but this did not persuade him to return to India; instead, he was caught up with the railway mania sweeping the country. In 1837 Mark was appointed secretary to the small 'Glasgow, Paisley and Greenock Railway' and, using his established skill as a manager, began a series of company mergers, first with the Grand Junction Railway (1841), then the Liverpool and Manchester Company (1845), and finally with the London and Manchester Company (1846). He was made general manager of the overall group which, at the time, was the largest company in the world.

Mark's somewhat abrupt style of management made him enemies on the board and in 1858 he resigned his post and moved to the Island, living at Bonchurch. He was soon made a director of the Island railways as well as acting as an advisor to a number of Government enquiries. He died at his Bonchurch home and is buried in the village churchyard.

Hutt, John (1795–1880)

Born in London, John was the eldest son in a family of thirteen. After early education at the family home at Appley House, Ryde, he studied at Christ's Hospital and then Trinity College, Cambridge, from where he graduated in 1827. As the eldest son, John had inherited Appley in 1815 on the death of his father, Richard (1764–1815) but sold it to his younger brother, William, some years later. With this brother, he was involved in establishing the colony of South Australia but, in 1839, was appointed as the Governor of Western Australia.

It is said of his period of rule there that 'he saved the infant settlement from utter disaster'. This was the result of his reorganisation of the system of land grants that was being corrupted through greed. John also had a benign approach to the Aboriginal people, implementing a policy for their protection and, where possible, their education. This enlightened approach did not endear him to the European settlers! He resigned his commission in 1846 and retired back to England. After some years spent in London, he went back to live with his brother William at Appley House, where he died. All that remains of the house is Appley watchtower on the Eastern Esplanade out of Ryde; the site is now a small estate of houses.

Even now the area known as 'Hutt River Province' (named after John), some 500 miles north of Perth on the West Coast of Australia, is a significant entity. A few years ago the area declared itself an independent principality, issuing its own currency and stamps, in order to avoid what were seen as draconian limits on wheat production!

Hutt, William (1801–1882)

William was born in Lambeth, London, the second son of the family and was educated privately at his family home of Appley House, Ryde, like his brothers, John and George. He graduated from Trinity College, Cambridge in 1827 and soon married a Durham heiress, the sister of a college friend. He moved north with his wife and, through her family connections, became an MP, first for Hull (1832–1841) and then Gateshead (1841–1874).

William was very interested in the development of new colonies. He served on the Commission for the Foundation of Southern Australia (together with his brother John) and was an active member of the New Zealand Company, being personally responsible for the annexation of New Zealand to Great Britain. His first wife died in 1860, and in that year he was made a Privy Councillor, became Paymaster General to the Board of Trade and was knighted in 1865.

With his second wife, Frances, Sir William moved back to the family home at Appley in 1871 and retained this as his principal home until his death. His wife died at the house in 1886. The house remained in the family, William leaving it to his next brother, Sir George Hutt (1809–1889), who had fought in both the Afghan Campaign (1839–1844) and the Anglo-Persian War of 1856–1857.

The huge unspoilt area known as Hutt Valley, some twelve miles north of Wellington, recalls William's close involvement with New Zealand. It was part of this valley that was used as the location for many scenes in the recent filming for J R R Tolkien's *Lord of the Rings*.

Keats, John (1795–1821)

Born in Moorfields, London, where he went to school, John spent some years at Guy's Hospital studying to be a surgeon and becoming a licentiate of the Society of Apothecaries in 1816. In this year, he was named by Leigh Hunt, the editor of *The Examiner*, as one of the three most promising writers of their generation. In early spring 1817, John stayed on the Island, first at New Village (between Newport and Carisbrooke) and later, and for longer, at Shanklin. During this stay, he wrote the play, *Otho the Great: A Tragedy in Five Acts*, the poem *Lamia* and *The Eve of St. Agnes*. In addition to works that progressed during his stay, he wrote to a friend about the area around Shanklin:

> *'A most beautiful place, sloping woods and meadow grounds reach around the church, which is in a cleft between the cliffs to a depth of nearly 300ft at least. This cleft is filled with trees and bushes in the narrow part, and as it widens, becomes bare, if not for premises on one side, which spread to the very verge of the sea, and some fishermen's huts on the other, perched midway in the balustrades of beautiful green hedges along their steps to the sands — But the sea, Jack, the sea — this little waterfall-then the white cliff — then St Catherine's hill'.*

He died in Rome. His writing was to be a significant influence on later writers such as **Tennyson** (see page 103).

Leeson, Henry (1803–1872)

Born in Nottingham but educated firstly in Hammersmith, London and then Ryton School, Henry went to Caius College, Cambridge in 1822. He received his degree of MA in 1839 and then moved to Oxford, taking the degree of MD in 1840. That year he was appointed Professor of Chemistry and Forensic Medicine at St Thomas's Hospital, London where he spent his professional career, retiring in 1852. During this time in London (when he became a member of the Royal Society, 1849), he worked with Gassiot, and this work led him to develop a goniometer, a device for measuring the angles of crystal surfaces. It is still in use today, known as a Leeson prism, and it is this for which he is best known.

Around 1862 he moved to the Island (because Gassiot was here?) settling at a villa at Pulpit Rock, Bonchurch. The road connecting Bonchurch and Ventnor, Leeson Road, is a fitting memorial of this versatile man.

Letts, Thomas (1803–1873)

Born at Stockwell, London, the son of a printer for the Royal Exchange, Thomas joined his father's stationary business on leaving school. On his father's death in 1835, he took over control of this small company. Very quickly, he popularized the idea of a personal diary and, together with other work related to the legal profession, Thomas soon established a successful business. He set up home on the Island at Chale in 1857, buying Southview House (the property was destroyed in the 1994 landslip). By 1885, the original company was liquidated, but Thomas's son Charles had set up his own company, Charles Letts and Co. in 1881, and this company continued to thrive through the next century. Although now eroded by the landslides in the area, Thomas had built a shrine on the old road above his house in commemoration of the tercentenary of the birth of Shakespeare, what survived of this monument has since been moved to Ryde.

Thomas died at Blackheath, London, but two of his sons died at Chale, George in 1883 and Albert in 1918.

Maund, Benjamin (1790–1864)

The son of a farmer, Benjamin was born in Tenbury, Worcestershire. Details of his early education have not been found, but in 1806 he was apprenticed to a stationer/printer in Ludlow, Shropshire. He remained there until 1813 when, the very day his father was buried, he purchased a printing and bookselling business in Bromsgrove, Worcestershire. Benjamin married a local girl there (Sarah Green) in 1817 and started a family of three girls and a boy. He had an abiding interest in flowers and, by 1825, produced the first volume of *Botanic Gardens* a thirteen-volume work, dedicated to the new **Queen Victoria** (see page 121), the last volume of which appeared in 1850. Its publication brought him much acclaim and, in 1827, he was elected to the prestigious Linnaean Society. Many eminent botanists of the time were pleased to be able to be associated with the work; such was the regard with which it was held. He published a range of botanical works while in Bromsgrove, many of them hand-coloured by his daughters, particularly by Sarah (1818–1909). His wife died at Bromsgrove in 1857 and, shortly after this, Benjamin retired, leaving his thriving business in the hands of a friend. Along with his three daughters, he moved first to Leamington Spa, then Folkestone and finally, in 1861, Sandown.

He died in Sandown, as did the three girls, the last two dying in 1909. Besides the wonderful prints for which he had responsibility, Benjamin is also remembered for introducing the plant Ribes oxyacanthoides (wild gooseberry) to England.

Nunn, Henry (1799–1876)

Henry's father was a wealthy banker in Nottingham and in 1811 was approached by two men who had invented a new way to weave lace but who lacked the funds to develop the idea. Finance was forthcoming but on condition that, once Henry reached sixteen, he was to become a partner in the business. Lacemaking with the machine (a traverse warp machine) began in Tewkesbury, and in 1827 part of the company moved to the Island, setting up as 'Freeman and Nunn' at Broadlands House, Staplers, near Newport. Henry himself purchased Great Briddlesford Farm and the Lordship of the Manor of Wootton.

The company thrived, lodging a patent for making 'French blond lace' in 1833. This material was both very fine and expensive. It helped business enormously when, in the early 1850s, **Queen Victoria** (see page 121) made much use of this Newport lace. At the peak of production, Nunn's factory employed around 250 hands. It was to help this business that the father of **Alexander Dabell** (see page 84) came to the Island. With failing health, Henry closed the business in 1870 and sold both the site and equipment. He retired to Great Briddlesford where he died. His daughter Mary (1835–1897) inherited his wealth and estates and became a generous benefactress, both to Wootton, where she provided land and the money to build a church, and to other Island appeals. She died at her seaside home in Shanklin.

Peel, Edmund (1798–1877)

Born in Wandsworth, Edmund graduated from Cambridge in 1820. Little is known about his life other than he served in the army before moving to Ventnor in 1846 and had a level of independent wealth from his Lancashire mill-owning family, being also a first cousin of Sir Robert Peel (1st Baronet Peel). He wrote a number of books and poems such as *The Return* but is best remembered for his work *The Fair Island*, which is a lyrical, romantic poem linked (but not obviously) to most places of significance on the Island.

In 1855, for some years, his younger brother, Sir Lawrence, joined him at his home in Ventnor on the latter's retirement from the Indian Civil Service. Edmund died at his later home in Newport and is buried at Carisbrooke.

Peel, Lawrence (1799–1884)

Like his brother **Edmund** (see page 97), Lawrence was born in Wandsworth and, after local schooling, went to St John's College, Cambridge, graduating in Law in 1821. He was called to the Bar in 1824 and then spent time as a circuit judge in Lancashire (the Peel family had made their fortune in Lancashire as they owned substantial calico mills). He became advocate-general at Calcutta in 1840. He was knighted in 1842 and became Chief Justice of the Calcutta Supreme Court that year. Sir Lawrence retained this post until he retired in 1855 and moved to Ventnor to live with his brother until the latter moved to Newport. He was made a member of the Privy Council on his return and, from 1857, was a director of The East India Company.

In 1864 he became President of Guy's Hospital, London and, from 1857 until close to his death, Sir Lawrence was a regular correspondent for *The Times* on a wide range of legal matters. He died at his home, Garden Reach, in Ventnor. The name came, not from the location of the property but, from the name of the district in Calcutta where he had lived for so long.

Pelham, Charles (1781–1846)

Born in Lincolnshire at the family estate, Charles became 2nd Baron Yarborough when he was thirteen upon the death of his father. After graduating from Cambridge, his family connections allowed him to be elected MP for Great Grimsby (1803–1807) and then MP for Lincolnshire (1807–1823). Always a keen sailor, he was one of the group who, in 1815, met in London at the Thatched House Tavern to form a club for those interested in saltwater yachting.

One of the club's annual meetings was to be at Cowes, and races in the Solent soon attracted the interest of the Prince Regent who, in 1818, became a member and so began the royal link with Cowes. The club was now entitled to be known as the Royal Yacht Club (1820). Only in 1825 did the club begin to formalise its activities, electing Charles its first commodore that year. He had married the niece and heiress of Lord Worsley, and, upon the death of her mother, sister of Lord Worsley in 1819, Charles became the owner of the Island estate of Appuldercombe where he and his growing family lived six months each year. This marriage also meant he owned many other parcels of Island land, many of which he sold off. Although his yacht, the 351-ton *Falcon*, was the pride of the club's fleet (built by **Thomas White** at Cowes in 1815, see Epoch 2, page 70) he sold the yacht in 1835, some two years later obtaining the King's permission for the club to be renamed, yet again, to become The Royal Yacht Squadron.

In 1837, Charles was elevated to become 1st Earl Yarborough. His stewardship of the club soon made it the premier gentleman's club in England and the list of club members grew steadily and included much of the nobility and people of senior military rank. It was whilst cruising off Vigo, Spain, in his brigantine *Kestrel* that he fell ill and died.

Squadron members had a monument to his memory erected on Culver Down, near Bembridge. By his thoughtful leadership, Cowes became the world centre for sea yachting and the close link with royalty remained until the 1970s.

Rylands, John (1801–1888)

John was born in St Helen's, Lancashire, where his father owned a small mill producing cloth. After his education at St Helen's Grammar School, he joined his father and two older brothers in the business. He very quickly demonstrated his skill as a salesman, and the company began to expand. Rylands and Company soon owned mills in other Lancashire towns and when his brothers retired, and then his father died in 1847, John became the sole proprietor of the company, which, in its heyday, employed 15,000 people and produced thirty-five 'long tons' of cloth a day!

John was a very generous benefactor of many charities and, when the construction of the Manchester Ship Canal seemed to face a lack of finance, John purchased £50,000 worth of shares in order to ensure its success. He moved to the Island in 1882, building a home at Havenstreet and calling it Longford House, after his Lancashire property. John also provided the village with the Longford Institute (originally housing reading and smoking rooms); it later became a restaurant.

John died at his Lancashire home and is buried in the Southern Cemetery, Manchester. In his time he was the richest textile manufacturer in the UK.

Seely, Charles (1) (1803–1887)

The Seely family came to live on the Island from Lincolnshire in 1861. Originally they were flour millers, but ownership of land in Nottinghamshire, that was found to hold rich seams of coal, made their fortune. It contributed to the development of a wide range of Midland-based industries. Charles bought Brook House and, over a period of time, other properties and land so that, by the time of his death, he was the biggest landowner on the Island. He had been MP for the city of Lincoln and kept up his political activities into his early eighties.

Smith, Charles (1807–1890)

Born at Landguard Manor Shanklin, Charles was the youngest of a brood of ten and in his early years he went to live with his maternal grandparents (the Roach's) at Arreton manor. He attended a school outside of Winchester and, in 1820, another in Lymington. In 1822 he was apprenticed to a chemist, firstly in Chichester and then in London where he lived until 1860, having set up in his own business in 1834.

Charles (usually referred to by his maternal name, Roach) had always had a passion for Roman and early English remains and he spent most of his free time scouring the areas of London then undergoing rapid development, as the groundwork regularly uncovered items of interest. His particular interest was early coinage and he was soon recognised as an expert in the field, being elected to Fellow of the Society of Antiquaries (FSA) in 1836. His private collection formed the nucleus of the National Collection of Romano-British Antiquities. In 1854, he published a catalogue of the antiquities in the Museum of London and was a regular contributor on the subject of early coins to the renowned *Gentleman's Magazine* as well as being a founder member of the Society of Numismatics and the British Archaeological Society.

Charles moved to Strood, Kent, in 1864 with his elder sister with whom he had lived. They both died there, she in 1874.

Snooke, William (Drew) (1788–1857)

With most of his family living in Brading, and Newport, where he was born, William had his home in Ryde where he was a teacher of mathematics. His hobby was botany, and he is remembered as being the first person to attempt the creation of a complete record of Island plants. In 1823, while still living in Newport, he had a small book published in London, *Flora Vectiana*. Although it provided information on more than 250 species, it strangely omitted some common ones that would have been present. He recorded sighting the rare cottonweed (Otanthus maritimus) that could not be found by later botanic searches. His wife Mary died at their Newport home in 1848. Soon after this he moved to Ryde.

Suffering from bronchitis, William died at his Ryde home and is buried in the cemetery there.

Spencer, George (1758–1834)

Born to a noble family at Wimbledon Park, Surrey, George had his early education privately until 1770. His tutor was the erudite Sir William Jones. He then attended Harrow School followed by Trinity College, Cambridge, from where he graduated in 1778. At this time, his father also owned Althorpe Estate in Northamptonshire and, by 1780, after returning from a two-year grand tour, George was elected MP for the borough. He withdrew from this position and became MP for Surrey in 1792.

His father died in 1783 and George became the 2nd Earl Spencer. His time as an MP was unremarkable, but he clearly made his mark because, returning from an abortive diplomatic mission to Vienna, the Prime Minister Pitt made him first Lord of the Admiralty in 1794 as well as making him a Privy Councillor. Despite having no knowledge of the Navy, George undertook a far-reaching reorganisation of the service and, perhaps most significantly, appointed capable commanders, amongst them, Jervis and Nelson (but he wasn't overawed by such people — George took Nelson to task because of the latter's long dalliances with Lady Hamilton whenever he visited Naples, where she lived at the time). He was concerned about technological innovations and did much to improve the work of the naval shipyards as well as being an early patron of the engineer Marc Brunel.

He was replaced as First Sea Lord in 1801 but continued to have an interest and influence in government until near his death. He bought land near the sea at Ryde and in 1808 had his marine residence built there, Westfield House, where he lived for three months each year; a location that allowed him to observe flag signals and ship movements in and around Portsmouth. As a result of his early private education, George had an abiding interest in early books, and, at one time, his library of over 40,000 volumes was the largest in Europe. Earl Spencer died at the family home, Althorpe, and is buried in a nearby village.

Stephenson, Robert (1803–1858)

Son of the George Stephenson, of railway fame, Robert, too, was a major contributor to the development of railways around the world. He became a member of The Royal Yacht Squadron (RYS) in 1850 after being 'black-balled' at his first attempt. His yacht was *Titania* and was unusual in that it was of iron construction rather than the usual wood. In 1851 he was asked to race his craft against the American-owned *America* for the 100-guinea Gold Cup on a course around the Island. He lost, and the cup was renamed The America's Cup some years later (this because of the name of the winning yacht, not because of the yacht's country of origin). Whenever he sailed he lived on board his boat and was a regular visitor to Cowes as, for the years up to his death, he attempted to win back the cup he had forfeited. His son George (1829–1905), named after his famous grandfather, continued the family engineering business, building railway systems in many parts of the Empire. He too became a member of the RYS in 1860. His yacht was a cutter, the *St Lawrence*, which was built at Cowes by Michael Ratsey. He was far more involved in the life of Cowes than was his father, living for the greater part of the year at Grantham House in the town. He is best remembered for his gift to the town of 'The Green' between the RYS and Egypt point.

Symonds, William (1782–1856)

This elder son of a naval captain was born in Bury St Edmunds where he received his early education. He joined the Navy in 1794 and was a lieutenant by 1801, having served during the Spithead Mutiny. From 1819 until 1825, he served as captain of the ports of Malta and, on his return to England, took out a lease on a Yarmouth property that had been the home of Captain John Urry and here set up home with his second wife, Elizabeth (1772–1851).

William had little interest in naval promotion but preferred boat design. Using a generous legacy given to his wife (!), he designed and built a number of craft, culminating in the corvette *Columbia*. In sailing trials in 1827 this craft demonstrated superiority over all others, and in 1831, through political machinations by some of his friends, he was asked to design a 50-gun frigate. So successful was this craft that, in 1832 when the Navy Board was abolished, William was appointed surveyor to the Navy.

He held this post until 1847 and in his time was responsible for 200 wooden sailing ships, each of a design that ensured British mastery of the sea. During this period he was made a member of the Royal Society (FRS, 1835) and knighted (1836). It was the advent of steam power and, more particularly, of propellers that signalled the end of his supremacy as wooden hulls could not withstand the strain of propellers. Made an admiral in 1848, he retained this rank until 1854 and, after the death of Elizabeth at their home in Yarmouth, he spent much of the year in Italy because of his declining health. Sir William died at sea off the coast of Sardinia and is buried in Marseilles.

Tennyson, Alfred (1809–1892)

Born in Lincolnshire, Alfred left Trinity College, Cambridge, in 1831 on the death of his father without completing his degree. He had begun writing poetry as early as 1830. These early attempts were not a great success but a revision of his earlier work, completed in 1840, established his reputation, and the elegy *In Memoriam* (1850), which mourned the death of his close friend Arthur Hallam, was his major poetic achievement. In that year he became poet laureate.

He first rented a house at Freshwater and, in 1856, purchased the property. This was the house, Farringford. It was during his time there that he wrote works such as *Maud, The Charge of the Light Brigade* and, in 1862, *Idylls of the King*, which was in memory of Prince Albert. So taken by this work was **Queen Victoria** (see page 121) that she arranged the first of her audiences at Osborne House with Alfred that year.

The public could not see enough of the somewhat retiring Alfred and he found that, whilst living at Farringford, tourists interrupted his solitude, so he and his wife began to split their time between Farringford and Aldworth, his other home near Haslemere, Hampshire. Few of his works relate directly to the Island, but *In the Garden at Swainston* was in memory of his Island friend Sir John Simeon (1815–1870), who had lived there. His total output of works was enormous yet he only accepted a baronetcy in 1884 after intercession by the Queen herself. Lord Alfred died at Aldworth and is buried in Poet's Corner, Westminster Abbey.

Wilberforce, Samuel (1805–1873)

Born at Clapham Common, London, Samuel attended Oriel College, Oxford, graduating in 1826. He was ordained in 1828 and given the living at Brighstone in 1830. He held this post until 1839. He quickly became significant, first by his appointment in 1841 as Chaplain to Prince Albert, and then in 1847, as Lord High Almoner to **Queen Victoria** (see page 121). He is best known as Bishop of Oxford, for his confrontation with the philosopher Huxley, over the Darwinian theory of evolution — a debate that he lost. While he lived at Brighstone, Wilberforce's father lived with him — none other than William Wilberforce (1759–1833), the man who had done so much for the emancipation of slaves. It was while he was Bishop of Oxford that Samuel returned to the Island to consecrate the newly built All Saints' Church in Ryde.

Interestingly, various rectors of Brighstone church became bishops over the years. This is why the public house in Brighstone has been, for many years, called The Three Bishops; these three were:

> Thomas Ken (1637–1711), Bishop of Bath and Wells (1667–1669)
> George Moberley (1803–1885), Bishop of Salisbury (1869–1885),
> Samuel Wilberforce, Bishop of Oxford, (1844–1873).

However, a fourth bishop seems to have been overlooked, **John Stokesley** (see page 37), who was Rector of Brighstone from 1518 until 1524. He was Bishop of London (1530–1539) and played a major role in freeing England from the domination of Rome. If the public house in Brighstone is ever renamed perhaps it should be called 'The Four Bishops'?

EPOCH 4, 1810–1830

Adams, William (1814–1848)

Born in St Pancras, London, the son of a judge, William entered Eton in 1826, and then went on to Merton College, Oxford, from where he graduated with an honours degree in Divinity in 1836. After further studies, he was appointed as vicar to St Peter's, Oxford. Together with lecturing fees he obtained, this stipend allowed him a comfortable degree of life. His Oxford lectures were soon summarised under the title 'Sacred Allegories'.

An ill-advised session of swimming in cold water near Eton gave him a life-threatening infection that led William, by 1842, to vacate his Oxford living and move to Bonchurch in 1843. He had already established himself as someone of note through *Sacred Allegories* (1842), so his series of lectures and other publications created whilst he rented the house known as Winterbourne were well received. By 1843 he knew he was dying, but he kept up his flow of work, most famous of which, perhaps, is *The Old Man's Home*, which contains many references to scenes of the Undercliff, an area of the Island of which William was most enamoured.

His last works were in collaboration with his neighbour **Elizabeth Sewell** (see page 124) and her brother, Rev. William Sewell (1804–1900), who jointly wrote stories for *The Sketches*, the proceeds from which helped establish the village school. He died at his home and is buried at Bonchurch.

Adams, William Davenport (1828–1891)

Born in London, the son of a naval captain, William was privately educated. He did not attend university and, when old enough, he gave private lessons, mostly teaching English. He married at Kensington in late 1850 and, very soon afterwards, moved to the Island, settling in Ryde and began work as a newspaper editor, most probably for the *Isle of Wight Observer*, which was first published at Ryde in 1852.

He was a prolific writer; his first notable work being *The History, Topography and Antiquities of the Isle of Wight* (1856) which became so successful it was reissued in 1877 and again in 1884. He wrote guides for Kent and Surrey and, in all, produced over 150 books covering a wide range of topics. William left the Island in 1870, moving to Scotland, where he founded and edited another newspaper, *The Scottish Guardian*. In 1878 he moved again, settling in Wimbledon where he died.

Boxer, Edward (1822–1897)

See the entry under **John Dennett** (see page 86) in Epoch 3.

Browne, Samuel (1824–1901) VC

Born at Barrackpore India, Browne was the son of an army surgeon and so, unsurprisingly, in 1840 he enlisted in the Indian Army. He was a captain by 1858 when he lost his left arm in some hand-to-hand fighting. In this skirmish, part of the Seeporah Mutiny, he and his men were able to prevent the reloading of insurgent's 9lb howitzers that were trained on advancing British infantry. His VC was gazetted that year. He was knighted in 1871. After a life spent in India, he moved to the Island in 1898, with the rank of general upon his retirement from the army.

The loss of his left arm made his use of his officer's sword cumbersome. It has been suggested, but disputed by others, that soon after the loss, he began to use a specially-designed belt to help him. It became known as 'The Sam

Browne Belt', initially only used by those that had known him in the Indian campaigns. It soon came into wider usage and became normal wear for officers. Sir Samuel died at his home in Ryde and is buried in the cemetery there.

Cambridge, Daniel (1820–1882) VC

Born in Carrickfergus, Ireland, Daniel spent his life in the British Army. He spent six years in Malta followed by seven in Canada (1846–1853). He became a celebrity as a result of amazing courage when fighting in The Crimean War, serving at Inkerman and the Redan. He had attained the rank of sergeant and won a VC (Victoria Cross). The London Gazette printed the citation:

> *'For having volunteered for the spiking party on the Redan, Sept 8, 1855, and continuing therewith, after being severely wounded and for having, in the after part of the same day, gone out in front of the advanced trench, under heavy fire, to bring in a wounded man, in performing such service, he was himself severely wounded a second time'.*

He received the VC from **Queen Victoria** (see page 121) herself at the very first investiture in Hyde Park, in June 1857. After serving some time back in Ireland, he was moved to the Island. Here, as master gunner, he was stationed at the Redoubt Battery, Freshwater, from 1868 (he appears in the 1871 census). In November of that year, he was awarded the rare privilege of being appointed to the Sovereign's bodyguard (Yeoman of the Guard). In 1880, he was recalled to service in London. He died at Plumstead, London, where he is buried.

Although the VC was created in 1857 it had been agreed that it should be awarded retrospectively for bravery in the Crimean War specifically to embrace such cases as this.

Cameron, Julia Margaret (1815–1879)

Born in Calcutta, Margaret moved to the Island in 1860 and lived at a house she renamed 'Dimbola' Lodge; this being the name of the family tea estate in Ceylon (now Sri Lanka). The family originally moved to London from Ceylon in 1848 and she quickly became part of the Kensington artistic community. This group included such notables as **Alfred Tennyson** (see page 103) and **George Watts** (see page 128). Her friendship with Tennyson was such that, in 1860, she was invited to his Farringford home near Freshwater.

Staying nearby, at the rented home of the artist George Watts, were members of the Prinsep family to whom she was related and with whom she had connections from her time in India and Ceylon. (Henry Thoby Prinsep had been a high court judge in the Indian Civil Service and had married Margaret's sister Sara; they later settled in Freshwater.) She was so thrilled with the area that, before she returned to London, she purchased two adjacent cottages near Freshwater Bay, added a tower, and so was born Dimbola Lodge.

By this time, her children had married and left home and her husband was often abroad. By 1863 she was thoroughly bored until her daughter, sensing this, bought her a camera and all the necessary chemicals that would enable her to create, and then develop, her own photographs.

Margaret threw herself into this novel (as it was then, particularly for a woman) activity but much of her early work was of poor quality. Her friendship with Tennyson gave her the opportunity to photograph him, and soon she was in demand for photographic portraits. The final accolade came when she was asked to go to Osborne and photograph **Queen Victoria** (see page 121).

Interestingly, it was at Dimbola Lodge that Virginia Woolf's parents first met, as Cameron and Woolf's mothers were related. It is a result of this link that Woolf wrote her only play, *Freshwater*, set mainly at Dimbola as it was in 1864. The house is now a museum dedicated to the remarkable Mrs Cameron.

At the height of her public acclaim in 1875, Margaret and her husband Charles left England to return to the family estates in Ceylon (they took their coffins with them!) She died there after a few years.

Clifford, Charles (1821–1895)

This third son of **Admiral Augustus Clifford** (see page 82), Charles was educated at home in Ryde before attending Charterhouse School and then Christ Church College, Oxford, from where he graduated in 1843. He was called to the Bar in 1846 and became MP for the Island, 1857–1865. He lived at the family home, Westfield, Ryde (the property built by Earl Spencer). After the reorganisation of the electoral system in 1865 he successfully stood as MP for Newport and retained this post for fifteen years. In his time he served diligently as private secretary to Lord Palmerston while the latter became Foreign Secretary, then Home Secretary and, finally, Prime Minister. Charles became the 4th Baronet Clifford on the death of his father in 1893. He died and is buried in London.

Coster, Guillaume (1826–1909)

Born in Amsterdam, Guillaume moved to London in 1848 as the representative of his (then) well-known diamond-cutting family. His claim to fame is that he alone had the responsibility of overseeing the cutting of the famous 'Koh-I-Noor' diamond, then the largest diamond in the world. Always a difficult task, this one was horrendous. Not only was the whole world watching but also, because the diamond had been given to **Queen Victoria** (see page 121) her consort, Prince Albert, took a keen interest in the work that began in 1851. Guillaume's planning managed to increase the 'brilliance' of the stone but did so by reducing its weight from the original 186.4 to 105.6 carats. He became world famous as a result as well as already having significant wealth.

Although he continued to oversee the family's London business, he purchased a shepherd's cottage and several acres of land in Shanklin in 1874. On the site of the cottage, but keeping one of its walls, he built Upper Chine House and had the grounds landscaped. The Dutch oak staircase that, along with a fireplace set with Delft tiles, is still to be found in the house and recalls his Dutch roots. He and his wife Edith regularly opened both the house and its grounds to the public to the benefit of local charities. Guillaume died at the house in 1909 and Edith lived there until her death in 1913. Both are buried at St Blasius Church, Shanklin. Soon after her death the house was sold and in 1914 was established as Upper Chine Girl's School.

Edwards, Edward (1812–1886)

Born to a bricklayer's family in London, little is known about his early life but for the fact that his local vicar, recognising his ability when Edward was about eighteen, gave him a pass that enabled him to use, what was then, the only free library in England, the British Museum.

By 1836 he was creating pamphlets on a range of subjects: universities, the British Museum and the Royal Academy among many others. His pamphlet on the British Museum created much interest and, in 1838, it led to him being appointed as an assistant in the printed book department. His monumental *Memoires of Libraries* eventually led to him working with William Ewart in the development of the Public Libraries Act (1850). As a result of this work, he was asked to become the Head Librarian of the first 'free library' in Manchester when it opened in 1852.

Edward stayed in Manchester until deafness forced him to retire and he took lodgings at Niton in 1879. Whilst there, he continued writing, including items for *Encyclopaedia Britannica* and even recast and improved his *Memoires of Libraries*. Unfortunately, he fell into arrears with his rent and was unceremoniously evicted! The local vicar took him in and he lived with the vicar's family until, out walking one bitterly cold day, he failed to return and was found on top of St Catherine's Down, suffering from frostbite. Though he survived this, it ultimately led to his death some months later. He was buried at Niton in an unmarked grave and only in 1902 was a monument added in recognition of the major role he had played in the creation of public libraries.

Fox, William (1813-1881)

Born to a family who farmed around the town of Mollom, Cumberland, William entered St Bees Theological College in 1835 (which closed in 1871).

He was ordained in 1843 and spent some years as a priest in Lancashire towns.

In 1862 he was appointed curate at Brighstone, living at Myrtle Cottage, not far from the shore. His move to the Island was doubtless inspired by his growing interest in palaeontology (possibly triggered by the work of Canon Buckland who, in 1829, described the first ever discovery of reptilian material found at Yaverland Point. Only in 1847 was this material named Iguanadon by Gideon Mantell in his *Geological Excursions Round the Isle of Wight*). William took every opportunity to beachcomb, looking for fossils, possibly to the detriment of his priestly duties. In his searches he was very successful and his possible dereliction of church work may be behind the Church's reason for relieving him of his living at Brighstone in 1867. He was in regular contact with luminaries such as Sir Richard Owen and Mantell and, during his searches, was responsible for a number of important discoveries, some of which were named after him, such as Iguanodon foxii.

He remained on the Island, and in 1875 was appointed as curate of Kingston, near Shorwell. From here, he continued his paleontological work until late 1880 when he left the Island. His considerable collection of over 500 specimens was acquired by the Natural History Museum in 1882.

The Island owes a debt of gratitude to Buckland, and particularly to Fox, for establishing the Isle of Wight as one of the world centres of dinosaur finds!

Gore-Browne, Henry (1830–1912) VC

Born in Ireland, Henry joined the army in 1846 and was posted to India. In 1857, he was a captain and charged with assisting the defence of the city of Lucknow. During the battle, the heavy guns of the insurgents were causing considerable damage to the defences of the Residency (that is the building or compound where the representative of the Queen resided). Gore-Browne was asked to lead a spiking party to stop the guns. With a small group of volunteers, he broke into the enemy battery, incapacitated their heavy weapons and killed over 100 of the enemy. His VC was gazetted in 1857. He remained in India until, in 1879, when retiring with the rank of colonel, he took the post of 'land agent' to the extensive Seely family estates on the Island.

In 1882 Henry married Jane, the sister of **Sir Charles Seely (1)** (see page 99), continuing his work as land agent. In 1886 he was honoured further by being made the Deputy Governor of the Island. He died in Shanklin hospital and is buried at Brook.

Gray, Valentine (1812–1822)

Valentine was born in Alverstoke, Hampshire and was brought up in the workhouse there. His parents were, needless to say, wretchedly poor and he was 'sold', aged eight, to a chimney sweep master in Newport, Benjamin Davies. Valentine died after cleaning a chimney at a house in Pyle Street, Newport (his malnourished and beaten body was found in an outhouse there), a site now marked with a blue plaque. There was a local outcry at the child's death and, eventually, Davies and his wife were jailed. Despite the imprisonment of his master, the outcry continued, so much so that the issue reached Parliament.

The MPs were slow to act; after all, they all had large houses, each with numerous chimneys — and all needed regular cleaning! Eventually, in 1840, an Act was passed, 'the climbing boys act', with the intention of banning the practice. Despite this, young boys (and girls) continued to be exploited and die. The original Act was ineffectual, as the penalties imposed by the legislation were derisory.

The publication of *The Water Babies* by Charles Kingsley in 1862, a story concerning the little sweep 'Tom', caused a great deal of public disquiet and led, in 1868, to a new set of legislation that banned the use of any climbing sweep under the age of twenty-one and, in 1875, a total ban on the practice.

Kingsley had written:

> *'(Tom) cried when he had to climb the dark flues, rubbing his poor knees and elbows raw, and when the soot got into his eyes, which it did every day of the week, and when his master beat him which he did every day of the week, and when he had not enough to eat, which happened each day of the week likewise.'*

Of Tom's master, Kingsley wrote:

'He lived in a great town in the North Country, where there were plenty of chimneys to sweep, and plenty of money for Tom to earn and his master to spend.'

There can be very few children whose short life finally brought about a major change of law and of public understanding that subsequently was of benefit to untold thousands who would have faced the same fate as Valentine.

Hadfield, Octavius (1814–1904)

Born at Bonchurch, where he received his early education as well as during his family's extended continental tour (1818–1824), Octavius was a sickly child, suffering from debilitating asthma. He went to Charterhouse School in 1829 and then Pembroke College, Oxford, in 1832 intending to join the priesthood. However, the regular attacks of his asthma meant he had to leave after only one year, returning to the Island to recuperate.

Octavius joined a missionary society in 1836 and was posted to New Zealand, arriving in 1839. There, despite having no degree, the bishop ordained him as a priest (he was thus the first person in New Zealand to be so ordained). He learnt Maori and soon became a close friend of local chiefs and became the major link between them and the Governor. In 1870, Octavius was made Bishop of Wellington, and in 1890, Primate of New Zealand, a post he held until his retirement in 1893. He died at his home at Edale, near Wellington, where he is buried.

Hartnall, Ebenezer (1814–1880)

The son of a pastor who had made his mark in Ipswich, Ebenezer was born in Portsmouth where he was apprenticed to a printer/publisher. He moved to the Island in the early 1840s setting up as a publisher, and in 1844 married a local (St Helen's) girl. That year he began the publication of *The Isle of Wight Miscellany*, but it lacked popular appeal and failed in 1846. Soon after this he moved to London and worked as secretary to the Hall of Commerce until

1858 when he returned to Ryde. For the next ten years he acted as editor of the *Isle of Wight Mercury* with some success. Around this time he was tried for libel at Winchester Crown Court and found guilty. The effect of this on his health was profound and he never really recovered from the shock, dying shortly afterwards. Ebenezer has been called the 'Father of IOW Journalism'.

Hassall, Arthur (1817–1894)

Arthur spent the early part of his career in Dublin and London. His particular field of interest was the study of the adulteration of food. He became well known for uncovering cases of malpractice and did so through good use of a high powered microscope as he admitted to 'having no Chemistry.' A significant event was his ability to diffuse an argument, then raging in Parliament, concerning the adulteration of coffee by the addition of Chicory. His work on food led to the 1860 Food Adulteration Act.

As a sufferer from tuberculosis, Arthur first visited Ventnor in 1866 as a direct result of **Sir James Clark's** (see page 81) report on the healthy nature of the locality. He made rapid improvement whilst there and this so caught his imagination he founded The National Hospital for Consumption and Diseases of the Chest, in 1867. After a campaign of fundraising, building began at Ventnor in 1869 with the Princess Louise (daughter of **Queen Victoria** (see page 121)) laying the foundation stone. It was visited by many luminaries and was declared a model for cottage hospitals, its design being copied in many countries. Patients included such notables as Karl Marx, **Alfred Tennyson** (see page 103) and Charles Dickens.

Arthur remained working in Ventnor, building a microscope laboratory in his home and regularly submitting his findings to scientific journals. He was also used as an 'expert witness' in court cases. For example, in 1876, he provided the petty sessions at Newport with his analysis of a sample of tea. A Miss Winifred Long of Calbourne was accused of supplying tea that had been adulterated with a range of materials. Hassall's certificate showing that, indeed, the tea was not pure was all the court needed to convict her. This disgrace may have contributed to her death the following year.

He remained as consultant physician to the hospital (given the appellation 'Royal' in the 1870s) until he retired in 1877. His life-long tuberculosis gradually got the better of him and he moved to warmer climes at San Remo where he died.

The hospital continued to provide palliative care to many hundreds of sufferers until the advent of appropriate antibiotic treatments. It closed its doors in 1964 and was demolished in 1969. Finally, Ventnor Town Council took over the site and it is now the Ventnor Botanic Gardens.

Hawkins, Thomas (1810–1889)

Born to a wealthy family, John lived at Sharpham Park, a 300-acre estate near Glastonbury, Somerset. He received his early education locally and by 1831 became a surgeon's pupil at Guy's Hospital, London. This clearly was not to his taste as, by 1833, he was back at Sharpham. This was the time when Mary Anning of Lyme Regis was establishing herself as a major fossil finder.

Realising that Sharpham was in an area of blue lias stone and doubtless, having found fossils there in his youth, Thomas began fossil hunting in friendly rivalry with Mary. He proved to be very successful, locating a number of complete Ichthyosaur skeletons. These he sold for considerable sums to the British Museum, the first collection in 1834 and the second, in 1840.

About 1860 he left Sharpham and travelled widely, always on the lookout for more fossils. Around 1875 he settled in Ventnor, perhaps attracted to the Island's south coast by the many reports of finds of dinosaur skeletons there. He died at his home in Ventnor and is buried at Bonchurch.

Hellyer, Thomas (1811–1894)

Little is known about Thomas's early life, particularly information about his training as an architect. He was born at Emsworth, Hampshire and came to the Island around 1838 on the advice of his brother Phillip who was a banker as well as postmaster for Ryde. Thomas set up business in Ryde and quickly attracted work. In all, he designed several Island houses as well as five Island churches:

Ryde Holy Trinity (1840),

St John's Oakfield (1841),
St Peter's Havenstreet (1842),
Binstead — a rebuild (1843),
St Saviour's Shanklin (1860).

He also designed Ryde County Hospital (1847), demolished in 1995, and the Royal National Hospital, Ventnor (1867), demolished 1969. He was also responsible for many buildings on the mainland, some as far away as Leeds. This busy man also designed the pavilion at the end of Ryde Pier as well as the pier's ornate railings.

Both Thomas and his wife, Harriet, died at Ryde, she in 1889 and Thomas five years later. Both are buried at Ryde.

Knight, Henry (1820–1895)

It is unclear where Henry was born but it has been suggested it was the south coast town of Worthing. He arrived in Ryde in late 1850. That he was wealthy is evidenced by his purchase of the Union Street Arcade there in 1856. His principle business was as an importer of fine Italian marble (at this time many grand houses were being built on the Island, as titled families needed a home close to the Queen's retreat at Osborne). In this, he enjoyed modest success, but his claim to worldwide fame rests with him having invented, and patented, the tin opener that, in its many forms, is now an everyday kitchen utensil. He sold the rights to the patent to Cross and Blackwell who, at the time, were Europe's largest producer of tinned goods. He seems to have made little profit from this transaction and by 1871 was a member of Ryde Town Council. He was a disputatious character and made many enemies on that body. His enemies were doubtless delighted when, in 1890, he was declared bankrupt, forcing him to sell the arcade. He died, and is buried, in Ryde.

Leith, Robert (1819–1892)

Born in India, Robert joined the Bombay Fusiliers as an Ensign in 1837. By 1845, he was a captain and, in 1849, led a storming party at the Siege of Multan. In this engagement he lost his left arm as well as suffering other serious injuries. He served in the High Command during the Indian Mutiny (1855–1859) and, during his later service in India, regularly took leave at the family home in Scotland. Immediate neighbours were the Gordons with their Scottish estate. Here he met the daughter of the house, Mary (1841–1926, grand-daughter of **Sir James Willoughby Gordon** (see page 47)). They married in 1865 at St Peter's Church, Shorwell. At this time, the Gordon family had inherited the Northcourt Estate and Mary lived there with her father, Sir Henry, son of Sir Willoughby.

It seems likely that when Robert had to return to his duties in India, Mary remained on the Island. It was this Mary who, as a young girl of seven, had befriended the eleven-year-old **Algernon Swinburne** (see page 148) when he was staying with the family of the Rector of Brook whilst being coached for a place at Eton. (The Swinburne and Gordon families were related, Mary Gordon/Leith was Swinburne's cousin, their mothers being sisters.) In 1917, Mary wrote *The Boyhood of Algernon Swinburne*, recalling many incidences in Algernon's early life.

Robert was promoted to full general in 1881 and retired back to Northcourt around 1886 by which time he had inherited the title of Lord Burgh. He and his wife played a significant part in the life of the village of Shorwell and did much to restore Northcourt House and its gardens. Mary gave the village money to establish and run a 'non-provided' primary school — that is, one that was not supported by County or other funds — and made her butler and his wife the school's first teachers! She lived on at the house after Robert's death, herself dying in 1926. Both are buried at Shorwell.

McDougall, Francis (1817–1886)

Born in Sydenham, London, Francis moved to Malta where his father was captain of the 88th Regiment. In 1835, he began his studies at the University of Malta, and then moved to King's College, London. There he trained as a surgeon, becoming a member of the Royal College of Surgeons in 1839. Thomas then moved to Magdalene College, Oxford and took holy orders in 1845. (Whilst he was at Oxford, he was a member of the winning Oxford 8 in the 1842 Boat Race.) Soon after this, in 1848, he and his wife Harriet accepted a missionary role and arrived in Sarawak. The local 'White Rajah', Sir James Brooke, gave him a swathe of land for construction of a church and hospital. Francis was appointed the first Bishop of Labuan and Sarawak in 1849, a post he held until 1868.

Husband and wife had a difficult time: not only did all four of their children die but regular wars interrupted their efforts. (In 1862, Francis wrote an account of a sea battle in which he was involved, and had it published in *The Times*.)

Both returned to England in 1868 and Francis was given a number of church posts until, in 1874, he was made Archdeacon of the Isle of Wight. By 1885, Francis was also Rector of Mottistone and Shorwell and they appear to have lived at Mottistone. Harriet died in 1886 and that year Francis moved to Winchester where he died and is buried. He was probably the only bishop who was also a surgeon!

Midlane, Albert (1825–1909)

Albert was born in Carisbrooke shortly after the death of his father. He attended schools in Newport and began work with a local printer, finally setting up in business as an ironmonger. He was deeply religious and a keen member of the Congregational Church but finally joined the Plymouth Brethren. He soon developed an interest in hymns, writing his first when he was only seventeen! (1842). His best known hymn, from a life's output believed to be around seven hundred works, is *There's a Friend for Little Children*, which was first published in 1859.

He would not accept payment for his hymn writing and, being a guarantor for an impecunious friend, became bankrupt. The Sunday School Union, which employed many of his hymns, together with donations from around the country, provided him with the money to annul the bankruptcy and also generate a small annuity for him and his wife. Albert died in Newport and is buried at Carisbrooke.

Ommanney, Erasmus (1814–1904)

Erasmus was born in London to a family with close ties to both the sea and to the Royal Navy. In 1826 he joined the Navy aboard the 74-gun frigate HMS *Albion*, captained by his uncle.

It was as a thirteen-year-old midshipman aboard HMS *Albion* that he took part in the famous naval Battle of Navarino (1827); the port is now known as Pylos (Greece). This was the last major battle between sailing ships: those of England, France and Russia successfully attacking those of Egypt and Turkey. The victory soon led to the Turkish evacuation from, and independence of, Greece. The Turkish commander's flag had been captured in this engagement and, as a matter of honour, the flag was passed from officer to officer as each died, in order of seniority. Erasmus, only thirteen at the time but nonetheless an officer, was the last to receive it. Before he died, he presented this symbol of oppression to the King of Greece.

Erasmus later served on the expedition to find evidence that would explain what happened to the ill-fated voyage of Sir John Franklin in his search for the Northwest Passage. He was personally responsible for finding the few clues that indicated that the expedition had found a winter refuge. In 1868 he was elected as a Fellow of the Royal Society (FRS) in recognition of the studies he had undertaken in the Arctic. In 1871, he was knighted in recognition of this earlier Arctic work. On his retirement as an admiral in 1875, he bought a property in Yarmouth overlooking the sea and lived there for some twenty-eight years (a road in the town is named after him). Sir Erasmus died at his son's home in Southsea, Portsmouth.

About 1840, Erasmus had served as an officer aboard the 36-gun frigate HMS *Pique* that was a ship renowned both for its officer's strict adherence to rules and for their brutality to the crew. It gave rise to a long sea shanty, the first verse of which runs:

> 'Oh 'tis a fine frigate, 'La Pique' is her name,
> And in the West Indies she bore a great fame
> For cruel bad usage of every degree,
> For like slaves in a galley we ploughed the salt sea'.

Parr, Harriet (1828–1900)

Harriet was born at York, one of six children. The unexpected death of her father in 1840 left the family destitute, and Harriet began work as a servant at a boarding school in the town in exchange for her education. She tried, unsuccessfully, to write poems but, in 1853, sent the draft of her first novel, *Gilbert Massenger*, to Charles Dickens. He was so impressed he arranged a publisher for her. As was often the case at this time as a woman, Harriet wrote under a male-sounding pseudonym, Holme Lee. The book was an immediate success (1855) and was quickly translated into French and Italian. This in turn led to lecture tours on the continent and a steady income. Harriet used this money in 1857 to buy a house she called Whittle Mead, just outside of Shanklin, on the Godshill Road. She lived there the rest of her life, taking on a local girl who became her devoted servant for forty years. It is where she did most of her subsequent writing.

Some of Harriet's works, such as *Her Title of Honour* (1870) were serialised in a number of magazines and this brought her work to the attention of an even larger audience. Many of her works concerned various imaginary lands or fairies. Her last work was *Loving and Serving* (1883) and, in total, she published over thirty novels as well as contributing to many magazines. She died at her home among all her cats, and she is buried at Shanklin.

Ponsonby, Henry (1825–1895)

Having served as a General in the Crimean War, Sir Henry served as **Queen Victoria's** (see page 121) Private Secretary from 1870 until his death. He met his wife at Court and the two were bound closely to life at Windsor, and then later, Osborne. This became quite onerous when, on the death of Prince Albert, the Queen made it difficult for government ministers and foreign dignitaries to meet with her. Henry's consummate skill in handling others made life (and business) at Osborne run smoothly during this period. Whenever the Queen resided at Osborne House, Henry and his wife Mary lodged at Osborne Cottage. He is best known both for the design of the Albert Memorial in London but also for his implementation of The Ponsonby Rule. This meant that Command Papers — that is, Government papers issued at the command of the Queen — had to sit before Parliament for a specified time, usually twenty-one days, before being ratified.

In 1883, he was pivotal in the establishment of the Royal Red Cross medal for army nurses. It was to be bestowed upon:

> 'any ladies, whether subjects or foreign persons, who may be recommended by Our Secretary of State for War for special exertions in providing for the sick and wounded soldiers and sailors of Our Army and Navy'.

King George V added the words 'or our Air Force', and it was later amended to include male nurses. The first recipient was, inevitably, Florence Nightingale and the second, an eighteen-year-old nurse, Sister Janet Wells (for service in 1879).

Unusually, Henry also acted as the head of the Queen's private office, Privy Purse, from 1878 on the death of the holder of that post, Sir Thomas Biddulph. Henry was, without doubt, the Queen's most trusted courtier, and when he died even the taciturn Queen was seen with tears in her eyes. The Queen's eldest daughter, speaking to her own daughter, said:

> 'Henry had been Grandma's right hand in so many things, and I do not know how she can replace him'.

Sir Henry died at Osborne Cottage and was buried at Whippingham Church.

Queen Victoria (1819–1901)

Victoria's first visit to the Island was for six months in 1831 when, as a twelve-year-old, she stayed with her mother (the Duchess of York) at Norris Castle. At the time, the castle was empty as the result of the death of the owner, **Lord Henry Seymour** (see page 66).

John Nash (see page 58), well known to the Royal Family, saw his opportunity and arranged for the Duchess and her daughter to attend the inauguration of St James's Church that he had just designed as a place of worship for East Cowes. It was Princess Victoria's first public engagement as she was asked to lay the foundation stone. The family stayed at Norris Castle again in 1833 by which time Victoria was becoming attached to the area.

Once Victoria became Queen in 1837 she asserted herself, to the extent of making her dominating mother live apart from her. Soon after her marriage in 1840 to Albert, Prince of Saxe-Coberg and Gotha, it became clear that there was no Royal residence suitable for their rapidly growing family. (Buckingham Palace had been a very expensive venture and, at this time, did not look out over a pleasant park as it does now, but faced a mass of squalid tenement buildings). She visited Norris again in 1843 as it was for sale but was unable to meet the asking price. Instead, Victoria took a lease (with an option to buy) on the next-door Osborne estate. After some haggling with the owner, Lady Blachford, over the price, Osborne was hers.

Although some sections of the original house were retained, Prince Albert, with the help of the architect and builder Thomas Cubitt, completely transformed the property, adopting the Italianate style. It was ready by mid 1846 and the Royal Family were regular visitors.

Prince Albert was also responsible for the rebuilding of Whippingham Church (the Nash building of 1813), and the restoration of the estate next door to Osborne, Barton. (This manor house was used by the Queen as 'overspill accommodation' for Osborne and was used, for example, by later Royals to house the Russian Royal Family, when they visited the Island in 1909). Osborne soon became the effective centre of the Empire on the death of Prince Albert in 1861. His death, soon after the death of other family members, made Victoria withdraw to Osborne where, for some weeks, she would meet no one, even eating all her meals alone. It was 1872 before Victoria really faced the public by going to a thanksgiving service to celebrate the Prince of Wales' recovery from an attack of typhoid that had killed some of his staff.

For over ten years, with some breaks on the mainland, the Royal Court had had to come to Osborne, and the business of government was conducted effectively but at some distance from Parliament. It also meant that most of the members of Europe's royal families visited Osborne, most doing so on several occasions.

The Queen died at Osborne. In an attempt to honour the terms of her will, King Edward VII offered the house to various members of the family, but no one wanted it. In the end, it was given to the nation. By 1903, at the insistence of Admiral Sir John Fisher, grounds at Osborne were used to build a college for training officers for the Royal Navy. It retained this function until 1921 when the college was closed. The staterooms of the house were thrown open to the public in 1904 as were part of the grounds. A large section of the main house was also used as a convalescent home for injured military officers. It retained this latter function into the 1990s even though the rest of the house was open to the public. Osborne House is now managed by English Heritage.

Rickard, William (1828–1905) VC

Born at Devonport in Devon, William was a quartermaster serving on board HMS *Weser* in the Crimean War in 1857. He was part of a small reconnaissance party charged with destroying an enemy food store, some miles inland from the area known as 'the Putrid Sea' (the Sea of Azov). They did this successfully, but the blaze they started alerted nearby soldiers and they came under heavy musket fire as they retreated. One of the seamen was badly wounded, and William, still under fire, retrieved the man and carried him over two miles, through deep mud, back to the ship. He received his VC while still on active service; the ceremony being carried out on board the *Weser*.

William retired to Ryde around 1864 where he became chief officer of the local coastguard station from 1865 until almost 1890. He died at his home and is buried at the town cemetery, Ryde.

Seely, Charles (2) (1833–1915)

Son of the first **Charles Seely (1)** (see page 99), this Charles continued the political involvement of his father, serving as a Liberal MP for the Island and initially used Brook House as a holiday home. He was knighted and also became a baronet.

Starting in the village of Brook, where he lived from 1875, Sir Charles began a lending library service but soon came to realise that the need for such a facility was Island-wide. He made a generous donation to begin just such a library service, based in Newport.

Living in Brook he was often reminded of the dangers presented to shipping by the nearby coast and, having a great deal of local influence, was instrumental in forming lifeboat stations at both Brook and nearby Brighstone. He died at Mottistone and is buried there.

Charles's second son, Frank, lived at Brook Hill House, one of the many properties built by Charles. It is this house that, much later, was owned by **Samuel Rowbotham** (see page 176), and then by the writer **J B Priestley** (see page 171). It was the third son, **John (Jack)** (see page 176), who became the most celebrated member of the family.

Sewell, Elizabeth M (1815–1906)

Elizabeth was the third daughter of a family of twelve born in Newport where her father, James, was a solicitor. She went to a local school until she was thirteen and then had two years 'of poor education' in Bath. Aged fifteen, she returned to Newport to help with the education of her younger three sisters. This formed the basis of her lifelong interest in the education of middle class girls based on strict Christian principles. Through her brothers, Henry (1807–1879) and William, she met members of the 'Oxford Movement' that was to colour her life's work. (This Henry became a solicitor and emigrated to New Zealand (1852–1875), becoming its first Prime Minister — if only for seven days. Another brother, Edward, became Warden of New College, Oxford, and was instrumental in the setting up of Radley College.) Through her father's contacts, the family were allowed to have an extended stay at Northcourt during much of 1835; the house being owned, but not occupied, by General Gordon.

The failure of two Newport banks in 1840 and 1842 led ultimately to her father's death in 1842, plagued by debts. By now, Elizabeth had begun writing; her first work, *Stories Illustrative of the Lord's Prayer* (1840) was a huge success, possibly more so in America, and it established her name there. In 1845, an American visitor to the Island told her that her book *Amy Herbert* had sold over 10,000 copies! On the death of her father, the family moved to Henry's home at Pidford (a house she clearly disliked — and not the

Georgian-style house with that name, but the much older cottage behind it) and, as Elizabeth's publications became popular, she and her sisters moved to Bonchurch, first renting, then in 1852, buying the house next door to Captain and Lady Jane Swinburne (Elizabeth later renamed her house 'Ashcliffe'). Her writing was in demand, and she generated a stream of works:

Amy Herbert (1844),
Gertrude (1845),
Margaret Percival (1847),
Laneton Parsonage (1848),

as well as a series of school textbooks, some twenty-seven publications in all. Her two-volume novel *Ursula* (1858) draws heavily on the topography of the Island where, thinly disguised, are descriptions of The Hermitage, Niton, Chale and Newport.

During her life, she travelled widely, particularly on the continent. Her friendship with the Swinburnes was such that they took her (along with Algernon) with them on a trip to the Lake District where she met Wordsworth.

In 1852, while still writing, Elizabeth, along with her elder sister Emma, opened a school for young ladies at their home in Bonchurch. Not only did she draw on the earnings from her publications but was given an unconditional gift of £500 by their neighbours, the Swinburnes (by now he was an Admiral), such was their close friendship. It was in this period that, particularly in America, her methods were widely copied such that she was seen as a latter-day 'Hannah More' as far as the education of girls was concerned.

In one of her works written at this time, 'The *Experience of Life*' (1853), she argued that girls should be prepared for a useful home life rather than a career! The school was a success, finally only closing its doors after nearly forty years.

After about 1870, her publications began to lose their appeal, and after the death of Emma, in 1897, she effectively withdrew from society, living with her remaining sister, Ellen, who also predeceased her. In her last years, Elizabeth received financial help from some of the many girls that had passed through her hands. She died at her home and is buried at Bonchurch.

Sewell, James (1810–1903)

This older brother of Elizabeth was also born in Newport and received his early education there. He went to Winchester School in 1821 and then New College, Oxford, where he obtained his degree of BA in 1832. He remained at the college fulfilling a range of posts until, in 1860, he was awarded the degree of Doctor of Divinity and made Warden of the College. James held this post until his death in his lodgings there. During his wardenship, the college moved from being one of the smallest colleges, open only to pupils from Winchester School, to become one of the largest establishments.

James was appointed University Vice Chancellor (1874–78) and was the first person to be secretary of the Oxford local examination delegacy. He is buried in the college cloisters.

Smith, Christopher (1817–1892)

Christopher was born in London and spent his career as a successful banker. He was deeply religious and, while still young, came under the influence of George Williams. This wealthy draper was appalled at the working conditions of young men and, in 1844, convened a meeting above his shop near St Paul's Churchyard, London, to plan ways in which their lot might be improved. This meeting was attended by, amongst others, Christopher, and the group of young men set up the Young Men's Christian Association (YMCA), an association whose intention was to provide 'support, accommodation, spiritual enlightenment and education'. YMCA associations quickly spread around the country and, through the activities of the London association during the Great Exhibition (1851) in London (in which Christopher played a major role), this soon led to associations being formed around the world.

Christopher retired to Bonchurch around 1875, continuing his links with the association and published a number of religious tracts. He is buried in St Andrew's churchyard in nearby Ventnor. His wife, Edith, continued to play a role in the management of the national YMCA movement until her death at their Island home in 1926.

Tancred, Henry (1816–1884)

Henry's father was the 6th Baronet Tancred and had a summer residence at Egypt House near Cowes where Henry was born. He attended the Godshill Free Grammar School and then Rugby School. He next appears in 1848 as an officer in the Imperial Austrian Army, serving in a regiment of Hussars and seeing much action fighting various renegade groups. Badly wounded when he fell off his horse, he returned to England to recuperate and there became interested in the Canterbury Association of New Zealand. He resigned his Austrian commission in 1850.

That year he moved to Christchurch, New Zealand, buying a large area of land. In 1856, he was appointed to the Legislative Assembly and in 1866 became Speaker of the Assembly, a post he held until 1876 when the provincial government was dissolved. He had had an abiding interest in education, working in support of Christ's College, Christchurch and, in 1859, was appointed Professor of History there. He died at his home and is buried at Christchurch.

Tombs, Henry (1824–1874) VC

Born at sea while his parents were returning to India, where his father was major general of the Bengal Cavalry, Henry entered the East India Military College in 1839. He was commissioned into the Bengal Artillery in 1841 and was soon involved in fighting the Gwalior Campaign (1843) and The First Anglo-Sikh War (1845). He enjoyed rapid promotion and, during the 'Indian Mutiny', his bravery was rewarded with a VC (1857). The commander wrote of him, 'The hero of the day was Henry Tombs, an unusually handsome man and a thorough soldier...'

By 1858, Henry was a Colonel and that year was praised by Lord Panmure, Secretary of State for War, in the House of Lords. He became a major general in 1868 and in the same year was knighted. Ill health forced his early retirement in 1872, and that year Sir Henry retired to Newport. He is buried at Carisbrooke.

Venables, Edward (1819–1895)

Related to the famous ecclesiastic family, Edward was born in Queenhithe, London, where his father (later to become Lord Mayor of London, 1826) was a papermaker. He graduated from Pembroke College, Cambridge, in 1845 and became Curate of Herstmonceux, Sussex, until 1853 when he moved to the Island where he had been given the living of Curate of Bonchurch. He lived there, at the house now known as Bonchurch Manor Hotel, until he left the Island, though his curacy only lasted from 1853–4. He was very active in Island church affairs until he was appointed Canon at Lincoln Cathedral in 1864. He is remembered not only for his *Guide to the Undercliff* (1867) but as the foremost authority of his time on church architecture. His classic *Episcopal Palaces of England* was published a year after he died at Lincoln.

Watts, George Frederick (1817–1904)

Born in Marylebone, George had very little formal education, it being limited partly through family poverty but exacerbated by frequent absences resulting from his poor health. He entered the studio of the sculptor William Behnes in 1827 having already demonstrated a remarkable skill at drawing. George studied intermittently at Royal Academy schools from 1835, having his first exhibition in 1837. Patronage by a number of wealthy middle class families enabled him to establish his practice as a portraitist when, in 1842, he won an important art competition; the cash award of £300 allowing him to travel to Italy.

In 1851, he moved to a London house owned by his friends, Thoby and Sara Princep (Sara was sister to **Julia Margaret Cameron** (see page 108) the photographer). Sara once said of him, with some exaggeration:

'He was invited for three days and stayed 30 years'.

(He stayed for twenty-four!)

There, he was an attraction at Sara's artistic 'salon'. It was whilst staying here that he met, and became firm friends with both Edward Burne-Jones, the Pre-Raphaelite artist, and the poet, **Alfred Tennyson** (see page 103). Another visitor to the salon was the sixteen-year-old actress, Ellen Terry.

(Interestingly, Ellen Terry's very first stage appearance was on the Island, at Ryde.) So taken by her was George that they married in 1864, only to separate a year later (but did not divorce until 1877). Ellen Terry visited the Island with him as indicated in her memoirs. Not only does Ellen appear in a leaded window in Freshwater church but also Virginia Woolf, in her comedy play *Freshwater* has her (as George's wife) as one of the people to be found at Julia Cameron's house, Dimbola Lodge. In 1867 George was elected to the Royal Academy.

In 1871, George purchased land in Freshwater and had a house built for his friends, the Princeps. The Briary, as it was called, was completed in 1873. This allowed him to spend the winter months with them as well as his other friends, the Tennysons and the Camerons, both of whom lived near-by. He used local celebrities for some of his paintings. In 1867, **Algernon Swinburne** wrote:

> *'It is a great honour for me to be asked to sit for him,*
> *now that he accepts no commissions and now paints*
> *portraits for only three reasons- friendship, beauty and*
> *celebrity.'*

Not only was George considered by many as one of the greatest English portrait painters but many of his historically-themed works, mostly large murals, will still be found in public buildings such as the Palace of Westminster and Lincoln's Inn.

With his second wife, he built a home, complete with a gallery, at Compton, Surrey, and this now holds many of his works. The Watts Gallery there recently received a valuable cash injection to ensure its maintenance. In 1902, George was awarded the prestigious Order of Merit (OM), being among the inaugural twelve recipients of the honour awarded personally by the King. George died at Kensington.

EPOCH 5, 1830–1865

Battenberg, Prince Louis (1854–1921)

This German prince was born in Gratz, Austria, and was part of the influential family that ruled the state of Hesse. This gave him a strong link to the English Royal Family and they helped him to join the Royal Navy in 1868, an action that also conferred British nationality. In 1884, he married Victoria, his second cousin and a granddaughter of **Queen Victoria** (see page 121). Louis served on a wide range of vessels — and travelled the world! By 1891, he was a captain and served aboard the massive HMS *Dreadnought* as part of the Mediterranean fleet. It is claimed that, in 1892, Lillie Langtry bore him an illegitimate daughter — a story given some credence by payments he made to the mother. He was a vice-admiral by 1907 and his very real skill in a wide range of naval matters saw him promoted to First Sea Lord in 1912. It was becoming clear at this time that trouble with Germany was looming, and Louis took important measures to strengthen the Navy. Despite his very real and applied skill, the rising anti-German sentiment of the country forced the government to demand his resignation from such a senior post and he complied in 1914, just before war was declared. In 1917, in an attempt to distance himself from his German roots, he changed the family name to Mountbatten and disposed of all the German titles that he held. The King honoured him by creating Louis 1st Marquis of Milford Haven and Earl of Medina.

Louis moved with his family (which included his son, another Louis, later to become Lord Mountbatten) to Kent House in East Cowes, which, up to this time, had been a 'grace and favour' house, part of the Osborne estate. He lived there for the duration of the war, only leaving in 1919 at which time he also retired from the Navy. He died in London.

Black, Frederick (1863–1930)

Born in Newport where he attended the (old) Newport Grammar School; in 1880 he entered the Civil Service by competitive examination. Frederick was particularly concerned with the Navy branch and was of sufficient seniority that, in 1915, he was given the vital wartime post of Director General of Munitions Supply, a position he held until 1919. That year he resigned from the Civil Service, was knighted in recognition of his wartime efforts and then took a degree in English at London University. Long before this, Frederick had an abiding interest and skill with the language and made his mark as a poet.

Upon graduation, Sir Frederick began a business career in London which only ended in 1928 when he returned to the Island, living at Carisbrooke. While still only seventeen he achieved the remarkable feat of rowing around the Island (about seventy miles!) in one evening. He is buried at Carisbrooke where there is a monument to him. His daughter Dora became well known, being the second wife of the philosopher, Bertrand Russell.

Cahill, John (1841–1910)

Though an Irishman, John was born in London and there he received his early education at St Edmund's College (1855–1863). He attended Old Hall Seminary and, in 1864, was ordained. He was made Curate of St Mary's, Ryde, in 1866 and, on the death of the priest there in 1868, was made Rector, a post he held until 1900.

John had worked closely with Elizabeth, Countess of Clare, both in building Island schools and the Carisbrooke seminary, and this may have played a part in John's elevation to become Bishop of Portsmouth (1900–1910), somewhat unusual for someone who had only served in one church. He is buried at Ryde Cemetery. His memorial in St John's Roman Catholic Cathedral, Portsmouth, has an incorrect year (1919) for his death.

Calthorpe, Somerset John (1831–1912) see also his son, Arthur Gough-Calthorpe (Epoch 6, page 164)

Born in London, Calthorpe joined the army as a cornet in the 8th Hussars in 1848. He was a lieutenant by 1851 and became ADC (aide-de-camp) to Lord Raglan during the Crimean War. During that conflict, he fought at the battles of Alma, Balaclava and Inkerman and at the Siege of Sebastopol. He was promoted to full colonel by 1859 and lieutenant general by 1892. He moved to Ryde in 1889, to the house, Woodland Vale, that he had purchased in 1869, and was soon elected as the first chairman of the newly formed Isle of Wight County Council, a post he held for eight years until 1898. He was made a Companion of the Bath (CB) in 1905 and, in 1910, succeeded to the title of Lord Calthorpe on the death of his elder brother. He died at his home in Ryde where there is a monument to him in St John's Church. The road between Ryde and Seaview is named after him.

Cayzer, Charles (1843–1916)

Charles was the son of a schoolmaster and born at Limehouse, London. Always intrigued by the ships busying around the port of London, it is little surprise that he soon joined the British-India Steam Navigation Company as its shipping agent at Bombay in 1861. By 1868 he was 'Master of Stores' for the whole company. He left their employ in 1877 and set up his own company in Liverpool selling ship's stores. This was so successful that, in 1878, Charles joined with a Captain Irvine, establishing Cayzer, Irvine and Co. and began the Clan shipping line, serving businesses in India and South Africa. By 1914, this company operated sixty-two steamers.

Charles became MP for Barrow-in-Furness (1892–1906), was knighted in 1897 and made a baronet in 1904. That year, he moved to the Island, buying the Old Park estate on the Undercliff. It was one of his daughters, Florence, that married **John Rushworth (Earl Jellicoe)** (see page 135) and who later came to live at the Undercliff.

Cayzer, Irvine and Co is still to be found on the Island but now deal with estate management.

Cottle, Ernest (1847–1919)

The Cottle family came originally from Somerset, and Ernest followed his father into the medical profession, completing his MD degree at Oxford in 1868 and winning first prize at the Army Medical School, Netley, in 1871. He took up the appointment of surgeon to the Scots Guards until 1877, when pressure of private practice forced him to resign his commission. He became a Harley Street specialist dealing with skin disorders and was the author of a number of medical works as well as being consultant dermatologist at St George's Hospital, London.

In 1870 his uncle, the vicar of Shalfleet, died and bequeathed Ernest Ningwood Manor and several hundred acres of surrounding land. Ernest let the estate until 1911 when he retired and then took up residence there until his death. In his will, he left the whole estate and most of his wealth to the Royal Society for Prevention of Cruelty to Animals (RSPCA) on condition both that his wife Sarah was allowed to remain in the house (she did so until she died there in 1932) and that the land and other buildings were to be used as a rest home for retired horses and ponies. He also paid for the building of four Almshouses nearby. The estate fulfilled these functions (except for the duration of the war) until 1975 when the RSPCA sold the whole estate. The Wyndham Cottle charity (Wyndham was Edward's middle name), part of the RSPCA, still maintains a rest home for retired horses at Milton Keynes.

Cowper, Frank (1849–1930)

With his origins uncertain, Frank clearly had training as an architect, as this was the business that allowed him, at the early age of thirty-four, to buy land at Wootton and design and build his own house, Lisle Court (that is, in 1883). However, it is not for his architecture that he is remembered but for being a trailblazer in the art of single-handed yacht cruising.

At this time, the 1880s, yachting was very much a sport of the wealthy who used craft that needed numerous members of crew, so to do so in (smaller) yachts that could be handled by one person was seen as unusual. In 1914, Frank was one of the earliest members of The Cruising Association and he made good use of his Island home. He was the author of a number of books, each of which is viewed as a classic: *Yachting and Cruising for Amateurs*, and *Sailing Tours* among them. He was a regular contributor to the *Smallcraft* magazine. He died at St Cross Hostel, Winchester.

De Vere Stacpoole, Henry (1863–1951)

A member of an aristocratic Irish family, Henry studied medicine at London University. His first posting was as a ship's surgeon, and in this role he visited most parts of the world. He began his writing as early as 1894 with *The Intended*, but his first work that relied on his travels was *Crimson Azaleas* (1907), which was set in Japan. His most famous work was *The Blue Lagoon* (1909). Henry moved to the Island in 1922, buying East Dene in Bonchurch, the old home of the Swinburne family, and where **Algernon Swinburne** (see page 148) had spent most of his childhood. There followed a spate of publications including, *In a Bonchurch Garden* (1937), his autobiography *Men and Mice* (1942), and the sea adventure, *Cruise of the Kingfisher* (1947). In all, he was responsible for over forty novels as well as translations of medieval French poetry (*Poems of Francois Villon* of 1456 is just one example).

Such was the success of his story *The Blue Lagoon* that it was made into a film three times, in 1923, 1949 and 1980. When his wife, Margaret, died in 1934, he donated Bonchurch pond to the village, in her memory (there is a plaque to that effect at one end of the pond), and in 1938, at Newport, married her younger sister, Florence. Henry died on the Island and is buried at Bonchurch.

Harrington, John (1837–1908)

The early history of John has yet to be uncovered, but he was born in Great Baddow, Essex. By at least 1870 he was living in Ryde where, in 1872, his daughter Agnes was born. On her birth certificate, he records himself as a 'Patentee' suggesting that, even as early as this, he earned his living through inventions. He established a small factory there producing cycles (the Penny-farthing variety) as cycling was becoming popular (even as late as 1894, tourist guides to the Island, such as that of M J Baddeley's, included maps designed to help cyclists). He had the foresight to send one of his 'Arab' cycles to the 1876 Expo in Philadelphia. There, the cycle came to the attention of Colonel A Pope, who came to England and met John, and subsequently imported some cycles to America. This was the beginning of the American cycle craze that lasted two decades, Col Pope setting up his own manufacturing business. In this, John can claim to have initiated the American cycle industry. By 1881 John was living in Kensington and, in that year's census, was recorded as a 'Cycle manufacturer' employing thirteen men and two boys.

His connection with the Island ended when the site and contents of his Ryde cycle works was auctioned in 1902. John and his wife, Eliza, retired to Brighton in that year, and he died and was buried there in 1908. One of the few known examples of an 'Arab' cycle can be seen in the Petersfield Museum.

Jellicoe, John Rushworth (1859–1935)

Born in Southampton where his family were iron and brass founders, John joined the Royal Navy in 1872 at Dartmouth and first saw active service during the 1882 Egyptian War. Made a commander by 1892, he was second in command of HMS *Victoria* when, as a result of the fleet admiral's obstinacy, she was rammed and sunk by HMS *Camperdown* off Tripoli. As a captain in

1897, John helped lead the land relief of Beijing during The Boxer Rebellion. By 1908 he was a rear admiral and was responsible for the construction of a new class of battleships — the 'Dreadnoughts'. Churchill (then First Lord of the Admiralty) promoted him to full admiral in 1911 and also gave him command of the renamed Grand Fleet.

His greatest moment came at the Battle of Jutland in 1916 when the British fleet under his command drove that of the Germans to disengage. This left the British with effective control of the sea for the rest of the war. It was this victory that propelled him to become First Sea Lord (1916).

Of Jellicoe, Churchill had written:

> *Jellicoe was the only man on either side who could lose the war in one afternoon'.*

This strange compliment was a way of saying that if John had made even one small miscalculation, then the potential damage would be irretrievable and lead, ultimately, to a German victory.

When his war service had finished, he was offered the post of Governor-General of New Zealand, a position he held with great honour (1920–1924). On return to England, he moved with his family to St Lawrence Hall, near Ventnor that had been the summer home of his wife's parents (before marriage, she had been Florence Cayzer (1875–1964), a member of the Cayzer ship-owning family). In 1925 he was created Earl Jellicoe. He became the first President of the British Legion from then until 1930. St Lawrence Hall was often thrown open to the townsfolk of Ventnor, and Jellicoe was a significant member of the local community. He died in London and his statue stands in Trafalgar Square, London.

Lemare, Edwin (1865–1934)

Born and educated in Ventnor, where his father was a church organist, Edwin won a scholarship when only thirteen years old, allowing him to study the organ at the Royal Academy, London. While still young, he built up a reputation as a supremely competent organist, touring far afield to Australia and Canada. He became Professor of Organ at the Royal School of Music in 1892. Edwin finally settled in America and was considered the most highly paid organist of his day. Few of his compositions are ever played today, but a version of one, written in 1892, is *Moonlight and Roses*. He died in America and in relative poverty.

Long, William (1839–1896)

Although born illegitimately at Calbourne, William took his mother's name and, when she left home to marry, he lived there on his grandparent's farm. He attended Calbourne National School where the Rector, Rev. Hoare, recognising his talents, provided him with extra tuition in return for work in the rectory gardens. He also secured William a place at Winchester Diocesan Teacher Training College in 1858, but William left within a year. He became an itinerant bookseller in Devon and, whilst living there, married Elizabeth Eustace, a local primary school teacher in 1863. A few years later, he worked as a bookseller's assistant in Bristol and by 1880 was established as a bookseller in Portsmouth.

During this time he had been collecting material for his first work, *Dialect of the Isle of Wight* (1886). To generate this, he must have made many visits across the Solent, not only to accumulate the list of words (for, despite living at Calbourne until eighteen, he was able to include a child's epitaph from a grave at Northwood Church) but to recount amusing stories from around the Island, such as that of Mr Dove, Inn keeper of The Star, Niton. Once this work had established him as a serious voice, he embarked on the classic *Oglander Memoires* (1888). This was followed by other works such as *Memoires of Emma, Lady Hamilton* (1891), and others.

He died at home on Portsea Island and was buried at Southsea. His widow, Elizabeth, settled in Ryde and continued his business with diminishing success until she died there in 1925.

Maudsley, Henry (1841–1926)

Henry moved to the Island in 1864 and settled in Seaview, near Ryde. He was a keen yachtsman and, using his cutter yacht *Spinx*, won the 1866 Solent race for the Albert Gold Cup. He used a special sail of his own design called a 'balloon sail'. This sail was run out from the yacht on a boom and, used as a foresail, allowed the yacht to make very good speed when running downwind. The sail type was immediately dubbed a 'Spinx Acre' because of its huge size, but some of the crew found this difficult to pronounce and it soon changed to the present 'Spinnaker.' Henry became the second Hon. Secretary of the Seaview Yacht Club in 1903 and served in this post until 1922 when he was elected commodore, a post he held until his death. Henry's sail is now a standard fitting on all racing yachts.

Maybrick, Michael (1841–1913)

Though born in Liverpool, Michael lived much of his life at Ryde. He was a singer and composer, being best known for the song *Blue Alsatian Mountains* and the hymn *The Holy City*, both very popular in Victorian times. He was sufficiently well known to be elected Mayor of Ryde four times in the period 1900–1911. He used the pseudonym Stephen Adams in his professional work conscious, perhaps, that his brother James Maybrick had been a major suspect in the infamous Jack the Ripper investigations. Michael died in London.

Milne, John (1850–1913)

Although his family lived in Rochdale, John was born in Liverpool while his parents were on a business trip. He went to local (Rochdale) schools and won a place at King's College, London. His particular interests were geology and mineralogy. He travelled widely: Iceland, Newfoundland and the Sinai desert and undertook further study at the Royal School of Mines, London and in Germany.

In 1875, John was invited to become the first Professor of Geology and Mining at Tokyo. He travelled overland through Russia and China and wrote a book about the journey. He undertook a wide range of research: prehistory of Japan, study of volcanoes and anthropology, but it was the Tokyo/

Yokohama earthquake of 1880 that set him on the track for which he was to become world famous. He soon formed The Seismological Society of Japan and began construction of devices, seismographs, to record and measure the intensity of the earthquake and associated shock waves. He also used his skill to improve what were appalling conditions endured by miners in the many coal and other mineral workings around Japan. In 1895, his house in Tokyo was destroyed by fire, along with his extensive library, and this persuaded him to return to England with his Japanese wife, Tone. He also brought with him Shinobu Horota ('Snowy') who was his devoted and very able assistant.

John settled in Shide, just south of Newport in 1895 and, from that moment until John's death, Shide became the world centre for seismology. Soon after this, in June 1896, Japan was struck by a tsunami whose waves reached an amazing height of 25 metres (80 feet). This tsunami, called the Sanriku tsunami, prompted John, in a paper read to the Royal Geographic Society, to say:

> *'The sea waves, which at about 8pm on 15th June, 1896, invaded the north eastern coast of Nippon (Japan) were as destructive to life as those which accompanied the well known eruption on 26 August 1883, of Krakatau, whilst one of the shocks by which they were preceded was of such severity that it was clearly recorded in Europe, and in every probability caused a disturbance over the entire surface of the globe. The magnitude of this disturbance, and the sub-oceanic changes by which it was probably accompanied, make it well worthy of record'.*

In making this statement, linking tsunamis with ocean floor movement, John did not realise he was, in fact, talking about plate tectonics, a subject that did not exist until the work of Alfred Wegener in 1915!

At John's suggestion, a worldwide series of stations was set up using his design for a seismograph and, by 1899, he was receiving data from around the globe. Beginning in 1899, and under the auspices of the British Association for the Advancement of Science, he published the famous *Shide Circulars*. These listed all records of contributing stations and they were issued every six months until the end of 1912, when he was too ill to continue. After his death at Shide, his wife moved back to Japan. John is buried at St Paul's, Barton.

Whilst he was active, his house at Shide received visitors from every corner of the globe, ranging from members of the Japanese Royal Family and Mrs Lou Hoover (whose husband later became the President of the USA, 1929 to 1933) to Captain Robert Scott (who took a seismograph with him to Antarctica — it was set up in Victoria Land, not far from Mount Erebus). Without the man, it became difficult to maintain the work and, in 1919, his 'observatory' was moved from the Island to Oxford University, later to Kew and finally, Edinburgh.

In 1974, the University of Tokyo presented a number of cherry tree saplings to be planted both at Shide and at the Isle of Wight College of Arts and Technology to be a 'living memorial' to this great scientist. The Japanese Ambassador to Great Britain carried out the ceremony and also placed a wreath on John's grave, such is that country's respect for him.

Morey, Frank (1858–1925)

Born in Newport, son of Henry Morey (1822–1906) the founder of the Morey timber company, still to be found in the town, Frank attended Portland House Academy, Dorset. He returned to the Island around 1875 and worked for his father. Frank had had an abiding interest in the natural world since the age of six, and it was not too long before he worked with other Island enthusiasts (including Professor Milne of Shide) to produce his magnum opus: *A Guide to the Natural History of the Isle of Wight* (1909). This work received much acclaim and helped Frank to be elected to the prestigious Linnaean Society of London. By 1919, Frank was a leading light behind the formation of the Isle of Wight Natural History and Archaeological Society and also became Curator of Carisbrooke Castle Museum. After the First World War, Frank took over the management of the family business and this, coupled with his increasing commitment to his hobby, meant he needed an assistant. Having met **James Jackson** (see page 164) on one of the latter's visits to the Island, Frank wrote to him, inviting him to come and work as his helper. Frank's home was Wolverton Manor, where he died. He is buried at Newport.

Poynter, Charles (1853–1929)

Likely to have been born in London, Charles came to work on the Island around 1878, joining the small but flourishing outfitters, Redfern of Cowes, a business begun by John Redfern (1819–1895). Much of this company's work centred on clothing the wealthy members of the Royal Yacht Squadron and their ladies, but Charles had flair! By the early 1880s, not only had he personally adopted the business name 'John Redfern' but had expanded the business such that he opened shops of that name in New York, Chicago, London and Edinburgh. In 1885 he was appointed dressmaker to **Queen Victoria** (see page 121) and, as such, was in demand from all sides. He made dresses for Lilly Langtry, the famous singer and mistress to the then Prince of Wales, as well as for such nobility as the Russian Royal Family (presumably at some time when they were visiting the Queen at Osborne). At the height of his success, his staff numbered seventy, of whom fifty were dressmakers, working either at his shop in the High Street or at Sun Hill, Cowes. This was a world-famous ladies' fashion house in its time and the business only closed in the 1920s, primarily due to the great depression. Charles does not appear to have married and he left the Island soon after the business closed.

Prothero, Rowland (1851–1937)

This third son (of four) was born in Clifton-on-Teme to the Rev. George Prothero. The family moved to Whippingham in 1853 when George was made curate of the parish. After an education locally, supplemented by tuition from his mother, Rowland went to Marlborough College in 1864. From there he won a place at Balliol College, Oxford, and graduated in 1875 with a degree in Modern History. In the meantime, his father, having been elevated to Rector of the parish, became Chaplain to **Queen Victoria** (see page 121) (1866) and then made Canon of the Diocese.

In 1878 Rowland was called to the Bar and became interested in farming matters. This led to his publishing, *English Farming, Past and Present* (1888) and, later, *Pioneers and Progress in English Farming*, a work that ran to fifty-four editions from 1912 to 1972. From 1898 until 1918 he acted as Land Agent-in-Chief to the Duke of Bedford.

In 1914 he was elected as MP for Oxford City and, with his knowledge of the farming world, it was natural for him to become President of the Board of Agriculture and Fisheries, 1916–1919. Elected to the Privy Council in 1916, he was further honoured by becoming Baron Ernle. Rowland's autobiography *From Whippingham to Westminster* recounted many boyhood happenings during his eleven years in the village.

Ratsey, Thomas (1851–1935)

The Ratsey family can trace their Island links back through many centuries and their story is more that of a dynasty. Thomas is possibly the most significant in the history of sail making, for which the whole of his side of the family is justly famous. Their history is complex because there are two branches to the family, both based in Cowes and both with strong connections to the sea. Thomas's side were linked to sails, the other, headed in his time by Michael Ratsey, were boat builders. They had a common ancestor in a Matthew Ratsey, born on the Island in 1650.

Thomas was the grandson of George Rogers Ratsey (1769–1851) who began the first Ratsey 'sail loft' at West Cowes in 1790. (A sail loft being the cavernous, open floor on which large areas of sail canvas could be laid out to be stitched together.) Incidentally, Thomas's mother was Elizabeth, daughter of Joseph White, the Cowes-based ship builder. The sailmaking business was slow to start, but once the Royal Yacht Club, later to be renamed as the Royal Yacht Squadron, was established and found an interest in yacht racing in the mid 1820s, business was assured. The Earl of Belfast had Whites build a racing brig, *Waterwich*, with sails made by Ratsey. It was so successful against all other craft that *The Times* reported:

> 'The Board of Admiralty having expressed its very great admiration of the symmetry and standing of the sails of Waterwich yacht made by Mr Ratsey of Cowes, have ordered that the sails of men-of-war should in future be cut in a similar manner'.

Times were difficult in the period 1850 to 1870, but in 1871 a Mr James Ashbury made a challenge for the America's Cup and used Ratsey's sails. Although his boat didn't win, the performance of the sails attracted widespread attention. From that time until the 1960s, every British challenger used sails from this company.

The American Civil War (1860–1866) stopped the flow of cotton from the Southern states, forcing Ratsey's supplier to use Egyptian cotton. In fact this proved to be stronger than any American material and gave Ratsey even better sails. Around 1892, Thomas recognised a sail as an aerofoil and devised diagonally seamed sails to provide even greater strength and also reduce stretching. By this time Thomas had merged his company with that of the Lapthorne family in Gosport and the new company trades under the joint names to this day, even opening a very successful New York branch, complete with an enormous sail loft, in 1902. With a break resulting from the First World War, Thomas oversaw a huge growth in the demand for his sails as yachting, and more particularly Cowes Week, became a significant social event. He spent most of the summer months aboard his yacht, *Dolly Varden*, and did so up to and including the 1934 season (by which time he was eighty-three!) He died at his home at Cowes.

Richards, John Morgan (1841–1918)

An American 'hustler' who specialised in patent medicines, John first visited the Undercliff area in 1872 and became a regular visitor to the Island, particularly the area around Ventnor. His attachment to the Island was such that, in 1898, he rented Norris Castle, East Cowes, for the whole summer. (At least one member of his family shared this attachment to the Island, his daughter, **Pearl Craigie** (see page 157), who wrote under the pseudonym of John Oliver Hobbes.) John was well known in fashionable London circles and, in 1902–3, was President of the American Society in London. He was so taken by the Island that, in 1903, he purchased Steephill Castle (between Ventnor and Niton) as his home. John was, in fact, the last private owner of the castle, living there until his death, as did his wife, Louisa, who lived only some months longer than John. While living at the castle, he published his reminiscences of the Island in his book *Almost Fairyland* (1914). In this very personal work, John never refers to 'the Isle of Wight' but always 'Almost Fairyland'! This deeply religious man also served on various local charities including the Ventnor Royal National Hospital.

Many American travellers visited Steephill: perhaps the most celebrated of these being Mary, the daughter of General Robert E Lee, the American Confederate Army's Commander in Chief, who stayed in 1912. The property became a hotel after John died, has since been demolished and the land used to build a small housing estate.

John has the dubious honour of being the person who introduced serious cigarette smoking to England (in 1877) through his London-based company. So popular were his Virginia-grown cigarettes that he very quickly amassed a fortune. Before his time, smoking was very much a habit indulged mostly by the wealthy, using cigars or packs of tobacco for use in pipes, although some cigarettes were imported from France. He first imported supplies of American cigarettes (a brand called Richmond Gem made by Allen and Ginster), and the idea caught on so quickly it was not long before British companies saw the market potential with cigarettes, in small packs of ten, bringing the habit of smoking into the reach of the working classes. Co-incidentally, from 1885, Allen and Ginster cigarettes used card to stiffen the packs and used the card to issue collectable card images. So, John was also responsible for introducing cigarette cards to us — a clever device — as it helped to develop 'brand loyalty' as smokers attempted to complete sets of picture cards.

Ritchie, Anne (1837–1919)

This eldest daughter of the poet W M Thackerey was born in London. She visited the Island regularly from 1862 and this may have been connected to her friendship with **George Watts** (see page 128) (there exists a voluminous correspondence between the two). In 1863 she published her first work, *The Story of Elizabeth*, in what was, at the time, the best outlet, *The Cornhill Magazine*, and this to huge public acclaim. It ensured continuing interest in her works, many originally published in the same magazine. In 1877 she married her cousin Richmond Ritchie and in the same year published *From an Island*, which was semi-autobiographical. Her husband was a significant figure in the India Office of the Government and, in 1907, he was knighted, having achieved the rank of Permanent Under-Secretary of State. Anne moved to the Island in 1916, some years after the death of her husband, living in Freshwater where she died in 1919. She is buried at Hampstead, London, next to her father.

Rogan, John Mackenzie (1855–1931)

John was born in Newport, the elder of two boys. His father was a master shoemaker at Hunny Hill, Newport, and much of his business would be the supply of boots to the nearby military at Albany Barracks, an army base next to Parkhurst Prison. In 1867, John joined the army at Albany as a band-boy. His early history in this service has not yet come to light but, by 1882, he was bandmaster to the Royal West Surrey Regiment, and, by 1896, he was a lieutenant and bandmaster to the prestigious Coldstream Guards, a post he held until 1920. He was the first bandmaster to be given a substantive officer's commission.

In 1903, he took the Coldstream band on a tour of Canada and on another tour, to France, in 1907. Sound recordings exist of John, in 1904, conducting the band playing works such as *God Save the King*, sung by Dame Nellie Melba. In Sir Henry Wood's autobiography, John is credited with introducing Henry (as he was then) to Tchaikovsky's 1812 overture by almost dragging him to the Queen's Hall (in 1897) to hear the Coldstream band play the work.

In 1918, by which time he was a major, the band held a concert in his honour conducted by, amongst others, Sir Thomas Beecham. When he retired in 1920, he held the rank of lieutenant colonel; no bandmaster had ever achieved such a high rank before. In his time John was the most famous military musician in the world. He died in London.

Saunders, Samuel (1856–1933)

The Saunders boatbuilding company began life on the River Thames in 1830 and, like the White company almost one hundred years before, saw advantage in relocating to the Island, at Cowes, a move which was accomplished in 1901. In 1898, they had patented a material they called 'Consuta', which was a laminate of plywood and waterproof calico and was used very effectively to construct the curved hulls of boats. Moving to the east side of the river Medina in 1909, they used this material with great success when they began the construction of airship units. They won the government contract to build the engine and crew pods for HM Airship 1, *Mayfly*.

Because of the interest in flying, Samuel decided to combine this with the company's skill with boat hulls and began production of planes that could land on water. His first success was 'The Bat Boat', a single-seater flying boat built for Thomas Sopwith, which, in 1913, won the Mortimer Singer prize for the first all British aircraft capable of six return flights over five miles in under five hours. Saunders still retained his interest in boat construction, and it was with this company in 1912 that the young apprentice **Uffa Fox** (see page 161) began work, on leaving school. In 1917 the Saunders Company developed its own aircraft, known as the 'T1' (named after it's designer, Henry Thomas, who is buried at East Cowes). Its first fight was from the company's Somerton airfield in November of that year.

Samuel purchased the Padmore Estate at Whippingham in 1915 but only moved to the house in 1920. As soon as the land was his, he sold over twenty acres of it to his own company. This was a stretch of land immediately north of the Folly Inn, bordering the river. He used the area to create a specialist factory with easy transport for both raw materials and the finished product. It became the country's largest manufacturing unit for military plywood and the composite material, Consuta, and remained so until the 1960s when the factory was destroyed by fire.

Samuel retired in 1929 and spent much of his time tending a large rose garden he had planted at Padmore. He paid for the construction of Whippingham Community Centre (and, in doing so, provided much needed employment during the depression). He died at a nursing home in Nettlestone and is buried at Whippingham, his coffin being specially made in the shape of a boat, using Consuta instead of wood.

Spindler, Theodor (1836–1889)

Born in Berlin, where, as an industrial chemist, Theodor ran a large dye works. He first came to the Island in 1872, staying at Ventnor in order to improve his fragile health. Having amassed considerable wealth, he returned to the Island in 1881 with his wife, Clara. He purchased Old Park at the Undercliff and very soon both he and his family became naturalised citizens.

Over the eight years he lived there, he not only transformed the area, by planting over a million trees and shrubs, but also laid out Ventnor Park and paid for piped water to be laid to nearby Whitwell Village (red standpipes can still be found). The drainage work carried out on his 144-acre estate coupled with the tree planting helped to stabilise the whole area, which sits on 'blue slipper' clay. After Theodor died, his wife and daughter lived at the house until their deaths (daughter Martha in 1900 and Clara in 1906).

Stone, Percy (1856–1934)

The son of an architect, it is perhaps not unexpected to find Percy following the same profession. Born in Marylebone, London, where he qualified, Percy's earliest major work appears to have been Nun's Acre (1886), a property in Goring, Oxfordshire, where, for some years, he lived. After designing other Oxfordshire properties (Pryorshurst, 1888 etc), he moved to the Island in 1890 with his wife, Francesca (Fanny). He used his architectural knowledge to undertake the first ever investigation of the ruins of the old Quarr Abbey (1896) and was responsible for the design of churches (Wootton and Cowes) as well as a number of significant memorials, most notably, that to **Queen Victoria** (see page 121) in Newport. Perhaps his most significant work was the design of the chapel of St Nicholas, Carisbrooke Castle. Percy's first wife (Fanny Powys) died in 1898 and two years later he married a Brading girl, Amelia Smith (1870–1953), and they lived in a rustic cottage at Merstone. He developed an abiding interest in the Island, producing two important publications: *Architectural Antiquities of the Isle of Wight* (1891) and *Legends and Lays of the Isle of Wight* (1912) as well as contributing to the *Victoria County History of the Island*. He died at his home in Merstone and is buried at Shanklin.

Swinburne, Algernon (1837–1909)

Born in London, Algernon spent much of his childhood at East Dene, Bonchurch, where his father had retired from the Navy. He went to Eton College in 1849 but left prematurely in 1856, moving on to Balliol College, Oxford. He left university without sitting for a degree.

In the winter of 1863/4 he stayed with his cousin's family, the Gordons, who lived at Northcourt, Shorwell. It was here that he wrote much of his first important work, *Atalanta in Calydon* (a play in the style of a Greek tragedy). He also collaborated with his cousin, Mary Gordon (who later married to become Mary Leith), helping her with her second book *The Children of the Chapel* (1864). It is, perhaps, Algernon's *Poems and Ballads* (1866) that assured his fame. It shocked society with its attack on kings and priests, rejection of Christianity and its celebration of what was seen as decadent sexual feelings. His total output of work was enormous; two later major works were *Bothwell* (1874) and *Tristram of Lyonesse* (1882).

Swinburne was an erratic character, given to heavy drinking and mood swings, and, from 1879, soon after the death of his father and the disposal of the East Dene house, he lived with his friend, the well-known literary critic Theodore Watts in Putney, London. Watts proved to be a calming influence on him, moderating his more extreme outbursts. Swinburne died while in the care of this friend. There is a blue plaque at his Island home at Bonchurch and Algernon is buried in the churchyard there — this despite his dying wishes to have no Christian service at his burial. The first chorus of his classic *Atalanta in Calydon* was the inspiration for the composer Arnold Bax (who, in 1942 was to become 'Master of the King's Musick') to write *Spring Fire* (1913).

Thornycroft, John (1843–1928)

Born in Vatican City, Rome, while his parents were on holiday, John was educated in London where his father, Thomas (1815–1885), had a studio (he later became a renowned sculptor, having commissions from **Queen Victoria** (see page 121)). John was more interested in engineering and, aged eighteen, joined the Jarrow shipbuilding yard of Palmers. A few years later, he studied at the University of Glasgow, obtaining a diploma in engineering.

He moved back to London and established a boatyard at Chiswick, around 1864. His particular interest was the construction of ship hulls that minimised friction, so yielding greater speed. In this, he was very successful and it led to the Royal Navy ordering from him its first high-speed, steam torpedo boat, in 1876, HMS *Lightning*. John then established a thriving boat business near Southampton and continued his research into hull design, as well as the idea of a hydrofoil. In 1891 he purchased Steyne House, Bembridge (the property still boasts the test tank he built there in 1910). John was knighted in 1902 and became a Fellow of the Royal Society in 1904. His businesses continued to thrive, making the name of Thornycroft respected in engineering around the world. Sir John died at his Island home.

Tuttiett, Mary (1846–1923)

Born in Carisbrooke, her father, Frank, was a GP based at Quay Street, Newport. Mary achieved instant fame with her first book, *The Silence of Dean Maitland* (1886) where much of the activity centred on the thinly-disguised Newport of her childhood, calling it 'Oldport'. As was often the case in these times, Mary wrote under a pseudonym: Maxwell Gray. Her output was prodigious. Not only did *The Silence of Dean Maitland* run to ten editions in eight years, but it was also made into a film (1934).

Her other works included:

The Reproach of Annesley (1889),
In the Heart of a Storm (1890),
The Last Sentence (1893),
The House of Hidden Treasure (1898),
Richard Rosney (1903),
The Suspicions of Ermengarde (1908).

Mary suffered a constant debilitating illness, rarely leaving the small house where she lived with her father. Most of her writing was carried out while she lay on a sofa, finding that sitting or standing was too painful. When she went to visit the American writer Wolcott Balestier, who was staying at

Bonchurch in 1891, she was taken there, lying on the floor of her carriage. Her book *The Last Sentence* was dedicated to this writer whom she greatly admired. When her father died in 1895, she moved to West Richmond to be with other family. She died at Ealing, London.

Webster, Richard (1842–1915)

Born in London, the son of a QC, Richard attended Charterhouse School and then Trinity College, Cambridge, from where he graduated in Law in 1865. He was called to the Bar in 1868 specialising in law relating to both business and railways. Unusually, for he was not yet an MP, he was appointed Attorney General in 1885 and only after this took a seat in the House, being first, the MP for Launceston then, later that same year, for the Island, a position he retained until 1900, when he entered the House of Lords. Around 1886 he purchased Alverstone Manor and a large tract of land (the Alverstone near Brading) and used this for pheasant and partridge shoots (**John Morgan Richards** (see page 143) was a keen visitor to these events). As a senior judge, he represented Great Britain in the Bering Sea Arbitration of 1903 (a boundary dispute between Canada and America which followed from America's purchase of Alaska from Russia) and was asked to settle the 1898 boundary dispute between British Guiana and Venezuela. In 1900 he was created Baron Alverstone and, later that same year, became both Lord Chief Justice of England and Master of the Rolls, posts he held until his death.

In 1905, Richard presented Shanklin with the Arthur Webster Hospital in memory of his son who had died at his Alverstone home in 1902. The building now operates as the Arthur Webster Clinic. When he retired, in 1913, Richard was elevated to the title Viscount Alverstone. He died, and is buried at Cranleigh, Surrey.

Worsley, Philip (1835–1866)

Philip was the eldest son of the Gatcombe branch of this notable Island family, his father being the Rev. Charles, vicar of that parish. He attended the Godshill Free Grammar School and then Cholmeley's School, Highgate, and matriculated from Corpus Christi College, Oxford, in 1853. He was a consumptive from an early age and this prevented him from acquiring a profession. Instead, he devoted himself to literature and in 1861 published his *Translation of the Odyssey*, which received widespread acclaim. This was followed by similar works while he lived at Freshwater where, in 1866, he died and is buried.

EPOCH 6, 1865–1899

Apperley, George (1884–2001)

Born in Ventnor, George's father died while he was still young and he and his widowed mother moved to Torquay when he was six. He attended a school in Devizes, and then moved to Uppingham School where he developed a growing interest in art. His first recorded work, *The Fleet in Torbay* was created around this time. In 1904 George holidayed in Italy and this fired his artistic ambitions. He married in 1907 and, in 1914, took a working holiday in Spain. Returning to England in 1916, he was declared unfit for military duties and he began a series of portrait works. Soon after the war was over, he divorced his wife somewhat unceremoniously and returned to Spain, creating many of his classic oils. The outbreak of the Spanish Civil War in 1932 drove him and his second (Spanish) wife to flee to Tunisia. After World War II, the Spanish authorities gave recognition to his work, not only giving him national honours but also holding exhibitions of his (mostly Spanish) work and calling him 'The English Painter of Granada'. He died and is buried in Tangier.

Baring, Godfrey (1871–1957)

Godfrey was born in London and, after an education at Eton College, threw himself into local Island politics. The family were wealthy; his father, having made his fortune in the developing oil business, and, in the year that Godfrey was born, had a house built, Nubia, just outside Cowes at Egypt Point, over-looking the Solent. This spot was chosen because the father (Lieutenant-General Charles Baring) was a keen yachtsman, owning the cutter *Mohawk* and, in 1889, becoming the first commodore of the newly formed Island Sailing Club.

Even as a young man, Godfrey was elected as only the second Chairman of the Isle of Wight County Council (in 1898 — he was twenty-seven!) and remained in this post for a quite remarkable fifty-one years. He also stood as Liberal MP for the Island (1906–1910) and worked as a Parliamentary Private Secretary for **Jack Seely** (see page 176) and others from 1908 to 1915. This remarkable man had also served as a Justice of the Peace for fifty-eight years (1894–1952) and Chairman of the Island RNLI for thirty-three (1923–1956).

The Baring family left Nubia House in 1955, the building was demolished in the 1960s, and the site is now occupied by modern housing. Godfrey died at a nursing home in Cowes.

Beken, Frank (1881–1970) and his son Beken, Keith (1914–2007)

The Beken family came to West Cowes from Canterbury, Kent, in 1888 when Edward Beken (1855–1915) relocated his chemist and druggist shop. His son Frank, working in their Island shop, which had a large rear window overlooking Cowes harbour, could not fail to be impressed by the to-ing and fro-ing of the numerous yachts such as the 154-ton *Susanne*. Using a quite unsuitable camera — one intended for use in a land-based studio (as most were at the time) — Frank took some remarkable photographs.

During WWI the Admiralty used him to photograph all existing naval craft and this gave him wider experience. Frank was also able to design his own cameras that met his very particular needs, as he tried to photograph a vessel moving at great speed while he bobbed about in a small motor launch.

After some lessons in racing technique from **Uffa Fox** (see page 161), Frank's son, young Keith Beken, began to experiment with photography and, with the help of an engineer who lived nearby, was able to construct a camera with a shutter speed of 1/500th of a second — just what was needed in the choppy conditions so often found at sea.

After war service 1939–45, during which Keith served in the air-sea rescue organisation, he returned to his father's shop and more seagoing photography. The work of both Frank and Keith in photographing both individual yachts and their massed ranks at the start of a race made the name of 'Beken' known around the world and the name will forever be associated both with Cowes and yacht photography.

Boissier, Arthur (1881–1953)

Born in Bloxham, Oxfordshire, and educated at St John's, Leatherhead, he preferred to use his middle name, Paul. He graduated from Oxford in 2001, and that year (and again in 1906) he played first class cricket for Derbyshire, as well as representing the University in varsity matches. He began teaching at Sherbourne School and in 1905 was appointed senior master at Osborne Naval College. In 1909 Paul married an East Cowes girl, Dorothy Smith. He remained at the college until 1919 when he was appointed house master and Head of Mathematics at Harrow School. In 1939 he was appointed to the headship of the school, a post he held until 1942 when he was asked to be Director of Public Relations at the Ministry of Fuel and Power. On the reorganisation of the ministries, Paul retired, going to live near the home of his Island-born daughter (Beatrice) near Aberdeen where he died.

Campbell, Robert (1885–1966)

Robert has a unique place in war history. Born at Gravesend, Kent, where he received his education, he joined the East Surrey Regiment at age sixteen. By the outbreak of World War I he was a captain, and when his battalion was attacked at the French Mons-Conde canal he was badly wounded and taken prisoner, being moved to incarceration at Magdeburg after treatment at a military hospital in Cologne.

Whilst in prison, he learnt that his mother was dying and he wrote a personal letter to the Kaiser asking for permission to visit her in Kent, promising to return to Magdeburg. Unbelievably, the Kaiser granted his request and, just before Christmas 1916, he spent a week with his mother before surrendering his liberty for honour and returning to Germany. Robert spent the rest of the war at Magdeburg.

He retired from the army in 1925, living at the family home at Gravesend. At the outbreak of war in 1939, he rejoined his old regiment with the rank of major and was posted to the Island as chief observer of the Royal Observer Corps. Robert's younger sister Gladys (1889–1972) was already living at Totland, having married there in 1923, and Robert used her home as his base whilst overseeing the operation of the Island's fourteen wartime Observer Corps sites. The wartime corps was stood down in 1945, at which time Robert finally retired and remained living with Gladys. He died at St Mary's Hospital, Newport, and is buried at Totland.

Campbell-Barnes, Margaret (1891–1962)

This writer of historical dramas is not as well known as many, despite her books being still in print. Margaret was born Margaret Campbell into a family of ten children in Rotherfield, Sussex. The family were reasonably affluent, allowing Margaret to have a private education in London and Paris.

Upon marriage in 1917 she settled in Epsom, raising two sons and writing short articles for a variety of magazines. The death of one of these, in a World War II tank battle and the death of her husband, soon after, made her, quite understandably, very introspective and, at the end of hostilities in 1945, she purchased a small thatched cottage (that had, at one time, belonged to a smuggler) in Shalfleet. There, at a friend's advice, she began writing. Her speciality was historical fiction with titles such as *The Tudor Rose*, *The King's Fool*, and *Mary of Carisbrooke*. Ten volumes appeared between 1954 and her death; two million of her books were sold worldwide. A curtain in Shalfleet church is dedicated to the memory of her dead soldier son.

Cocks, Arthur Somers (1887–1944)

Arthur was born in Freshwater but, being orphaned in 1895 on the death of his mother (his father had died in 1894), was reared by a succession of family members. He went to school at Charterhouse and, after some time farming in Canada, joined the Life Guards (part of the Household Cavalry) in 1906. By the end of the First World War he was in command of the 6th Tank Corps and, during his various engagements, was awarded both the DSO (Distinguished Service Order) and MC (Military Cross). In 1922, he retired from the army with the rank of lieutenant colonel, having that year inherited Eastnor Castle in Herefordshire along with the title 6th Baron Somers. In 1926 he was made Governor of Victoria, Australia, a post he held until 1931. Soon after his return to England, he was made Lord Lieutenant of Herefordshire, a post he held until his death. He had always been active in the Boy Scout movement and became more and more involved in its management until, in 1941, on the death of Lord Baden-Powell, the movement's founder, Gerald, was made Chief Scout of Great Britain and the Commonwealth. He died at his home, Eastnor Castle.

Cotter, William (1866–1940)

Born in Cloyne, Co. Cork, William was educated at St Colman's College, Fermoy, and studied for the priesthood at Maynooth, Ireland. He was ordained at Portsmouth in 1892 when he was appointed Curate at St Mary's, Ryde, a post he held until 1900 when he was promoted to Rector of the parish. He was appointed Canon in 1902 and then Titular Bishop of Clazomenae in 1905. In 1910 William was appointed 3rd Bishop of Portsmouth, a post he held until his death in 1940. He is buried in the grounds of the Waterlooville Convent.

Craigie, Pearl (1867–1906)

Born in America, Pearl was the daughter of **John Morgan Richards** (see page 143). In 1867, he brought his family to London where he took up a post selling patent medicine. Pearl was educated mostly in London, culminating in a period of private study at London University. In 1887 she married Reginald Craigie, but this proved a mistake, leading to separation in 1891 and divorce in 1895. (She later said of her marriage that it was like 'living with a boa constrictor'.) Because of Craigie's society connections, Pearl became well known in London literary circles and soon began writing articles for a variety of magazines. The strain of her separation led her, in 1892, to convert to Roman Catholicism and, by 1895, she was recognised as one of the most important Catholic novelists of her day. Her works, all written under the pseudonym of 'John Oliver Hobbes', included:

> *Some Emotions and a Moral* 1891,
> *The Sinners Comedy* 1892,
> *A Study in Temptations* 1893.

Many of her quotations suggest she had little faith in men, probably the result of her rather messy divorce:

> *'A man with a career can have no time to waste upon his wife and friends, he has to devote it to his enemies'.*

> *'Men heap together the mistakes of their lives and create a monster they call destiny'.*

Pearl became president of the Society of Women Journalists (1895–6), and her father who was the proprietor of the well-known *Academy Magazine* made her its editor. It was under her leadership that this publication achieved its longest period of success.

Before her father purchased Steephill Castle in 1903, she had leased nearby St Lawrence Lodge and did most of her later writing there (1899–1902) then later, at the castle. In total she wrote more than seventeen works as well as numerous articles in a wide variety of magazines. During this time she also wrote a number of plays that ran successfully in London:

The Ambassador played in 1908,
The Flute of Pan played in 1904.

It is worth noting that the play *The Ambassador* produced the longest run for a play then known at St James's Theatre, London.

Some of her better-known books are:

Love and the Soulhunters 1902,
Tales About Temperament 1902,
The Vineyard 1904.

She died in her sleep in London having left the Island that morning. Her father purchased St Lawrence Lodge from the owner's executors soon after her death and renamed it 'Craigie Lodge' in her memory.

Damant, Guybon (1881–1963)

Born in East Cowes the second of five sons, Guy (as he was always known) entered the Royal Navy as an apprentice in 1895. He was an expert swimmer, perhaps the influence of the Solent, so close to his parent's house in Cambridge Road. He quickly became interested in naval diving and, in 1905, worked with the famous physiologist, Professor J S Haldane. Haldane's interest was to confirm his idea of 'staged decompression' for divers as a means of preventing the fatal 'bends' when they resurfaced from a deep dive. Guy (by then a lieutenant) and Haldane experimented in a Scottish loch and established the concept of staged decompression, still used to this day. Using the system, Guy established a world record of a safe dive to 200 feet in that year. By 1906, he was appointed an experimental officer to the Navy with responsibility for deep water diving. He was promoted to captain by the outbreak of World War I, but his most significant work, for which he later became justly famous, began in 1917.

The 14,000-ton White Star liner *Laurentic*, which had been modified to be an armed merchant cruiser, was sailing from Liverpool to Halifax, Nova Scotia, when, within sight of the Irish coast, she hit two German mines. The *Laurentic* sank very quickly in 130 feet of water with the loss of 354 lives (it was the largest ever loss of life at sea resulting from a mine explosion, only

121 on board survived). But, on board were also 3211 bars (35 tons) of gold valued, in 1917, at £25 million. (As an interesting aside, it was the *Laurentic* that, in 1910, carried Inspector Dew to Canada when he was chasing Dr Crippen and Ethel le Neve. *Laurentic* arrived ahead of the murderer's ship so that Dew was waiting for them on the quayside when they docked.)

Guy was asked to organise the salvage of the gold and to do so in utter secrecy. This gold represented a significant part of the remaining British war chest, and if the Germans had realised its presence on the seafloor they would have ensured its removal was made impossible.

Salvage work began within a week, with Guy using a salvage vessel disguised as a trawler. What the divers found was worrying. The ship was on its side and much of it in a state of near collapse with the strongroom deep inside the ship. Doors had to be dynamited and piles of debris cleared. Work was further complicated by the weather that, during most of late 1918 and early 1919, was too rough to allow safe diving. Work continued until 1924, by which time all but some three gold bars had been recovered (the three are still at the wreck site). Only after salvage work had ceased were the public informed of Guy and his team's heroic undersea struggle. In the interwar years he and his team were kept busy diving and, where possible, salvaging WWI sunken ships and their cargoes.

Guy later became the Royal Navy's first Inspector of Diving. He lectured and wrote about deep-sea diving and underwater natural history. He retired in 1945 with the rank of commander. He died at his home in East Cowes and is buried at Kingston cemetery there.

Dixon, John (1897–1958)

John was born near Keighley, Yorkshire. At the early age of twleve he was apprenticed to his father's printing business in the town. He spent four years in the Navy during WWI and, after demobilisation and further work with his father, he moved to Shanklin in 1926. There he used a small gravure machine that allowed him to create a range of both publicity and everyday working documents to the rapidly growing number of Shanklin Hotels and Boarding Houses. His business quickly prospered and, in 1935, was elected to the Council of British Master printers. John married a Brading girl, Barbara

Cooper (1908–1999), in 1936 and it was with her, sailing off the Needles in a small dingy, that he took a photograph of that landmark. The image was a huge success and led, ultimately, to John creating images for use on Christmas and other greeting cards — the birth of the company that became nationally famous in this field. Business continued to grow and machines were set up at the best-known site of the works, to the south of Parkhurst Forest. After the Second World War, business continued to expand, and a second works was set up at Inverness, Scotland. At the height of its success, the company produced over thirty million postcards each year. John died in 1958 at The County Hospital, Ryde, and is buried at the Old Church, Shanklin. His wife, Barbara, took over running the business for some years and, after many changes of ownership, 'J Arthur Dixon' ceased trading in 2000.

Eley, Frederick (1866–1951)

Born in Shrewsbury, where he went to school, Frederick joined the local National Provincial Bank at age sixteen. He clearly showed much promise because he quickly rose through the bank, being the manager of the Leeds branch by 1903 and had a seat on its board of directors by 1916. Frederick became a baronet in the 1921 New Year Honours list.

His link to Leeds allowed him to be asked to be a director of John Waddington (a printing company based in Leeds), just before that company chose to publish the game of Monopoly. He also acted as chairman of Crosse and Blackwell (1932–1946) and the Bank of British West Africa (1942–1948).

Frederick purchased Southview House, Chale (the old home of **Thomas Letts** (see page 95) and his family), in 1938 and lived there during spring and summer each year until just before his death. In his time, he was a renowned racehorse owner. His ashes are interred at Stoke Poges, Buckinghamshire.

Fleming, Arthur (1881–1960)

Arthur was born in Newport where he received his basic education. At sixteen, he went to Finsbury Technical College, London and studied electrical engineering. After further specialist training in America, he worked for the British Westinghouse Company at their Trafford Park works. By 1913, he was superintendant there, beginning the systematic training of new recruits and, by 1917, was manager of the company's education department. This department was soon recognised around the world for the quality of training given and Arthur's impact on the world of industrial training was profound. In 1924, he became a member of the Council of the University of Manchester and later served on the Governing Body of Imperial College, London. He was elected President of the Institute of Electrical Engineers in 1938 and knighted in 1945. He returned to the Island in 1947. Sir Arthur died at Ryde Hospital after a short illness.

Fox, Uffa (1898–1972)

Born in East Cowes and educated at the primary school at nearby Whippingham, he began work as an apprentice (1912–1919) with S E Saunders, the local shipbuilder. Later in life, he was to express great pride in having worked, in 1912, on the motorboat *Maple Leaf IV* as his first apprenticeship task. This craft became the first boat to attain a speed of fifty knots and later won the Harmsworth Trophy. As soon as his apprenticeship was complete, he borrowed money from his father and initially set himself up in the business of boat repair at the early age of twenty-one. His early work was aboard a decommissioned steam-driven, 'chain ferry' that had seen service since 1896 and had run (as they still do, although now they are diesel-electric) between East and West Cowes. He converted one side of the ferry into living accommodation, the other into a design area, and the centre section, covered over, was the repair/construction bay. After only some six years, he moved from repair work to the task of hull design.

His first significant design was created in 1928, a fourteen-footer, *Avenger*. This craft was an instant success, winning the Prince of Wales Cup that year as well as all the Cowes Week races in her class (twenty in all). His various racing victories led him to America where, in 1933, he won the 'canoe' championship of the USA in the name of the Humber Yawl Club (it is worth remembering that an American 'canoe' is what we call a yacht, with certain technical variations!) As a consequence of his victory, the American Canoe Association paid him the very rare honour of making him an 'Honorary member for life'.

On the death of Sam Saunders in 1935, his house at Padmore, Whippingham, with all its land, was put up for sale. Uffa purchased twenty acres that ran down to the river, some two hundred yards south of the Folly Inn. He moved his floating bridge workshop there and built a quite remarkable house — appropriately called Twenty Acres.

He seemed incapable of creating a poor design. In his autobiography, the naturalist and artist Sir Peter Scott (who was also an Olympic yachtsman!) wrote:

> '(the dinghies) were built with the precision and artistry
> of a violin; Uffa had set new standards of workmanship
> in boatbuilding, and to own one of his fourteen footers
> in the 1930s was to own the most perfect little boat in
> the world'.

In 1938, Uffa purchased Medina Yard. This was an area that had Cowes High Street on one side and Cowes Harbour at the other. Whilst building boats was clearly the love of his life, there was one creation of which he was most proud: In 1941, he had listened to one of his recently RAF-enlisted apprentices (who was Bobby, his stepson) describe the problems faced by air-sea rescue teams. Some months later, Bobby was himself lost at sea whilst trying to save a downed airman (but the boy eventually turned up as a prisoner of war).

Uffa decided the answer to saving downed airmen lay with a lifeboat dropped by parachute. His staff set to designing a lifeboat that could be carried, like a torpedo, on the underside of an aeroplane and dropped to people in the water. The craft was to have sails and a motor as well as a supply of emergency food and water. However, this was wartime and to get anything done needed official permission. This, Uffa got, by going direct to the Minister with responsibility for supply, Lord Brabazon (whom Uffa knew personally, as Brabazon was a yachtsman) in London. Uffa's staff worked in two teams each serving twelve-hour shifts so that there was no cessation of

effort. The first lifeboat was completed, from initial design to finished construction, in three weeks. After extensive trials, the lifeboats were accepted
and used on a range of different aircraft. They saved many airmen's lives and
it is significant that Uffa's tombstone in Whippingham churchyard displays,
not a 'flying fifteen' or one of the other yachts of his design for which he is so
famous but, an airborne lifeboat.

With his second wife, he purchased a property at Puckaster, on the coast,
not far from St Catharine's Lighthouse and lived there until 1950. When he
sold this property, he purchased a derelict warehouse that faced into Cowes
harbour. This was his final home and the scene of many parties that included
many famous people, including the yachtsman and his good friend, yachting and drinking companion, Prince Phillip. Strangely, perhaps, this sea dog
died, not on the Island but at a friend's house in Worcestershire.

Prince Philip said of him:

> *'There is a tendency nowadays to imagine that
> everything new must be scientific or rational. Uffa as
> a helmsman in his day was a world-beater, and as a
> designer of boats he was also a world-beater. I can state
> categorically that there is nothing scientific or rational
> about Mr Fox. Like all great designers his genius is
> entirely human.*

Gamage, Ernest (1875–1959)

Born in London, just before his father, Albert, opened a shop in Holborn,
Ernest soon became a significant figure. Gamage Bros., the shop, became
known around the globe after Ernest created what was the British Empire's
first mail-order business. (Albert began his shop in Holborn because nearby was William Hamley's very successful toyshop, opened in 1760, called
Noah's Ark.) The shop grew by Albert buying up nearby properties until,
by the 1940s, the premises were a veritable rabbit warren. Ernest purchased
The Old Grange in Wroxall in the early 1930s and it remained his principal
home until his death there. He used his huge wealth to travel the world and
indulge his passion for collecting. When he died and the house contents

sold in 1960, museums descended on the auction, as so much material was unique. The shop of Gamage Bros. finally closed in 1972, principally because, sited in Holborn, it was away from the main London shopping areas around Regent Street to where Hamley had moved long ago.

Gough-Calthorpe, Arthur Somerset (1864–1937)

Unlike the rest of his family, Arthur joined, not the Army but the Navy, enrolling at Dartmouth in 1878. His promotions came quickly, being a commander by 1896 and, after serving as naval attaché to Russia, Norway and Sweden, was a Rear Admiral by 1911. At the outbreak of World War I, Gough-Calthorpe was in command of the First Battle Squadron. Later he was asked to command the Mediterranean fleet and, in 1918, asked to negotiate the peace treaty with Turkey. Arthur achieved the rank of Admiral of the Fleet in 1925 and retired to the family home at Woodland Vale, Ryde in 1930. He died at the family home.

Jackson, James (1894–1966)

James was born in Mold, in present-day Clwyd, Wales. His father deserted the family while James was still young and, in 1901, his mother moved the family to her hometown of Hunstanton, Norfolk, where she ran a boarding house. James was a sickly child and so his mother undertook home tuition for him. Her father had been a keen archaeologist and this interest soon passed to James who spent much of his free time on the beach, searching for fossils. This interest in nature was further excited through his contact with the Argentinean-born, world-famous naturalist and writer, W H Hudson — who just happened to be one of his mother's guests! Writing his first book at the age of fifteen, the local paper rallied to his cause and, with help from interested archaeologists, paid for him to attend a local college. After some years as a dealer in fossils and rocks, he worked as a geological assistant at the National Museum of Wales, Cardiff, and then, in 1924, answered

Frank Morey's (see page 140) invitation to come and work with him on the Island, living in Newport.

By this time, James was a Fellow of the Geological Society of London and was well regarded in university circles. On the death of Frank Morey (1925), Morey's sister, Catherine (1855–1943), continued to support James who, in that year, took up the post of Curator of Sandown Museum. He published *The Geological Story of the Isle of Wight* (1942) as well as contributing many papers to learned journals. Shortly after Catherine's death, he moved briefly to Wales and then Torquay and, finally, Lyme Regis where, after making many geological discoveries, he died.

Jones, Penrhyn (1878–1945)

Known as Penrhyn, although his birth is registered with the name Penellyn, he was born at Cowes while his mother and father (the proprietor of Sandrock Hotel at Niton) were on holiday. After a local education he attended Malvern College and whilst there was successful in the competitive Consular examinations.

Penrhyn was posted to the British Consul Office in Shanghai, China, in 1902 and worked there, taking legal qualifications and joining Inner Temple as a barrister, in 1910. In 1926 he was appointed British Consul at Harbin, North China, and awarded a CBE in 1928. Penrhyn returned to Shanghai in 1931 being appointed a judge at the British Supreme Court there. He became Chief Judge at the court in 1933 and served in that post until 1937 when he retired. He still lived in Shanghai when, in 1941, the Japanese invaded China and he was interned by them. Penrhyn was repatriated after five months, and he returned to England in 1942, settling at Ticehurst, Sussex, where he died and is buried.

Ketelbey, Albert (1875–1959)

Born and educated at schools in Birmingham, Albert became the organist of St John's Church, Wimbledon, at the remarkably early age of sixteen! He took up a music scholarship at the Trinity College of Music, beating Gustaf Holst into second place in a competition. Whist in London, he became the musical director to the Vaudeville Theatre and it was in this post that he composed much of his music — mostly overlooked today. His works included *In a Persian Market, In a Monastery Garden, Bells Across the Meadow* and some forty others. He moved to Egypt Hill, Cowes, in 1948 and, whilst not well known in this country, he was highly thought of on the continent where, for example, he was a regular conductor for the Amsterdam Concertgebouw. His music had such popularity in the 1930s that he is believed by many to have been the first-ever British music millionaire. Most of his time at Cowes he dedicated to his passion for billiards. Albert died in London.

Marconi, Guglielmo (1874–1937)

Born just outside Bologna, Italy, Guglielmo had an Italian father and an Irish mother (she was a member of the wealthy and influential Irish Whiskey family of Jameson). Having finished his studies, and whilst on holiday in the Italian Alps, he read of Hertz's early experiments on radiation. On his return home, he began experimenting in the attic of his home. One evening in 1895, he showed his mother what he had achieved: a transmitter at one end of the room, a receiver connected to a bell at the other. Pressing a switch on the transmitter made the bell ring, a separation of nine metres. By mid 1895, he was able to send Morse code signals over 2 km. His father saw no value in his work and nor did the Italian Post Office when they were approached. His mother, however, believed in his work and persuaded him to take his ideas to England where her family had a degree of influence.

With the help of his family, he moved to England in February 1896 and quickly sought a patent for his idea. The patent (British Patent 12039) was filed in June 1896. In September 1896, Marconi gave a demonstration of his 'spark gap' system at Three Mile Hill, Salisbury; this to an audience of Post Office engineers and Army and Navy personnel. It was a great success, and he obtained official backing (and finance!) to extend his research.

After further work on Salisbury Plain, he moved to the Island at Alum Bay. Working in the grounds of the Needles Hotel, he was able to transmit a Morse code message some twenty miles to a receiver set up in the Haven

Hotel, Poole. His work was creating a great deal of interest in the scientific world such that, in June 1898, the great scientist Lord Kelvin made a special trip to witness the experiments. At one stage in the year he was asked by The Prince of Wales to create a link between himself, aboard the royal yacht *Osborne*, riding off the north of the Island, and **Queen Victoria** (see page 121) herself, then in residence at Osborne House.

Such was the interest occasioned by his findings, and so large was the number of people wishing to 'see for themselves', that the proprietor of the Needles Hotel asked Marconi for an increase in his rent. The timing of this request could not have been more opportune. With the success of cross-Solent transmissions, he had for some time been thinking of the next step. The demand from the hotel was the spur, and he simply moved on, going to stay at the Sandrock Hotel at Niton and setting up experiments at Knowles Farm, Niton (next door to St Catharine's Lighthouse and close to sea level), in early 1900. From here he was able to communicate with France. All this time, he had been improving his equipment and, in April 1900, he filed the famous Patent '7777'. This explained how, in future, he would be using tuned circuits, the very basis of radio signalling today. This enabled stations to transmit at a particular frequency so that their signal did not interfere with other transmissions that had been the case with the spark-gap system.

In the four years whilst living on the Island, Marconi had developed systems so that, instead of short distance, untuned spark-gap transmissions, he was able to send frequency-specific messages (in Morse code) across the English Channel. Small memorials mark the two Island sites where this work was conducted. That at Knowles farm simply reads:

> *'This is to commemorate that Marconi set up a wireless Experimental station here in 1900 AD'.*

Marconi went on to found the famous company of that name and his invention transformed the world in which we live. He was awarded the 1909 Nobel Prize for Physics in recognition of his work. He died in Rome and, as a unique gesture and mark of respect, the World's radio transmitters closed down simultaneously for five minutes at the time of his funeral so that the ether was silent.

Mason, Alfred (1865–1948)

Alfred was born in Dulwich, London, and attended the prestigious Dulwich College before graduating from Trinity College, Oxford, in 1888. His interest was English and it was not long before he assumed an acting career in London. He had begun writing on a small scale before his 'magnum opus', the adventure story, *The Four Feathers* (1902), which was subsequently turned into a successful film.

He became MP for Coventry (where he lived at the time) during the 1906–1910 Parliament and then recommenced his writing career, making a significant contribution to the detective fiction genre by creating Inspector Hanaud of the French Surete, the first book of a series, *At the Villa Rose*, appearing in 1910.

At the outbreak of war, Alfred joined the army with the rank of captain and saw service in France and later served as a counter-intelligence officer, working first in Spain and, later, Mexico. When his service was completed, he resumed writing and moved to the Island, Kite Hill House, just outside of Wootton. He wrote a number of plays, the most successful of which, *Open Windows* was performed at St James's Theatre, London. In all, Alfred wrote over thirty books, many of them during his residence on the Island. He died in London.

Noyes, Alfred (1880–1958)

Alfred was born in Wolverhampton and entered Exeter College, Oxford, in 1898. He very quickly established himself as a writer. Most notable of his early works include:

The Loom of Years (1902),
The Highwayman (1904),
Forty Singing Seamen (1907).

It is the second of these that established him, and for which he is most famous; to quote:

'The road was a ribbon of moonlight over the purple
moor And the highwayman came riding, Riding, riding
The highwayman came riding, up to the old inn-door'.

In 1907, Alfred married the daughter of the United States Consul and, through her father's contacts, undertook a very successful lecture tour in the USA. Following on from this he was offered a Princeton University Professorship in 1914. He stayed in the USA until 1926, shortly after his wife's death. Moving back to England, he settled on the Island (in 1929) at Lisle Combe, St Lawrence, with his second wife. While there, he wrote:

The Torch Bearers (1930),
A Biography of Voltaire (1936).

Interestingly, *The Torch Bearers* is not a poem but a three volume History of Science!

At the outbreak of war in 1945, he took his family back to the safety of the USA only returning to St Lawrence in 1949 where he lived until his death. He died at Ryde hospital but is buried at Totland. In 1990, his son Hugh became High Sheriff for the Island.

Odell, Noel (1890–1987)

Noel was born at St Lawrence where his father was Rector. After local primary education, he studied first at Brighton College and then the Royal School of Mines, London. During the First World War, he served as a lieutenant in the Royal Engineers, mostly in France. He worked as a geologist for the Anglo-Persian Oil Company both in Persia and, later, in Canada. He soon turned to academic work, first at Harvard University (1928–30) and then Clare College, Cambridge. At the outbreak of the Second World War, he re-enlisted and served as a major in the Bengal Sappers.

In 1946, he was appointed Professor of Geology at Calgary, Canada, and took similar chairs in New Zealand and India. One of his abiding passions was mountaineering and, in this arena, his greatest claim to fame was to be the first person to climb to the summit of Nanda Devi, India, that reaches

25,695 ft. It was in this mountaineering role that he was the last person to see George Mallory before he disappeared, climbing Mount Everest.

Noel died in Cambridge.

Pollard, Albert (1869–1948)

Albert, the second son of a family of six, was born in Ryde where his father was a teacher of Chemistry. After primary education in the town, he went to Felsted School, Essex, and then Jesus College, Oxford, from where he graduated with a first class History degree in 1891. As early as 1893 he was the assistant editor of the *Dictionary of National Biography* and in this post was responsible for over 400 entries. He became Professor of History at University College, London, from 1903 until 1931 and became well known with the publication of many books on the Tudors, a field in which he was a recognised expert. His books included biographies of Henry VIII, Cranmer and Wolseley and the classic *History of the English Parliament*.

Albert formed the History Association in 1906 and was the editor of the *Bulletin of the Institute of Historical Research* from 1923 until 1939. His work was fundamental to raising the status of History such that it became seen as an academic subject, particularly in schools. He retired to Milford-on-sea, near Lymington, Hampshire, where he died and is buried.

Pound, Dudley (1877–1943)

Dudley was born in Wroxall, the son of a barrister. Although his American mother was in a position to see that he could take employment in a well-known New York bank, he chose to join the Royal Navy as a cadet at Dartmouth in 1891. By 1909 he was a commander and, by 1913, an instructor at the Naval Staff College, Greenwich. Made a captain by 1916, he had command of the battleship HMS *Colossus*. This ship was in the thick of the Battle of Jutland (1916), sinking two German cruisers.

By 1930, he was a vice admiral and, in 1936, as a full admiral, had command of the Mediterranean Fleet. He was knighted in 1937 and became First Sea Lord in 1939, just in time for the Second World War.

Sir Dudley's prime concern in the Battle of the Atlantic was the war against the menace of German submarines, the U-Boats. These presented a severe threat to the British war effort as the German High Command had realised that, even if not defeated in an armed struggle, England could be starved into submission by cutting the country's many sea routes, through which so much material flowed. Sir Dudley died in London before seeing the ultimate success of the plans he had laid to defeat them. As may befit such a senior naval officer, he died on Trafalgar Day and is buried in London.

Poynder, John (1866–1936)

John was born in Ryde and received his education, first at home and then at Harrow school, followed by Christ Church, Oxford, in 1885, but he left before completing a degree. John inherited extensive properties in Wiltshire and was soon elected MP for Chippenham, serving three terms. In 1920, after notable service both in Parliament and on the London Council, he became Baron Islington and was appointed as Governor General of New Zealand. He resigned this post in 1912 and from 1915 until 1918 was Under Secretary of State for India. He died at his home in London.

Priestley, John B (1894–1984)

John was born in Bradford where he also went to school. Against his father's wishes he went into the local wool trade and, as a salesman, travelled widely in Europe as a result. During World War I he was injured serving on the western front and, upon demobilization, used the generous terms to obtain a place at Trinity Hall, Cambridge. He was a prolific writer, producing his first work, *English Journey*, in 1934. There followed a huge output that also produced the story for a Gracie Field's film, *Sing As We Go*, in the same year. The year 1939 saw an autobiography entitled *Rain Upon Godshill* (but it was published in 1941). His study, built on a flat roof on the east face of the house, would have provided him with a clear view towards that village. However, this autobiography has little connection with the Island, apart from its title!

Soon after the outbreak of war in 1939, John was asked by the government to provide a regular Sunday evening broadcast. He did so under the title *Postscripts*. At the time, Priestley's broadcasts were second only to those of Churchill in terms of audience rating and importance. A transcript of part of one of these evening monologues, broadcast in 1940, just after Dunkirk, was as follows:

> *'Among the paddle steamers that will never return was one I knew well, for it was the pride of the ferry service to the Isle of Wight — none other than the good ship 'Gracie Fields.' I tell you, we were proud of the 'Gracie Fields' for she was the glittering Queen of our local line and, instead of taking an hour over her voyage, used to do it, churning like mad, in 45 minutes. And now never again will we board her at Cowes and go down to her dining room for a fine breakfast of bacon and eggs. She has paddled and churned away-for ever. But now-look-this little steamer and all her brave and battered sisters is immortal. She'll go sailing proudly down the years in the epic of Dunkirk. And our great-grandchildren, when they learn how we began this war by snatching glory out of defeat, and then swept on to victory may also learn how the little holiday steamers made an excursion to hell and came back glorious'.*

(The *Gracie Fields* was a paddle steamer that brought holidaymakers to Cowes from Southampton and, having saved over 280 troops, was later sunk leaving Dunkirk with another group during the wartime evacuation of troops.)

At the height of his fame, in 1948, he moved to Brook Hill House, atop the hills at Brook, overlooking the Military Road. His output of work was prolific; one of the first stories from his new home was *The Linden Tree*, but he also provided the libretto for the Arthur Bliss Opera *The Olympians*.

After a series of affairs, he and his wife divorced rather messily and, in 1953, he married Jacquetta Hawkes, the well-known broadcaster and archaeologist. As if it was a celebration of their marriage, they were joint authors of *Journey Down a Rainbow*. They stayed at Brook Hill House until they finally left the Island in 1959. John had over seventy of his works published during his twenty-six years based on the Island. He moved to a house just outside Stratford-on-Avon, Warwickshire, where he died after some twenty-five years.

Rawlins, Horace (1875–?)

Born in Ryde, Horace moved to America in January 1895. His particular claim to fame is that he was the first ever winner of the American golf Open Championship (played in 1895) and that when he was only just twenty-one! At the time, he was the assistant professional at the host course: The Newport, Rhode Island, Golf and Country Club. This first competition was thirty-six holes but was played by eleven competitors, on a 9-hole course! His prize was $150 and a gold medal.

Roe, Alliott Verdon (1877–1958)

Born in Manchester, Alliott declined to follow his father's profession in medicine, leaving for Canada, aged only fourteen, for work in civil engineering. This proved to be unsatisfactory, and he soon returned to England and took a number of posts, including one as an apprentice in Portsmouth Dockyard, and later as a designer for the Sheffield Simplex Car Company. Whilst working as 3rd engineer on an ocean-going steamship he developed a keen interest in building model aircraft. In 1906, seeing that the *Daily Mail* was offering a first prize of £150 for the first model aircraft to demonstrate sustained flight, he submitted an entry and won the competition easily, but the judges saw fit to award him only half the advertised prize money (despite being a competition for model aircraft, the judges seemed more interested in balloon flight).

This success was the turning point of his life, and Alliott decided, together with his brother Humphrey, to begin the construction of aircraft. The recent successful heavier-than-air flight by the Wright brothers in America acted as a spur to this venture.

Howard Pixton (Roe's chief mechanic) had written:

> *'In the early days of fight, Brooklands was the hub of nearly all experimental flying in Great Britain. Brooklands was the home to a handful of "intrepid birdmen" with primitive planes of wood and glue. Prior to 1910, there was practically no flying on English machines and, if you wanted to fly, you had to go to France and buy a French aeroplane. It was due to people like A V Roe that this was to change.'*

AV (as he became known) was the first Briton to construct and fly an aeroplane, at Brooklands in June 1908, a year before the first officially recognised flight in Great Britain by John Moore-Brabazon. (This first aircraft of AVs, a triplane, is kept at the Kensington Science Museum.) AV exhibited a Roe Triplane at the 1910 Boston USA Airshow but failed to win a significant prize. In January of that year, he formally registered AV Roe as the first company to become an aircraft manufacturer. The famous AVRO 504 made its first significant appearance in the 'War of the Roses' air race in 1913 at Moortown, near the centre of Leeds. It clocked a speed of 66.5 mph, coming fourth but nonetheless created a great deal of interest with a succession of design and engine changes. The '504' fulfilled many First World War roles and was still in use as a basic trainer in 1941! In the 1920s, C G Grey, the authority on early aviation, wrote:

> *'The modern aeroplane is the direct descendent of Roe's machine and not, as many think, of the Wright's machine, a design which was long ago discarded as inefficient'.*

AVRO 504 was sold to Armstrong-Siddeley in 1928 and AV and his associates moved to the Island and purchased the boatbuilding company of S E Saunders at East Cowes. As early as 1929, a new company, Saunders-Roe, had been formed and began construction of 'flying boats', seen at the time as a good way to link the various parts of the British Empire, much of which was either bounded by open sea or close to large rivers. AV was knighted for his services to aviation at this time. From 1930 until just before the outbreak of war in 1939, Saunders-Roe made a name for themselves in both the design and the construction of seaplanes and motor yachts.

During the war, Saunders-Roe (SARO) moved some of its operation to Beaumaris, Anglesey, although the East Cowes works were able, despite bomb damage, to complete construction (under licence) of much needed aircraft: 461 Supermarine Walrus and 290 Sea Otters were built. This freed the Supermarine factory to concentrate on the building of Spitfire fighters.

Development work continued and, in 1947, SARO unveiled the world's first and only jet seaplane, the SR. A/1. Only three prototypes were built, one of which is in the Southampton Hall of Aviation. The project was abandoned in 1951 after one of the craft sank in the Solent after hitting a floating log.

During the war, the design team had begun work on a large troop, or passenger-carrying, seaplane and, in 1953, the first SARO Princess flying boat was shown at the Farnborough air display. Ultimately, this magnificent craft was not a success and it was the last of a long line of flying boats.

In 1952, the Government were looking for an interceptor that would cope with a possible threat from Russian highflying bombers, and Saunders-Roe was one of two companies to win a development contract. This led to the creation of the SR53, a fighter that used a rocket engine. It could climb at the amazing speed of 25,000ft/sec and reach a speed of 1.33 mach (1.33 times the speed of sound). It first appeared in public at the 1953 Farnborough air display (an example of this aeroplane is kept at the RAF Museum, Cosford). The Government lost interest in this development in 1957, and further work ceased.

In 1951, SARO bought the rights to the Spanish-designed Ciervo Skeeter helicopter and began its manufacture. The first prototype had flown in 1947 and, with a degree of updating and alteration, Skeeters entered UK military service in 1957. It was not a huge success and manufacture soon ceased. Around this time, work began on the design of analogue computers at the 'Electronics' division at Osborne, with the intention of using such systems to help with the control of flight in ever-faster aircraft.

After early development work with small hovercraft, SARO received a contract to develop a full size machine in 1958, and this led to the creation of the SR-N1 hovercraft, the design of which led to a series of similar, passenger and car-carrying, craft that plied across, both, the Solent — between Cowes and Southampton, Ryde and Gosport — and between England and France.

In 1955, SARO was commissioned to develop a missile capable of delivering Britain's recently developed A-bombs and H-bombs, and this led to the development of the rocket-testing site at the Needles Headland. This was the Black Knight rocket. Local testing was needed before full trials were conducted at Woomera, Australia. The secure, easily guarded underground accommodation at The Needles, originally constructed as a defensive measure in the Napoleonic War, was ideal.

In 1959, soon after AV's death, Westlands, based in Yeovil, bought SARO, and AV's link to the Island was broken. He had lived with his family at Rowland's Castle, Hampshire, since 1945 and died in hospital, in Portsmouth. In its thirty years on the Island, the company had lived up to the sense of adventure that first made Sir Alliott 'take to the skies'.

Rowbotham, Samuel (1880–1946)

Samuel's father, Thomas, was a civil engineering contractor who built much of the infrastructure of the east side of Birmingham. Born in Birmingham, Samuel took over the business in the 1930s and, in 1937, sold the family's 300-acre Gilbertstone estate (in what is now South Yardsley) to Birmingham City Council for a huge sum, together with the proviso that his company could be responsible for building the houses on the land. At this time he was already living at Brook Hill House on the Island and, because of the extent of the work he had done in Warwickshire and the area to the east of Birmingham, was honoured by being elected High Sheriff of Warwickshire that year. In his will, he made a donation to Birmingham University that established a prize. He spent a good deal of his time on the Island breeding horses, Suffolk Greys in particular. This was not easy in the war years because of the general shortage of feed. He died at his home and is buried at Brook.

Seely, John Edward (Jack) (1868–1947)

Born in Nottinghamshire, where Jack grew up at the family estate of Sherwood Lodge, he nonetheless spent many of his holidays on the Island.

At the age of seventeen, he was given a place on the crew of the Brook life-boat, a position that he retained until the mid 1930s, this despite his military and political duties. He showed his mettle during a violent storm in October 1891:

> *'The Brook lifeboat, with Jack on board, was launched to go to the aid of the French ship Henri et Leontine. However, the sea was so ferocious that the lifeboat was thrown back on the beach. Undaunted, Jack tied a rope around his waist and swam to the stricken craft, gave the horribly injured captain first aid, and then used a breeches buoy to get him to land.'*

Jack had been to school at Harrow where, in addition to befriending Stanley Baldwin, the future Prime Minister, he met, and formed a life-long friendship, with Winston Churchill. He studied Law at Cambridge and, while there, enrolled in the Hampshire Yeomanry, training with them in his vacations.

The Boer War (1899–1902) saw him in command of the Isle of Wight troop and it was during this hostility he was awarded the DSO (1900). While he was still on the battlefield, he was elected as Liberal MP for the Island.

On his return, disgusted with the Government, he 'crossed the floor' and was joined in doing so by Churchill. By 1912 he was Secretary of State for War and did much to prepare the country for the looming troubles. Unfortunately, in the run up to the war, Jack was, in part, responsible for an unwarranted delay in the development of the British aircraft industry as, in his role in the Government, he agreed that French aircraft should be pur-chased rather than British, on 'the grounds of safety'. This despite evidence from **A V Roe** (see page 173) to the contrary.

Soon after the 1914 outbreak of hostilities, Jack resigned from Government and was appointed a lieutenant colonel. He was involved in many of the ter-rible battles of the conflict and, in 1918, was gassed, ending his remarkable service with the rank of general. After the war, he returned to politics, first in the Ministry of Munitions and then as Under-Secretary for Air. He resigned this post in 1919 but remained as an Island MP until 1924.

His wartime experiences left an indelible mark such that, in the early 1930s, he was seen by many as pro-Nazi or at least as an appeaser. In fact, he was simply horrified at the thought of another 'Great War' and, until about

1938, did what he could to counter some of the worst of allied propaganda, having widely publicised meetings with Hitler, Mussolini and their associates. Early in 1939 he came to realise the danger posed by the Axis forces, and was bitterly upset that he had been so easily duped by them, offering his services to the military. He died at the family home of Mottistone Manor.

Earl Birkenhead wrote of him:

> *'In fields of great and critical danger he has constantly, over a long period of years, displayed a cool valour which everyone in the world who knows the facts freely recognises'.*

Selincourt, Aubrey de (1894–1962)

Aubrey's father owned the famous London store known as 'Swan and Edgar' and he was brother-in-law to A A Milne. Born near Broadlands, Hants, Aubrey took a Classics degree at Oxford. He served at Gallipoli with the N Staffs regiment and obtained a transfer to the Royal Flying Corps later in 1916. Serving as a pilot with the 52nd Squadron, he was shot down in May 1917 (by the German 'Ace', Werner Voss) and saw the war out as a prisoner of war.

On demobilization in 1919, he moved to Niton. This was his permanent home, despite working in Dorset, first as a teacher and, by the 1930s, as head teacher. The school faced financial problems, and Aubrey resigned and moved back to his home on the Island. He immediately continued writing; his first Island publication, *Isle of Wight*, appearing in 1948, using the same format as his first book on Dorset (1947). Once established as an author, he employed his skill as a classicist to translate works such as:

Herodotus' *Histories*,
Livy's *Early History of Rome*,
The War with Hannibal,
Arrian's *Life of Alexander the Great*.

All of these, and many others, came out as part of the 'Penguin Classics' series. In addition to writing, he also gave poetry recitals, **Mimi Khalvati** (see page 197), recalling these in one of her poems.

Aubrey died at his home just outside Niton.

Shedden, Roscow (1882–1956)

Roscow was born in East Cowes, the eldest of a family of six. He went to school there and later attended a church seminary, joining the priesthood. The family were wealthy: one earlier member having been a successful merchant in Virginia and then making a further fortune in London through marine insurance. When this relative died in 1826, the family estates (then in Northamptonshire) came to Roscow's grandfather on the Island. Roscow had been brought up at his father's large house, Millfield, in Old Road.

Roscow was appointed Bishop of Nassau (West Indies) in 1919 and, before he left the Island, gave a service in Whippingham church. He made many valuable improvements in his bishopric, including the quality of education provided by the schools. He wrote a book about his experiences, *Ups and Downs in a West Indian Diocese*. Roscow served as Bishop there until 1931 when he returned to England. He then served as Honorary Assistant Bishop for Oxford until his death at Chipping Norton where he is buried. The Shedden family extended the esplanade at East Cowes seafront from the junction with Cambridge Road up to the wall marking the start of the Norris Castle estate. Until 1939, this stretch was known as Shedden Esplanade.

Smith, Clement (1878–1927) VC

Born in Romsey, where his father was church canon, Clement moved to the Island with his family in 1895, when his father gained the living at Whippingham. He lived at the rectory until 1900 when he joined the army, being commissioned in the Duke of Cornwall's Light Infantry. After service in South Africa, he joined the force defending British Somalia against local tribesmen. It was here, at Jidballi, that he was awarded the VC for his single-handed attempt to defend two wounded colleagues. He became a major by 1916 and, while fighting in the Juba Mountains (in what is now South Sudan), was awarded The Military Cross (MC).

In the First World War, he commanded the Imperial Camel Corps, based in Egypt. He returned to the Island on the death of his father (1921) and the village of Whippingham presented him with an engraved cup. When he retired from the army in 1922, with the rank of brigadier general, he moved to Italy where he died. He is buried in the English Cemetery, Alassio, Italy.

Vereker, John (1886–1946) 6th Viscount Gort, VC

Born in London, but with the family home of East Cowes Castle (to which the family had moved in 1861 when the third Viscount Gort married the widowed owner), John joined the army in 1905, gazetted into the Grenadier Guards. By the outbreak of war in 1914 he was a captain and an aide-de-camp to Sir Douglas Haig. He held a variety of staff posts until, in 1917, he was given command of the 1st Battalion, Grenadier Guards.

It was in this post that he won a bar to his DSO at the 3rd Battle of Ypres. In 1918, John was awarded a VC at the Battle of Cambrai when, having been severely wounded, he climbed off his stretcher and refused to leave the field until the position had been taken. In 1937, he was made Field Marshal and Chief of the Imperial General Staff, the highest military post of the Empire. He is probably best known for being in command of the BEF (British Expeditionary Force) that, in 1939, was sent to France to try and stem the German advance. The British High Command's failure to appreciate the scale of the German's massive onslaught, coupled with vacillation by the French High Command, put John in an impossible position. It led to the scramble that became the evacuation from Dunkirk. After this, John, the 6th Lord Gort as he is now, was effectively sidelined for the rest of the war, being given the Governorship, first of Gibraltar and then Malta.

Not sufficiently recognised is the fact that he was responsible for the wartime large-scale extension of runways at RAF Gibraltar. These proved to be of inestimable value later in the war as they allowed refuelling of aircraft on their way to both the defence of Malta and the later landings in the North African campaign. In 1942 he was made Governor of the beleaguered Island of Malta and, under the most difficult circumstances, saw that the population of over 200,000 were adequately fed despite severe rationing, water shortages and regular bombing. His final posting was as High Commissioner for Palestine (which at this time had been mandated to Britain by the defunct League of Nations). He was drafted back to England in 1946, suffering from cancer. He died soon after at Guy's Hospital, London.

While they lived at East Cowes Castle, the family did much to improve East Cowes town. Lady Vereker paid for East Cowes to have its own Town Hall. The family were also generous beneficiaries to the local church and gave some four acres of land to the town to create the Jubilee Recreation Ground. They also made significant changes to the castle itself as well as building Castle Farm, which made good use of the fertile fields to the southwest of the main building. John was a keen sailor and loved his yacht *Carlotta* to the extent that, in 1925, he stayed aboard her while he wrote *The British Army Training Manual*.

When the Verekers left the Island, in 1933, they were the last private owners of East Cowes Castle, this wonderful creation of the architect, **John Nash** (see page 58). The castle has since been demolished and the whole estate is now occupied by housing; only the north gatehouse and the icehouse remain.

Whitchurch, Harry (1866–1907) VC

Born in Sandown, Harry received a wide medical education, studying in England, France and Germany. After qualifying as a doctor and further training at St Bartholomew's Hospital, London, he joined the Indian Army in 1888. He served in a number of engagements including the Looshai Expedition. Whilst serving at Chitral Fort, Harry was with a small scouting party that was attacked by a large force. The Captain in charge was badly wounded and several Ghurkhas killed. Having to make a wide detour to avoid the worst of the fire, Harry carried the officer on his back for three miles. Several times, to overcome some obstinate enemy, he had to lay down the officer and lead the remaining men in a charge, after which he would again pick him up and move on.

His VC was gazetted in 1895. He went on to serve further in India and, in 1901, was involved in the relief of the Peking Legations (China). Harry rose to the rank of Surgeon-General and died of fever at Dharmsala, India, where he is buried.

EPOCH 7, 1899–1990

Abraham, Gerald (1904–1988)

Born and educated in Newport, Gerald had hopes of joining the Royal Navy but ill health prevented this. After a few piano lessons, he taught himself both the theory and practice of music and, in 1927, produced his first book, on the composer Borodin. He then taught himself Russian and followed this with *Studies in Russian Music* (1935) and *On Russian Music* (1939). In 1939, Gerald became the deputy editor of the BBC magazine *The Listener* and remained as that publication's music editor until 1962. In that year he became Assistant Controller of Music for the BBC.

Gerald was made the first Professor of Music at Liverpool University in 1947 as well as occupying similar chairs at other universities. In 1969 he was elected as President of the Royal Music Association, a post he held until 1974. His output of publications was enormous, culminating in *The Concise Oxford History of Music* (1979). He died in hospital at Midhurst, Sussex.

Aisher, Owen (1900–1993)

Born in Bulford, Wiltshire where he went to school, Owen worked for a range of building companies until, in the early 1930s, he joined with his father and began making concrete roofing tiles. These were so successful, Owen set up a company, Marley Ltd, in 1934. The business grew quickly such that, during World War II, he helped make parts for the famous 'Mulberry Harbours'. He was made chairman of the company in 1945, a post he held until 1982.

Owen had become interested in sailing in the early 1930s when he joined the Putney-based Ranelagh Sailing Club. He was soon attracted to the yachting scene at Cowes and won many awards, the most prestigious, perhaps, being the gruelling 'Fastnet' race, which he won in 1951. HRH Prince Philip was a regular member of his crew, and Owen was elected 'Yachtsman of the Year' in 1958. Around this time, he purchased a property in Cowes. Owen's successful business allowed him to accept significant other roles such as President of the Royal Yachting Association (1970–1975) and Admiral of the Royal Ocean Racing Club. Owen became a member of the exclusive Royal Yacht Squadron in the 1970s. He was knighted in 1981. He died at his other home at Godstone, Surrey.

Armitage, Michael (1930–)

Born in Oldham, Lancashire, Michael moved to East Cowes with his family in 1937. He went to the local (Grange Road) primary school and then to Newport Grammar School. He enlisted in the RAF in 1947 as a Halton apprentice and won a scholarship to the Royal Air Force College, Cranwell, from where he was commissioned in 1953. He then served first as a fighter pilot in Hong Kong, and then in a series of staff, academic and flying, training appointments in the UK and Germany, before commanding RAF Luqa in Malta and, later, RAF Bruggen, Germany, one of the RAF's premier operational stations at this time.

His later and more senior appointments included Director of Forward Policy in the Air Force department, Director of Service Intelligence during the Falklands conflict in 1982 then Chief of Defence Intelligence responsible for all military intelligence. Michael's final post was Commandant of the Royal College of Defence Studies from where he retired in 1990 having achieved the rank of 'Air Chief Marshal'.

He was appointed CBE in 1974, knighted in 1983 and made a Freeman of the City of London in 1996. Sir Michael retained a link to the Island as, upon retirement, he was, for some years, President of the Isle of Wight Aircrew Association.

Attrill, Louis (1975–)

Born and educated in Shanklin, Louis began his rowing career there when he joined the local rowing club. It was natural therefore that, on obtaining a place at Imperial College, London, in 1993 (where he read Civil Engineering), he joined the college rowing team. In his first year in this 'eights' team they won first place at the Henley Regatta. In the 1999 World Championships in Canada, the team were awarded a silver medal, and in the 2000 Sydney Olympics Louis' team were awarded gold.

Louis still lives on the Island where he works for the family civil engineering company.

Bate, Anthony (1927–2012)

Born and educated in Stourbridge, Worcestershire, Anthony moved to the Island in 1945 when his parents took over the running of the Northbank Hotel, Seaview. It was whilst he worked in this trade that his girlfriend (Diana Watson, a local girl who later became his wife — they married at St Peter's, Seaview in 1954) persuaded him to join the local amateur dramatic group, a move that he relished to the extent that, in 1951, he decided to make acting his career and Anthony enrolled at the Central School of Speech and Drama, London.

Anthony began acting professionally in 1953 and by the end of his career had performed in well over 100 films and plays. He made his mark in the 1977 spy drama, in the role of Kim Philby, in *Philby, Burgess and Maclean*, playing against Derek Jacobi. He used his air of authenticity, coupled with an undertone of subtle menace, to good effect in further spy dramas, particularly in the 1979 BBC TV production *Tinker, Taylor, Soldier, Spy*.

Beken, Keith (1914–2007)

See the Entry under his father, Frank in Epoch 6 (see page 153).

Bottomley, Virginia (1948–)

Born Virginia Garnett in Danoon, Scotland, her parents holidayed at Nettlestone where they owned a property, and this is where Virginia was christened. She attended Putney High School for Girls, graduated at the University of Essex and then the London School of Economics (LSE). She celebrated her marriage to her long-standing friend Peter Bottomley at the Nettlestone house and she clearly developed an attachment to the Island because, in the 1983 General Election, she made an (unsuccessful) bid for the Island seat. Undeterred, she became MP for SW Surrey the following year, a seat she held until 2005 when she was raised to the peerage when she adopted Nettlestone as her title. She had worked as Private Secretary to Chris Patten when he was Minister of State in the Department of Education and Science (1985–6) and became Minister of State for Health in 1989. She was elected to the Privy Council in 1992.

Baroness Bottomley (of Nettlestone) is Chancellor of the University of Hull and a Governor of London School of Economics. Although she lives in Surrey, she retains the house in Nettlestone.

Britten, John (1928–1977)

See under **Norman, Desmond** in this epoch (see page 202).

Cockerell, Christopher (1910–1999)

Christopher was born in Cambridge, the only son of the Director of the Fitzwilliam Museum there. He attended Gresham's school in Norfolk, winning a place to Peterhouse, Cambridge, from where he graduated with a degree in engineering in 1931. He joined the **Marconi** (see page 166) Company in Chelmsford and was involved in both experimental outside radio broadcasts and early work on television. Just before the outbreak of World War II, he developed a direction finder for use on the Cunard liner *Mauretania*. This proved so successful that, in 1939 at the request of the RAF, he devised a radio-homing device for use on aircraft, thousands of which were employed to very good effect during World War II. By 1948, Christopher had thirty-six electronic patents to his name.

Despite numerous offers of promotion, he left the Marconi Company in 1951 and set up a small boat hire business with his wife at Lowestoft. Feeling that a ship's motion could be made more energy-efficient, he experimented at his home and, using a domestic fan and two tin cans, he created the first amphibious hovercraft, patenting the idea in 1955. He found it difficult to interest companies in his idea until a friend arranged for the idea to be shown to **Lord Louis Mountbatten** (see page 201).

Eventually, in 1957, the Saunders-Roe Company at East Cowes took up the work, having received Government financial backing to develop the idea. In that year, Christopher moved to live at 'The White House' near to the Osborne works of Saunders-Roe, his home there also serving as his office. The first 'hovercraft', called the SR-N1, left the works in 1959. He lived in East Cowes for the rest of his life, overseeing the gradual development of his idea, culminating in the production of a cross-Channel hovercraft that could carry over 400 passengers and up to sixty cars. Hovercrafts are still in service in many countries where there is a need to cross difficult terrain such as marshland. The link to the Island is maintained by the hovercraft service that still operates between Ryde and Southsea. Christopher was awarded the CBE in 1966, became FRS in 1967 and was knighted in 1969. Sir Christopher died at a nursing home at Sutton Scotney, Hampshire.

Compton, Violet (1904–1944)

Violet, later known by her stage name of 'Betty', was born in Sandown, and she and her family moved to Canada around 1912, settling in Toronto. It was here that she began her career in the theatre. After some minor success, she moved to New York and joined the famous 'Ziegfeld Follies'. The peak of her career came in 1927 when she was given a leading role in the original stage production of *Funny Face* in which she was the dance partner to Fred Astaire. In 1929, she took a leading role in Cole Porter's *Fifty Million Frenchmen*. The 1957 Bob Hope film *Beau James* chronicled the life of James Walker who, after resigning as Mayor of New York, married Betty in Cannes, France, in 1933 (he was her fourth husband). She died in hospital in Manhattan, USA.

Ellis, Mary (1917–2018)

Born at Leafield, Oxfordshire, where her father was a well-to-do farmer, Mary and her family moved to a larger farm adjacent to Brize Norton airfield in 1928. Here, she doubtless developed her interest in flight, having already flown, aged eight, through Alan Cobham's 'flying circus' when it ran pleasure flights from Witney. Mary (born Mary Wilkins) attended Burford Secondary School and, on leaving, helped on the farm. She had her first flying lesson in 1937 and attained her pilot's licence in 1938.

She responded to a wartime call for qualified pilots to join the newly-formed Air Transport Auxiliary (ATA) in 1941 and was based at Hamble, Hampshire. The ATA's task was to ferry aircraft from factories (or repair facilities) to RAF bases, so freeing up aircrew for active service. During the war, 161 women fulfilled this role, and Mary's log-book shows, that in the five years she served, she had ferried seventy-six different types of aircraft, including over 400 spitfires and forty-seven Wellington bombers. On landing one Wellington at an RAF base, the officers could not believe that a 5ft 2in tall 'girl' could have flown the plane alone, until they searched for, and failed to find, 'the pilot'!

After acting as pilot for a wealthy businessman (who, at the time, owned Sandown Airport), in 1950, he asked her to manage the establishment. It was here that she met her future husband (Dennis Ellis) who was an instructor there. They married in 1961, and Mary oversaw the growth of Sandown Airport until she retired in 1970. She lived near the airfield until her death.

Fewtrell, Ernest (1909–2005)

Ernest had the rare distinction of being born in the police station at Ryde where his father was a constable. He had his schooling in Ryde and, as soon as he was old enough, went to work on a sheep farm in Australia. On his return to England in 1927, he joined the Buckinghamshire police force. By 1950 he was Detective Inspector and, by 1954, Detective Superintendent and head of the Buckinghamshire CID. He came to wide public notice in 1963 because the 'Great Train Robbery' was on his patch. He was closely involved in tracking, arresting and sentencing the twelve men responsible. Upon retirement in 1964, he wrote a book of the event, *The Train Robbers*. He died at his home at Poole, Dorset.

Fleming, Victor (1901–1991)

Victor was born in London where he went to school. His music-loving parents introduced him to the violin at which he soon became a master. He played in a number of orchestras around the country and, in 1948, after a tour to the Island, he settled in Ventnor. He came to prominence in 1967 when he was made conductor of the British Concert Orchestra, working with notable musicians such as Semprini.

Victor helped to establish the Welsh National Opera Company and was in demand in radio programmes. He became Mayor of Ventnor in 1979, his house on the promenade being distinguished by having an ornamental fence sporting musical notes. He died at his home and is buried at Ventnor.

Francki, Wojciech (1903–1996)

This Polish officer was commander of the destroyer ORP *Błyskawica* when it came into her homeport of Cowes in 1942 (ORP is the Polish equivalent of our HMS). The ship had been ordered by the Polish government and had been built at White's at Cowes in 1935 (see **Thomas White**, Epoch 2, page 70). Having escaped the German forces when they overran Poland in 1938, the ship worked in tandem with the Royal Navy as part of the Free Polish forces.

In May 1942 ORP *Błyskawica* came back to Cowes to have her armaments improved. It was standard practice for naval vessels to be allowed to dock in port and retain their stock of armaments in wartime. But, as a 'foreign' ship, ORP *Błyskawica* was asked to disarm when she docked. Her commander, Captain Francki PN, luckily, chose to ignore this order from the Admiralty and, realising that Cowes was a possible target for an attack, actually took more armaments on board! Whilst undergoing her refitting, the Germans decided to bomb a number of sites including Cowes, knowing that the town and its environs housed ship, submarine and aircraft manufacturing facilities. Captain Francki and his men provided the principal defence to the surrounding area (supported by 'bofors' gunfire from Free-French minesweepers that were also in the river), the attack lasting so long that ORP *Błyskawica's* guns had to be drenched regularly in buckets of seawater to prevent overheating.

Although ORP *Błyskawica* did not 'down' any aircraft, her fierce defence of the town, as part of which Francki ordered the use of smoke flares to obscure the area, meant that the bombers had to fly higher than they had planned and so much of their bombing fell away from its intended targets. Many incendiary devices fell in Parkhurst Forest, the fires they started misleading subsequent waves of aircraft, over 160 in all. Once the attack was over, Francki had his men help the civilian population deal with the fire and other damage to the town. There is no question that Captain Francki and his men saved much of Cowes from severe damage, as well as saving many lives. Because he had deliberately ignored an Admiralty order, he received no award for this action, though many senior officers thanked him for his bravery.

ORP *Błyskawica* served valiantly in other wartime operations including North Sea convoy work and the Dunkirk evacuation. Francki was awarded the DSC for his part in this latter engagement. He was also the recipient of the Polish Order of Merit, the Polonia Restutia Cross, twice, and the Polish Cross of Honour, four times!

The ship and its crew are remembered by a number of plaques in the town of Cowes, as well as a square named after Captain Francki himself, recalling the stout defence provided by the ship and her crew under his command. The ship was handed back to the Polish communist government in 1946 and only withdrawn from their service in 1967. ORP *Błyskawica* is now a Polish national treasure, conserved as a museum ship (like our HMS *Victory*) in Gdynia, Poland.

Francki was born in Warsaw and initially fought in the Polish Army's successful defence against the Russian Bolsheviks at the Battle of Vistula (1920). He joined the Polish Navy in 1921 and was in command of his first ship, ORP *Wilja*, by 1934. He was given command of ORP *Błyskawica* only three days before the fateful attack on Cowes. After the war, he took his family to New Zealand and finally settled in Australia. He continued with a life at sea until he was seventy-three. He died in Australia, but his ashes were buried, with full military honours, at the Powązki Cemetery, Warsaw.

Fuchs, Vivian (1908–1999)

Born in Freshwater, Vivian's family faced disruption at the outbreak of World War I with his father, a German national, being interned on the Isle of Man for the duration of hostilities. The family remained on the Isle of Wight until 1918. Vivian then attended schools in Kent followed by study at St John's, Cambridge. His tutor there was James Wordie who had been a senior scientist on Sir Edward Shakleton's *Endurance* Expedition (1914–17). Graduating as a geologist in 1930, Vivian took part in expeditions to East Africa, generating material he used to gain his doctorate. He reached the rank of major during World War II (1939–45) and, upon demobilization in 1947, was appointed Field Commander for the Falkland Island dependencies survey.

It was in this post that he devised a scheme to cross the Antarctic using Sno Cat Tractors. A successful crossing was made in 1957 with the expedition proving, amongst other things, the existence of a landmass under the ice. Vivian was appointed Director of the British Antarctic Survey, 1958–73. On his return to England, he was knighted. He retired in 1973.

Gale, Patrick (1962–)

Patrick was born in Newport where his father was Governor of Camp Hill Prison. After his primary education, he attended Winchester College and then graduated from New College, Oxford, in 1983.

He began writing upon leaving college, earning his keep as a waiter in an all-night restaurant. His first work was *Aerodynamics of Pork*, which was published in 1985 to critical acclaim. Patrick has since produced a novel each year, one of which, *Notes from an Exhibition*, being crowned with the 'Best Read of the Year' award in the television programme *The Richard and Judy Show*. He now lives in Cornwall and is still busy writing.

Galsworthy, Jocelyn (1942–)

This Hampshire-born artist, a member of the well-known literary family, studied first at Winchester and then the City and Guilds School of Art, Kennington. She later worked in Paris and Munich and had her first exhibition at the Winchester Guildhall in 1964. Since 1985 she has made a world-acclaimed name for herself, specialising particularly in painting English and international cricket scenes. She has published two books, *Lords of Cricket* (2005) and *White Hats and Cricket Bats* (2000), and continues her work from her studio in St Helens, having moved there in 1991.

Gascoyne, David (1916–2001)

Born at Harrow Middlesex, David attended Salisbury Cathedral School and then Regent Street Polytechnic, London. He was only sixteen when he published his first work, *Roman Balcony*. He was an early champion of writing in the surrealistic style and his work soon attracted interest. The publication of *Poems 1937–1942* came with images by Graham Sutherland. He spent many years in Paris and Southern France (1937–1939 and 1953–1964), making friends with luminaries such as Salvador Dali. Seen as someone who had made significant contributions to French culture, David was made 'Chevalier dans l'ordre des Arts et Lettres' by the French Ministry of Culture. David moved to Northwood with his wife in 1985, where he died.

Goring, Marius (1912–1998)

Marius was born in Newport, his father being a local GP. Being of German extraction, the family followed the actions of members of the Royal Family and, in 1917, modified the original spelling of the name (which had been Goering). Marius attended Perse School in Cambridge and it was there that he made his first stage appearance (in 1925).

From 1932 to 1934 Marius was stage manager at The Old Vic Theatre and, at very short notice, in 1934, was asked to play Romeo to Peggy Ashcroft's Juliet. The performance earned him critical acclaim and he subsequently took many Shakespearean leads in the 1930s.

At the outbreak of war, he joined the Army and had the responsibility for broadcasts to Germany (he was fluent in both German and French). From 1947, he led a group of Shakespearean actors on tour to various French and German cities. His most memorable film roles were under the direction of Powell and Pressberger, the film moguls, when he took leads in films such as *A Matter of Life and Death* and *Red Shoes*. TV work included roles in *The Scarlet Pimpernel* (1955), *Edward and Mrs Simpson* (1980) and *Old Men at the Zoo* (1983).

Having helped to form English Equity, the actor's union, he became its president, (1963–65). In 1991, Marius was awarded the honour of Commander of the British Empire (CBE). He died at his home at Heathfield, East Sussex.

Green, David (1961–2013)

Born at Winchester where he attended Bishop Wordsworth's School, David had an abiding interest in outdoor activities. As soon as he was able, he became a ski instructor in France but soon returned to England, setting up a windsurfing school on Southampton Water.

In 1987, the National Sailing Centre at Cowes was purchased and re-named the United Kingdom Sailing Academy (UKSA) with David as wind-surfing coach. It was established to provide training in all aspects of sea craft. His enthusiasm and boundless energy soon saw him promoted to be the UKSA's chief executive and, under his stewardship, the charity expanded until it was catering for 9000 students a year and had a staff of 200.

Prompted by an article in the magazine *Yachting Monthly*, David became instrumental in the purchase and restoration of Sir Francis Chichester's fa-mous yacht, *Gypsy Moth IV*, bringing it to Cowes after it had re-enacted the original round-the-world trip. He resigned from UKSA in 2006 and set up his own Cowes-based marine consultancy. He died at his Cowes home.

Hancock, Sheila (1933–)

Sheila was born at Blackgang where her parents were publicans. The family moved to run a public house on Kings Cross Road, London, while she was still very young, and she went to Dartford Grammar School before winning a place to study at the Royal Academy of Dramatic Art (RADA).

Her acting debut was in her hometown of Dartford in 1950 when she played Beth in *Little Women*. She has subsequently had a very busy acting ca-reer that encompasses stage, screen (in *Carry on Cleo*, for example), TV (*The Rag Trade* as well as other series) and radio (the game show, *Just a Minute*). She became the first female artistic director of the Royal Shakespeare Company (RSC) and currently undertakes a leading role in various charities, as well as continuing with a busy acting schedule, recently in *The Sister Act* at the London Palladium (2009–2010).

Harris, Michael (1933–1994)

Born and educated in Belper, Staffordshire, Michael attended the London College of Art from 1959. He returned there in 1967 starting the hot glass facilities. After a range of disagreements with the college authorities, he re-signed his lectureship and, with his wife, took the brave step of starting a glass manufactory at Mdina, Malta — doubtless tempted by the generous tax arrangements available to new ventures.

This venture, Mdina Glass, was an immediate success and Michael stayed there, training locals and attracting worldwide notice. This business thrived until 1972 when the government of Dom Mintoff made it clear that he wished to sever all links with the English. This forced Michael to move his business, and he settled at St Lawrence. He also opened a sales outlet at Alum Bay and so benefitted from the huge tourist trade there. In 2013, some years after his death, his sons moved to new studios at Arreton where the business continues.

Hughes, Geoffrey (1944–2012)

Born in Wallasey, Cheshire, and educated at Abbotswood School, Liverpool, Geoffrey began work as a car salesman, who spent his free time performing with the Merseyside Unity Theatre and then the Victoria Theatre, Stoke-on-Trent. Around 1965, he was 'spotted' by an agent and, in 1966 made his debut in a minor role in the television comedy *The Likely Lads*.

He soon began attracting 'character' roles such as that of 'Eddie Yeats' in the long-running *Coronation Street*. He also took more significant roles in other TV comedies such as *The Royle Family* and *Keeping Up Appearances*.

Geoffrey and his wife moved to Newport in 2003 where they ran a timber supply company. He was a keen supporter of Island charities and this work was recognised in 2009 when he was elected Deputy Lord Lieutenant of the Island. Geoffrey died at Newport, having suffered from cancer.

Imrie, Celia (1952–)

Born in Guildford where she went to the Guildford School of Acting, Celia made her television debut in *Upstairs Downstairs* in 1972. Though famous for her television work, Celia has also made her mark on stage where, in 2006 she was awarded an Olivier Award for her part in the stage musical *Acorn*

Antiques. Her many film roles include being one of the ladies in *Calendar Girls* (2003) and matron in *St Trinians* (2007).

Celia has a home in London and has had a second home in Cowes since 1989. She has been heavily involved in the appeal for the establishment of an inshore lifeboat for Cowes.

Irons, Jeremy (1948–)

Jeremy was born in Cowes and received his early education in St Helens. He went to Sherbourne School where he was an indifferent student but, towards the end of his time there, was offered the part of Mr Puff in Sheridan's *The Critic*. This set him on his career of acting and he studied at the Bristol Old Vic theatre, his stage debut there being in a production of *Hay Fever*. This was followed by playing John the Baptist, opposite David Essex in the London production of *Godspell* (1971–1973). He first came to critical notice in 1975 when he played Frantz Liszt in *Notorious Woman*. Jeremy's major breakthrough came in 1979 when he played the part of Charles Ryder in the television adaptation of *Brideshead Revisited*. This was soon followed by a major part in the highly successful film *The French Lieutenant's Woman* and in 1980, Jeremy won Best Actor Oscar for his portrayal of Claus von Bulow in the film *Reversal of Fortune*. More recently he appeared in *The Time Machine* (2002), *Casanova* (2005), and *Kingdom of Heaven* (2005). His most recent major role was as 'Pope Alexander VI' in the 2011 television production of *The Borgias*. He still mixes his film work with regular stage productions.

Jupitus, Phillip (Phill) (1962–)

Born Phillip Swann at Newport where his unmarried mother had fled to escape her irate father, Phillip took the name of his stepfather. He left school early and obtained a post with the Department of Health and Social Security, a post he held for five years. Such work didn't suit him and he decided, in 1984, to become a support act for local touring bands. His performances as a comedian soon brought him to the notice of others and, early in the

1990s, he began to appear on television. By 1996, he was a regular on comedy programmes such as *Never Mind the Buzzcocks*, *Just a Minute* and *I'm Sorry I Haven't a Clue*. He also works on stage in the West End in *Hairspray* and in the touring version of *Spamalot*. Phillip, who currently lives in Leigh-on-sea, Essex, was awarded an Honorary Doctorate from the University of Essex in 2010.

Kendall, Kenneth (1924–2012)

Born in southern India, where his father worked as an engineer, Kenneth's family moved to Cornwall when he was ten. He was educated at Felsted School, Essex, and won a place at Corpus Christi College, Oxford, to read English. However, the war interrupted his studies and he was called up, serving as a captain in the Coldstream Guards in time to be involved in the D-Day landings.

On leaving the army, he began teaching in Essex when a colleague suggested he should apply to the BBC because of his clear diction. This he did and became an announcer for BBC radio in 1948. He changed to television in 1954 and, in 1955, became the first 'in-vision' newsreader. Kenneth retired from newsreading in 1981 but continued TV work as a freelance, his most memorable appearances being as host to the BBC Channel 4 programme *Treasure Hunt*, which ran from 1982 to 1989.

Kenneth set up home in Cowes in 1990, seeing that this gave him easier access to London (and continuing BBC work) than his family home in Cornwall. Initially, he opened a restaurant but finding this too taxing he opened a successful marine art gallery in the same premises. He died at Cowes shortly after suffering a heart attack.

Khalvati, Mimi (1944–)

Mimi was born in Tehran, Iran, and came to the Island as an eleven-year-old pupil at Upper Chine Girl's School in 1955. Although she clearly had visits home, she stayed at this school into its sixth form by which time she was eighteen. After working for an oil company in Iran she studied at Neuchâtel, Switzerland, and then at the London School of Oriental and African Studies.

She began writing collections of poetry in 1985 with *I Know a Place*; since then she has created several poetic works. Among them are:

In White Ink (1991),
Mirrorwork (1995),
The Chine (2002).

The Chine draws on her time on the Island where Shanklin Chine was a short walk from her school. Her work is highly regarded, as is her teaching of creative writing at universities in both the UK and the USA. Mimi was asked to be 'Poet in Residence' for the Royal Mail as part of the Poetry Society's Poetry Places scheme. She continues this and other work. One of her most recent publications is a translation, together with Choman Hardi, of Kurdish poems by Kajal Ahmad.

Krishnamma, Suri (1959–)

Born in Shanklin to an Indian father and English mother, Suri and his family moved to Carisbrooke when he was three. He had his education there, leaving for London at eighteen, having completed his A levels at the local college. He began work at a printing house in the East End of London but, after some years, took up a place at the Bournemouth Arts Institute, studying photography. After one year, he changed again, moving back to London to the National Film and TV School, studying the art of directing.

In 1986, whilst still a student at the school, Suri created his first film, *Mohammed's Daughter*, a production that won him a BAFTA nomination. He has subsequently produced over thirty films including *A Man of No Importance* (1994) and a version of *Wuthering Heights* (2003). Suri has also worked as director in TV series' such as *The Bill* (1991) and *Casualty* (2008). To date, his only film created on the Island is *A New Year's Day* (2000).

Macarthur, Ellen (1976–)

Born just outside of Matlock, Derbyshire, Ellen developed an early interest in sailing, buying her first dingy by saving her school dinner money. She first sailed alone in a race when she was eighteen, circumnavigating England. Taking part in other gruelling yacht challenges, her sailing skills were recognised in 1998 when the Royal Yacht Association made her 'Yachtsman of the Year'. She wrote her first book *Taking on the World* in 2002, and in 2003 set up the Ellen Macarthur Trust, a charity to help eight to twenty-four year-olds suffering a range of illnesses by introducing them to sailing.

2005 saw her achieve the remarkable feat of completing the fastest solo circumnavigation of the world (though she began the voyage in November 2004). In the New Year Honours that year she was created a Dame. In 2001, Dame Ellen settled in West Cowes where her two charities are based.

Meek, Elizabeth (1953–)

Despite having a surname that has been common on the Island for centuries, Elizabeth was born and educated in London. At the insistence of her parents, she trained there as a nurse and for some years worked as such at Westminster Hospital. She had always enjoyed painting and took this aspect of her life seriously in 1978. Only after some years did she concentrate on one aspect of this skill, the painting of miniatures, the first of which she created in 1990.

Her work was of such high standard that she was quickly recognised as a leading exponent of the genre, receiving commissions from around the country, including one from Prince Charles. She was elected as Fellow of the Royal Society of Artists (FRSA) in 2000 and Elizabeth became President of the Society of Women Artists (2000–2005) and President of the Royal Miniature Society (2004–). She moved with her husband to the Island in 2006, living at Shanklin. In 2012 she was awarded Prince Charles' award for the most outstanding work of miniature painting.

Michelmore, Arthur (Cliff) (1919–2016)

Born in Cowes, where he went to the local secondary school until he was sixteen, becoming head boy, Cliff joined the RAF in 1936 as an apprentice at RAF Halton. He reached the rank of squadron leader (ground) and, soon after the war, became involved with the British Forces Network (BFN), both as an organiser and, in a broadcast of *Robin Hood*, as one of the cast. Cliff left the RAF in 1949 and became freelance. His lucky break came when the Germany-based broadcaster for *Two Way Family Favourites* fell ill and he was asked to take over. This radio link between British troops in Germany and their families in England had an enormous following and made Cliff, and Jean Metcalf, the presenter of the English side (the lady that Cliff eventually married), household names.

His first BBC television programme appearance came in 1955 with the evening slot *Highlight* and, in 1957, began *Tonight*. He became so well known that he was soon a familiar face, presenting anything from General Elections to Apollo moon landings. In 1969, Cliff left the world of current affairs to front the BBC *Holiday* programme that ran for almost twenty years; the travel involved taking him to virtually every corner of the globe. He retired to his house in West Sussex where he died.

Minghella, Anthony (1954–2008)

This Island-born member of the well-known Island ice cream making family went to Fairway Grammar School, Sandown, and then Hull University. There he first studied, and then taught, drama. By the mid 1980s, he was a script writer, first for the ITV *Magpie* programme and then for the BBC, with *Grange Hill*.

Aiming at yet more television work, Anthony wrote and directed the story *Truly, Madly, Deeply* (1990) which eventually appeared as a film. So successful was it that it won him a BAFTA award and this, in turn, led to him being asked to direct the film *The English Patient*. The film won nine Oscars. As a consequence, he was in great demand by other filmmakers, leading to further acclaim with *The Talented Mr Ripley* and *Cold Mountain*.

Awarded a CBE in 2001, Anthony became the chairman of the British Film Institute in 2003, a post he held with great success for four years. Only his 2006 film *Breaking and Entering* was seen as a commercial failure. His last film was a television adaptation of McCall Smith's stories, broadcast by BBC television in 2008, *The No.1 Ladies' Detective Agency*, which received much acclaim. He died in hospital, having suffered a haemorrhage after a simple operation on his neck.

Mountbatten, Louis (1900–1979)

Although not born on the Island, Louis had numerous, lengthy and close connections with it. His father, Prince Louis Battenburg (1854–1921), and his family, lived at Kent House, East Cowes, and from 1913 until 1919; Louis himself was a cadet at the Osborne Naval College, only a mile or so away. In 1917, some time after the outbreak of World War I, the family renounced all its German titles and anglicized the name, an important move, as Prince Battenburg was the First Sea Lord in the British Navy! (he had married a daughter of **Queen Victoria** (see page 121)). Young Louis (now 'Mountbatten') served first as a midshipman, then as a sub lieutenant aboard the submarine chaser *P31* by 1919 and, by the start of hostilities in 1939, was a commander aboard a destroyer, HMS *Kelly*.

HMS *Kelly* was attacked off the coast of Denmark and badly damaged, and Mountbatten blamed, as he was cruising where he should not have been. The incident was made into a film, *In Which We Serve*, starring Noel Coward.

When Louis was only forty-one, Churchill promoted him to vice admiral (the only other person attaining this rank at so early an age was Lord Nelson) and appointed him as Chief of Combined Operations. A major turning point came in 1943 when he was appointed Supreme Allied Commander, South East Asia Command. Louis oversaw the defeat of Japanese forces in Burma (now called Myanmar) and, by 1945, the surrender of the Japanese in Malaya. He was made the last Viceroy of India and helped to arrange the partition that created present-day India and the new state of Pakistan.

In 1965, having refused the governorships of both Malta and Australia, Admiral of the Fleet, Earl Mountbatten, as he now was, was offered and accepted the governorship of the Island. He had always had a soft spot for the Island and undertook the duties with relish. He was murdered along with some of his family while holidaying in his boat while off the Northern Ireland coast.

Murphy, Brian (1933–)

Brian was born in Ventnor where he received his education. He was drafted into the Royal Air Force at RAF Northwood for his war service and, soon after demobilization, joined the Joan Littlewood Theatre Workshop. In the 1960s and 70s he was a jobbing actor, taking any role that came his way. He had parts in television programmes such as *The Avengers* and *Dixon of Dock Green*. He became immensely popular playing the part of George Soper, first in *Man About the House* (1973–1976) and then the spinoff, *George and Mildred* (1976–1980). In both television sitcoms he played against the actress Yootha Joyce. Since 2003, Brian has played the part of Alvin Smedley in the long running television sitcom *Last of the Summer Wine*. He lives near Bromley.

Norman, Desmond (1929–2002)

Born in London, his family moved him to America for the duration of the Second World War. When he returned, he attended Eton College and, because of an interest in aircraft, he went to the de Havilland Technical School where he became friends with **John Britten** (see page 186). These two formed the Island company of Britten-Norman, based at Britten's home at Bembridge. The company was formed in 1951, but the first attempt at building an aeroplane attracted no buyers, so the two turned to the conversion of war-surplus aircraft, such as Tiger Moths, so that they could be used for agricultural crop spraying. This led them to realise there was a need for a light plane suitable for inter-island work. 1965 saw the maiden flight of the first 'Islander', a model that was to see service in well over 100 countries. In 1979, Britton-Norman was bought by a Swiss company and, in 1981, they moved manufacture, under licence, to Romania, with the Bembridge works retained for specialist customisation work and from where the Trislander model is sent worldwide.

Norman, Philip (1943–)

Born in London, Philip's family moved to Ryde where his father ran the ballroom at the end of Ryde Pier. He attended Ryde School until he was eighteen, and after some experience on the Island, took up a post with the *Sunday Times* in London in 1965, writing the influential 'Atticus' column. He is better known for his insightful profiles of a wide range of public figures, the first of which, 'Shout', the 1981 profile of the Beatles, established him on the world stage.

Philip's publications centred round the world of popular music, Elton John, the Rolling Stones and others, including, rather oddly, Colonel Gadaffi of Libya. His total list of works is now extensive. He lives in London.

Raymond, Claud (1923–1945) VC

Born in Mottistone and educated at his local primary school and then Wellington College, Raymond joined the Royal Engineers, being commissioned in 1943. In 1945 he was attached to a group sent to assist with the re-conquering of Japanese-held Burma (now called Myanmar). As a lieutenant, Raymond led a charge from their landing craft and was confronted by a strongly-defended force. Despite being wounded at least three times, he continued to run forward, killing the enemy as he passed them. The main group of Japanese hastily withdrew and this gave the allied troops a chance to withdraw with the wounded. Raymond refused treatment until others had been attended to, but he died of his wounds returning to their landing craft. He is buried in Taukkyan Cemetery, Myanmar, and his VC was gazetted in 1946. (The earlier, original, citation prepared soon after the battle was with General Wingate when his plane was shot down.)

Robertson, Shirley (1968–)

Born near Dundee, this remarkable woman began her sailing career at the age of seven, most of it in nearby lochs. Shirley began competitive sailing in 1983 and graduated from Herriot-Watt College in 1990. By 1995, she represented this country in a variety of international sailing competitions, and by winning gold medals in two Olympic sailing events (Sydney 2000 and Athens 2004) she became the only woman ever to do so. Shirley has had many honours bestowed on her: International Sailing Federation World Female Sailor of the World (2000) and OBE (2005) among them. She has worked closely with the UK Sailing Association since 1998 and this, perhaps, drew her to live in Cowes in 2000. Shirley has been a regular presenter/host for the CNN television programme *Mainsail* since 2006. She became UKSA ambassador in 2006 and continues to promote sailing amongst the Island Schools.

Seely, David (1920–2011)

Like most of this family, David was not born on the Island and, unlike his father ('**Jack' Seely** (see page 176)), he joined the Navy (rather than the army) becoming a cadet at Dartmouth in 1925. At the outbreak of World War II, he was serving on board the battleship HMS *Repulse*. Despite his famous quote, 'I had a rather dull war, I never got sunk', he served with distinction on six warships and in a number of engagements, most notably as part of 'Force H' which was charged with the destruction of the German battleship *Bismarck*.

David achieved the rank of captain aboard HMS *Ajax* in 1963 and played a major role in Britain's defence of Malaysia against infiltration from Indonesia. He succeeded to the Barony of Mottistone in 1966 and resigned from the Navy the following year. Lord Mottistone took up a number of directorships and, in 1986, was founding chairman of the mental health charity SANE, overseeing its growth and development 1986–1995. He was Lord Lieutenant of the Island (1986–1995) and then Governor (1992–5), the first such appointment since the death of Lord Mountbatten in 1974. He had always had an interest in the sea, being Commodore of the House of

Lords Yacht Club and a member of the Royal Yacht Squadron. He died at his Mottistone home.

Simpson, Doris (1913–2006)

Born in Guildford where she was educated, Doris trained as a nurse and spent most of her working life in hospitals in Hampshire. On retirement, she moved to Yarmouth in 1980 and, clearly not fulfilled with her gardening, she began writing. Her first book, *Angel of Vengeance*, was a huge success, drawing on her wide experience of nursing and hospitals. It was written, as were all of her books, using the nom-de-plume of Anthea Cohen. It was immediately followed in 1983 with *Angel Without Mercy* and ultimately to the series of eighteen 'Angel' books, the last of which appeared in 2005. Doris died and is buried in Yarmouth.

Sotherton, Kelly (1976–)

Although born at Newport Hospital, Kelly lived and was educated in Ryde. Her very real expertise with various forms of athletics became obvious when she was a pupil at Ryde High School. While she was at Brunel University, she represented the Island at the 1997 Island Games held in Jersey. There she came first in six events making it clear that her athletic efforts should be directed at the demanding heptathlete event.

In 1998, Kelly moved to the Midlands where she joined the renowned Birchfield Harriers club. She crowned her career by winning a bronze medal for the event at the 2004 Olympics and then gold at the 2006 Commonwealth Games held in Melbourne.

Stigwood, Robert (1934–2016)

Robert was born in Adelaide, Australia, and came to England in 1955 having hitchhiked his way on land and working on oil tankers at sea. Based in London, he made friends with a number of people connected to the growing music industry. By 1967, he had merged his company with that of Brian Epstein and was promoting performers such as Mick Jagger and Eric Clapton as well as managing pop groups such as the Bee Gees. He also had responsibility for a range of popular theatrical works such as *Evita*, *Hair* and *Jesus Christ Superstar* as well as the films *Saturday Night Fever* and *Grease*. This placed him at the pinnacle of the British pop industry. After a serious row with the group, *The Bee Gees*, he left England and ran his empire from his 126 foot yacht in the Bahamas. Robert returned to England in 1992 and purchased Barton Manor, next to Osborne House, using the manor as his company headquarters, flying to engagements by a helicopter kept in the grounds. For several years while he lived there, Robert allowed the grounds to be used for local charitable purposes, four times each year. He died in London.

Taylor, Shaw (1924–2015)

Born in Hackney, London, Shaw served his military service in the RAF, based initially at Ventnor but by 1944 was in Burma (Myanmar). After the war, he spent time studying at RADA (Royal Academy of Dramatic Art) and then returned to the Island as part of the 'Gateway Players', based, of course, at Ventnor! By1962 his was a familiar face through the very successful BBC *Police 5* programme. He was made an MBE in 2000 and, upon retirement, moved to Totland where he died and is buried.

Titchmarsh, Alan (1949–)

Born in Ilkley, Yorkshire, Alan left school at fifteen and began an apprenticeship with the local town as a gardener. He undertook evening study at

Shipley Institute, studying horticulture and then moved to the Royal Botanic Gardens, Kew where, after further study, he became one of their staff. Alan made his first significant breakthrough in 1983 when he fronted the televised *Chelsea Flower Show*, and has done so up to the present. He then appeared regularly with the television series *Pebble Mill* which ran from 1991 to 1996, then starred in *Gardeners' World* (1996–2003). In 2000, Alan was awarded an MBE for services to horticulture.

In 2004, the Royal Horticultural Society awarded him their highest honour, the Victoria Medal of Honour. Alan has a second home in Cowes, is a patron of the Cowes Inshore Lifeboat and, for the year 2008, was elected 'High Sheriff of the Isle of Wight'. In all, Alan has published over forty gardening books, and, so far, eleven novels.

Toynbee, Mary (Polly) (1946–)

Mary, but known as 'Polly', was born at Yafford and lived there until her parents divorced when she was four years old. She moved to London with her mother and, after a somewhat lacklustre education both there and at Badminton school, obtained a scholarship to St Anne's College, Oxford. She remained there for only eighteen months and left, embarking on a number of menial posts before beginning a career in journalism. By 1990 she had a regular feature in *The Guardian* newspaper and then moved to the BBC in 1998, returning to *The Guardian* more recently. Polly has been awarded a number of honorary doctorates by English universities for her contributions to the well-being of society.

Trevor-Roper, Richard D (1915–1944)

Richard was borne in Shanklin and received his primary education there. He attended Sherborne School in Dorset and then served in the Royal Artillery (1936–1939). Richard joined the Royal Air Force Volunteer Reserve in 1939 and was posted to RAF Cardington in that year. He clearly showed skill because, by 1943, not only had be been promoted to flight lieutenant, but had come to the notice of Wing Commander Guy Gibson. This officer had been given the task of combing all other squadrons to create a team for an unspecified, secret mission. It turned out to be the well-documented 'Dam Busters' raid. Richard took part in this attack as rear gunner in the lead bomber, flown by Gibson himself. In this action, he was awarded the DFM (Distinguished Flying Medal) and in later action, also in 1943, the DFC (Distinguished Flying Cross).

In 1944, Richard was shot down and killed in action near Munich and is buried at Durnbach. He is listed on the Shanklin war memorial.

Upward, Edward (1903–2009)

Born in Romford, Essex, though with family living on the Island at Newport, Edward attended Repton School, Derbyshire, and then Corpus Christi College, Cambridge. (The Upward family can be traced in Newport back to 1682 and possibly earlier.) He taught English in a number of prep schools in Scotland and then Cornwall until, in 1932, he took a post at Alleyn's School, Dulwich, eventually retiring from that school as Head of English in 1961.

He then moved to the Island, living at Sandown. Edward was an influential writer: W H Auden citing him as a crucial influence on his early works. His first novel *Journey to the Border* appeared in 1938, though his material had been published in a variety of magazines before this, such as *The Island* (1935).

Once retired, he again began writing, beginning with, in 1962, the first volume of a trilogy *In the Thirties* and then *The Rotten Elements* in 1969. He often found that his somewhat extreme leftist views (until 1948 he had been a significant member of the Communist party) made it difficult for him to find a publisher.

Unusually, the bulk of his publications were created in his last fifteen years, some twenty works in all. He died at Pontefract, Yorkshire, at the home of a friend.

Wilson, Eric Charles (1912–2008) VC

Eric was born in Sandown where his father was priest. After his primary education there, he went to Marlborough school and then the Royal Military College, Sandhurst, from where he was commissioned into the East Surrey Regiment in 1933. He had always had an interest in things African (his grandfather had founded the Church Missionary Society station in Buganda in 1876) and, at the first opportunity, he volunteered for service, first with the Kings African Rifles, and then, in 1939, with the Somaliland Camel Corps.

In July 1940 Mussolini ordered his Abyssinian-based troops to attack the British garrison in Somaliland, which they did with an overwhelming, mechanised force. Eric was in command of a machine gun post on 'observation hill', defending the port of Berbera. After a fierce fight, the post was overrun. So certain were the brigade staff that Eric had been killed in the final attack, in which he manned the last of three machine guns single-handed, it was arranged for him to be awarded the first VC of the African campaign, posthumously. The citation for his VC, gazetted in October 1940 said:

'For most conspicuous gallantry on active service in Somaliland….. The enemy finally overran the post when Captain Wilson, fighting to the last, was killed'.

In fact, Eric had been taken to the prisoner of war camp at Adi Ugri in Italian Eritrea and was freed when the 5th Indian Division overran the area. Once free, he joined the Long Range Desert Group in the Western Desert and, at the end of that campaign, transferred to Burma, helping to establish a bridgehead over the Chindwin River at Kelawa. He retired from the Army in 1949 with the rank of lieutenant colonel.

After twelve years service in Tanganyika, as part of the Overseas Civil Service, he made good use of his fluency in Kiswahili and Gikuria, working to help overseas students through the London Goodenough Trust for Overseas Students. He died at his home in Dorset.

Bibliography

1. The Boyhood of **Algernon Charles Swinburne** by Mrs D Leith (1917).

2. **John Milne**: the man who measured the shaking earth by Paul Kabrna, (2007).

3. **John Milne**, Father of Modern Seismology by L Herbert-Gustar and P Nott (1980).

4. The Scandal of **Sophie Dawes** by Marjorie Bowen (1934 and reprints)

5. **White's** of Cowes by David Williams (1993).

6. **Joseph Nye**; From East Cowes to St Petersburg By Rob Martin (2004)

7. Isle of Wight by **Aubrey de Selincourt** (1948).

8. Rain Upon Godshill by **J. B. Priestley** (1941).

9. The Curious Life of **Robert Hooke** by Lisa Jardine (2003).

10. By Candlelight, the Life of **Dr Arthur Hill Hassall** J.R. Soc. Med. (1983, 76,p990).

11. Narrative of a Busy Life by **Arthur H Hassell** (1893).

12. Place Names of the Isle of Wight by Helge Kokeritz (1940).

13. Will of **Thomas Erlesman**, 1531,Public Record Office ref: prob11/24.

14. Will of John Erlesman, 1600, Public Records Office ref: prob 11/95.

15. Will of **William Keeling**, 1620, Public Record Office ref: prob11/136.

16. Will of **Robert Newland,** 1637, Public Record Office ref: prob11/174.

17. Will of **Robert Newland,** 1644, Public Record Office ref: prob11/192 (son of the above Robert).

18. Will of **Robert Holmes,** 1692,Public Record Office ref: prob 11/412.

19. Will of **Thomas Auldjo,** 1816, Public Record Office ref: prob 11/1678.

20. East Cowes Castle, the Seat of **John Nash** esq. By Ian Sherfield, (1994).

21. Air Bird in the Water: The Life and Works of **Pearl Craigie** by Mildred Harding (1996).

22. **Thomas Arnold** by T W Bamforth (1960).

23. East Cowes and Whippingham, 1303–1914 By Rosetta Brading, (1990).

24. East Cowes and Whippingham, 1914–1939 By Rosetta Brading (1992).

25. West Cowes and Northwood, 1750–1914 By Rosetta Brading, (1994).

26. Newport in Bygone Days by J Eldridge (1952).

27. Lords, Captains and Governors of the Isle of Wight HMSO, (1974).

28. Remarkable Islanders by Ian Williams (2006).

29. Pushing up the Daisies by Jan Toms (2006).

30. The Beken File by **Keith Beken,** (1980).

31. A Bibliography of **George Brannon**'s Vectis Scenery, by P Armitage (1974).

32. The Challenging Sky – The Story of **A V Roe** by L Ludovici (1956)

33. Dear Osborne by John Matson (1978).

34. Man of War; **Sir Robert Holmes** and the Restoration Navy by Richard Ollard (2001).

35. The **Oglander** Memoires Ed W H Long (1888).

36. The Dairyman's daughter and other annals of the poor by **Legh Richmond** reissued by Gospel Standard Trust Ltd (1976).

37. The Chine by **Mimi Khalvati** (2002).

38. Galloper Jack (The Story of **Jack Seely**) by Brough Scott (2003).

39. Launch by General **Jack Seely** (1932).

40. Classic Sails, The **Ratsey** and Lapthorne story by William Collier (1998).

41. Insula Vecta, The Isle of Wight in the middle ages by S F Hockey (1982).

42. Hearth Tax returns for the Isle of Wight, 1664–1674 IOW Records Series, Vol 1 (1981).

43. Autobiography of **Rowland Prothero**, *From Whippingham to Whitehall*

44. Alfred the Great (contains the whole of Asser's 'Life of Alfred' as well as Alfred's will) translated by Simon Keynes and Michael Lapidge, (2004), Penguin Classics series.

45. People of Wight by Angela Wigglesworth (1996).

46. Two-Way Story by **Cliff Michelmore** and Jean Metcalfe (1986).

47. An Autobiography of **Elizabeth M Sewell** edited by her niece, Eleanor (1907).

48. Freshwater – a Comedy by Virginia Woolf edited by L Ruotolo (1976) (this edition contains the two versions of the comedy, that of 1923 and of 1935).

49. The Baronet's Tale by Sir Charles Baring (1983), pub. IWCC.

50. Almost Fairyland by **J M Richards** (1914).

51. Man of Valour; **Field Marshall Lord Gort** VC by J R Colville (1972).

52. The **Watts** Gallery, a visitor's guide by Underwood and Jefferies (2004).

53. Flora Vectiana by **William Drew Snooke** (1823).

54. Flora Vectensis by **William Bromfield** (1856).

55. Pigot's Hampshire Trade Directory, 1830 (this includes information on the towns and environs of East and West Cowes, Ryde, Brading, Newport and Yarmouth).

56. Shalfleet, Isle of Wight by R F Sprake (1967).

57. Just Me; the autobiography of **Sheila Hancock** (2009).

58. Phillimore's Parish Records for Hampshire, Vol. 12 (this covers Marriages, many from as early as 1547, in the parishes of Brading, Calbourne, Freshwater, Niton, Whitwell, Yaverland) and Vol. 14 (covers Newport, also from 1547) (1910) (S and N Genealogy supplies have recently cre-

ated a searchable DVD version of the whole 16 volumes of Hampshire marriage records).

59. Hakluytus Posthumus by Samuel Purchas (1625). With a reissue in 1925 from which electronic copies are available.

60. The Royal Yacht Squadron, 1815–1985 by Ian Dear (1985).

61. Article on **William Fox** in Archives of Natural History (1983) 11(2) pp299–313.

62. Taking on the World by **Ellen Macarthur** (2002).

63. **Michael Hoy,** The Man and his Monument by Dorothy Wright.

64. A Guide to the Natural History of the Isle of Wight by **Frank Morey** (1909).

65. The Geological Story of the Isle of Wight by **James Jackson** (1942).

66. Architectural Antiquities of the Isle of Wight by **Percy Stone** (1891).

67. Legends and Lays of the Isle of Wight by **Percy Stone** (1912).

68. Geological Excursions Round the Isle of Wight by Gideon Mantell (1847 and later editions).

Index of Locations

Location	Notable (bold IOW born)	Epoch
Carisbrooke	**Midlane, Albert**	**4**
	Ross, Alexander	1
	Tuttiett, Mary	**5**
Carisbrooke Castle	Carey, George	1
	Fortibus, Isabella de	1
	King Charles I	2
	Mohun, Phillipa de	1
	Reviers, Baldwin de	1
	Seymour, Margaret	1
	Stuart, Princess Elizabeth	2
Chale	Eley, Frederick	6
	Letts, Thomas	3
	Selincourt, Aubrey de	6
East Cowes	Armitage, Michael	7
	Auldjo, Thomas	2
	Battenberg, Prince Louis	5
	Boissier, Arthur	6
	Damant, Guybon	**6**
	Fox, Uffa	**6**
	Nash, John	2
	Nye, Joseph	2
	Roe, Alliott Verdon	6
	Saunders, Samuel	5
	Seymour, Henry	2
	Shedden, Roscow	**6**

Location	Notable (bold IOW born)	Epoch
	Vereker, John	6
	White, Thomas	2
Farringford	Tennyson, Alfred	3
Freshwater	Cameron, Julia Margaret	4
	Cocks, Arthur Somers	**6**
	Fuchs, Vivian	**7**
	Hooke, Robert	**2**
	Ritchie, Anne	5
	Watts, George Frederick	4
Gatcombe	**Worsley, Philip**	**5**
Godshill	**Cole, Henry**	**1**
Great East Standen Manor	Cecily, Plantagenet (Cecily of York)	1
	Wriothesley, Henry	1
Great Park	Keeling, William	1
Haseley	Horsey, Edward	1
Havenstreet	Rylands, John	3
Hermitage	Hoy, Michael	2

Location	Notable (bold IOW born)	Epoch
Knighton	Morville, Hugh de	1
Lisle Court	Cowper, Frank	5
	Lisle, John	**2**
Merstone	Stone, Percy	5
Mottistone	Gore-Browne, Henry	4
	McDougall, Francis	4
	Raymond, Claud	**7**
	Seely, John Edward (Jack)	6
Nettlestone	Bottomley, Virginia	7
Newport	**Abraham, Gerald**	**7**
	Black, Frederick	**5**
	Buncombe, John	2
	Edes, Richard	**1**
	Erlesman, Thomas	**1**
	Fleming, Arthur	**6**
	Fleming, Thomas	**1**
	Gale, Patrick	**7**
	Goring, Marius	**7**
	Gray, Valentine	4
	Hughes, Geoffrey	7
	Jackson, James	6

Location	Notable (bold IOW born)	Epoch
	James, Dr John	1
	James, Dr Thomas	1
	Jupitus, Phillip (Phill)	7
	Newland, Robert	1
	Rogan, John Mackenzie	5
	Sewell, Elizabeth M	4
	Sewell, James	4
	Sotherton, Kelly	7
	Tombs, Henry	4
New Village	**Dennett, John**	3
Ningwood	Cottle, Ernest	5
	Pinhorn, John	2
Niton	Edwards, Edward	4
	Pittis, Thomas	2
	Selincourt, Aubrey de	6
Northcourt	Leith, Robert	4
Northwood	Gascoyne, David	7
Norton	Crozier, Richard	3
	Hammond, Graham	3

Location	Notable (bold IOW born)	Epoch
Nunwell	**Oglander, John (1)**	**1**
	Oglander, John (2)	**2**
Old Park, Undercliff	Cayzer, Charles	5
	Cheape, John	3
	Spindler, Theodor	5
Osborne	Cockerell, Christopher	7
	Mountbatten, Louis	7
	Ponsonby, Henry	4
	Queen Victoria	4
Quarr	Cochrane, Thomas	3
Redoubt Battery	Cambridge, Daniel	4
Ryde	Adams, William Davenport	4
	Boxer, Edward	3
	Bromfield, William	3
	Browne, Samuel	4
	Cahill, John	5
	Caldwell, James	2
	Calthorpe, Somerset John	5
	Clifford, Augustus	3
	Clifford, Charles	4
	Cotter, William	6

Location	Notable (bold IOW born)	Epoch
	Wilkes, John	2
	Wilson, Eric Charles	7
	Whitchurch, Harry	6
Seaview	Bate, Anthony	7
	Maudsley, Henry	5
Shalfleet	Campbell-Barnes, Margaret	6
Shanklin	Coster, Guillaume	4
	Dixon, John	6
	Keats, John	3
	Khalvati, Mimi	7
	Krishnamma, Suri	7
	Meek, Elizabeth	7
	Parr, Harriet	4
	Smith, Charles	3
	Trevor-Roper, Richard D	7
Shide	**Worsley, Henry**	2
	Milne, John	5
Shorwell	**Hareslade, Robert de**	1
	Henday, Anthony	2
St Helens	**Dawes, Sophie**	3

Location	Notable (bold IOW born)	Epoch
	Murphy, Brian	7
	Peel, Edmund	3
	Peel, Lawrence	3
West Cowes	Aisher, Owen	7
	Arnold, Thomas	3
	Baring, Godfrey	6
	Beken, Frank	6
	Beken, Keith	7
	Christian, Hugh	2
	Davenant, William	2
	Jones, Penrhyn	6
	Macarthur, Ellen	7
	Fellows, Charles	3
	Francki, Wojciech	7
	Green, David	7
	Imrie, Celia	7
	Irons, Jeremy	7
	Ketelbey, Albert	6
	Kendall, Kenneth	7
	McBride, John	2
	Michelmore, Arthur (Cliff)	7
	Poynter, Charles	5
	Ratsey, Thomas	5
	Robertson, Shirley	7
	Stephenson, Robert	3

Index of Notables

T

Lightning Source UK Ltd.
Milton Keynes UK
UKHW011247051019
351070UK00010B/183/P